THE AGAMEMNON

OF

AESCHYLUS.

T0371096

THE AGAMEMNON

OF

AESCHYLUS

WITH A METRICAL TRANSLATION AND NOTES
CRITICAL AND ILLUSTRATIVE

BY

BENJAMIN HALL KENNEDY, D.D.

REGIUS PROFESSOR OF GREEK,
AND HONORARY FELLOW OF ST JOHN'S COLLEGE, CAMBRIDGE;
CANON OF ELY.

EDITED FOR THE SYNDICS OF THE UNIVERSITY PRESS.

SECOND EDITION.

Cambridge:
AT THE UNIVERSITY PRESS.

London: CAMBRIDGE WAREHOUSE, 17, Paternoster Row.
Cambridge: DEIGHTON, BELL, AND CO.
Leipzig: F. A. BROCKHAUS.
1882

CAMBRIDGE UNIVERSITY PRESS
Cambridge, New York, Melbourne, Madrid, Cape Town,
Singapore, São Paulo, Delhi, Mexico City

Cambridge University Press
The Edinburgh Building, Cambridge CB2 8RU, UK

Published in the United States of America by Cambridge University Press, New York

www.cambridge.org
Information on this title: www.cambridge.org/9781107621008

First published 1882
First paperback edition 2013

A catalogue record for this publication is available from the British Library

ISBN 978-1-107-62100-8 Paperback

HONORI · ET · MERITIS

ALMAE · MATRIS · CANTABRIGIAE

CVI · QVANTVM · IPSE · DEBEAT

TESTES · SVNT · ANNALES · ACADEMICI

HOC · OPVSCVLVM · QVALECVMQVE · SIT

VERECVNDE · DEDICARE · VELIT · EDITOR

INEVNTE · ANNO · AETATIS · SVAE · SEPTVAGESIMO · OCTAVO

A.D. VIII. ID. NOVEMB. A.S. MDCCCLXXXI.

INTRODUCTION

TO THE FIRST EDITION.

I. 1. The *Agamemnon* is the first play in the Trilogy called 'Ορεστεία, acted B.C. 458, *Ol.* 80, 2, in the archonship of Philocles, three years before the death of Aeschylus. The other two tragedies which follow it are the *Choephoroe* and *Eumenides :* with them was acted the Satyric drama *Proteus*, probably at the great Dionysia (τὰ κατ᾽ ἄστυ) ; and the prize was awarded to our poet. He had a patriotic motive, arising from his strong conservative opinions, for the constitution of the plot of the third play. The authority of the ancient court of Areopagus was menaced with diminution, if not extinction, by a law which Ephialtes brought forward, on the instigation of Pericles, who led the democratic party in opposition to Kimon, the son of Miltiades. Aeschylus, a stern aristocrat, desired by his *Eumenides* to support the dignity and power of this venerable institution, which he there represents as holding a solemn trial of Orestes under the presidency of Pallas Athene, the tutelar of Athens.

2. These three tragedies must be regarded as constituting one great whole; three acts, as it were, of one plot. In the first play, the *Agamemnon*, is 'the Crime.'

The victorious king, returning from Troy, is murdered by his wicked wife Clytaemnestra with the help of her paramour Aegisthus. In the second, the *Choephoroe*, is 'the Vengeance.' Orestes returns from his retreat in Phokis, circumvents Clytaemnestra and Aegisthus, and puts both to death: but, having thus contracted the guilt of matricide, he becomes a victim to the haunting torture of the Furies (Erinyes or Eumenides). In the third—the *Eumenides*—we have 'the Avenger's Trial.' Orestes flies to Delphi, there obtains the protection of Apollo, who procures for him a trial before the ancient court of Areopagus, under the presidency of Pallas. The Furies plead against him, Apollo speaks for the defence : at the close Orestes is acquitted by the casting vote of the goddess, restored to his civil rights, and freed from the persecuting power of the Furies, whom Pallas consoles with the promise of a grove and sacred rites at Colonus near Athens.

II. 1. Aeschylus, like his contemporary Pindar, is a strictly religious pagan. But his religion is of a sterner and gloomier cast than Pindar's; probably chequered by his philosophic studies in the schools of Sicily and Italy. He may well be called a pessimist, nay, the very patriarch and first preacher of pessimism. Look at his *Prometheus*. In that drama, man born to trouble, as the sparks fly upwards (450 &c., τὰν βροτοῖς δὲ πήματα κ.τ.λ.), has gained through Prometheus all that is to raise him from his low estate; natural science, letters, numbers, medicine, arts, with their ministers, fire and metals :

βραχεῖ δὲ μίθῳ πάντα συλλήβδην μάθε,
πᾶσαι τέχναι βροτοῖσιν ἐκ Προμηθέως.

And with what issue? For these benefactions to men

the benefactor is expelled from heaven, chained on Cau-
casus, and tormented by command of the divine ruler
Zeus. True it is, a hope is held out of better things
(521 &c.), but a very distant, a very indefinite one. Art,
says Prometheus, is weaker than Necessity. Who, asks
the Chorus, guides the rudder of Necessity?—The Fates
and the Furies.—Is Zeus then weaker than these?—He
cannot escape Destiny.—What is destined for him, but to
reign for ever? To this question Prometheus refuses a
reply: the season is not come. The Προμηθεὺς λυόμενος
is lost, and we cannot take the answer from the modern
voice of Shelley.

2. The supreme power then, according to Aeschylus, in human affairs, is Μοῖρα, τὸ πεπρωμένον, Fate or
Destiny. In the *Prometheus* he expands this power into
that mythic trinity (Μοῖραι τρίμορφοι, Clotho, Lachesis
and Atropos) which Rome adopted with the title of
Parcae, but also with that of Fata, afterwards Fatae, from
whom we get our Fays or Fairies. Again, he recognises
them in the *Choephoroe*, ὦ μεγάλαι Μοῖραι (304); and
thrice in the *Eumenides*, where he calls them half-sisters
of the Furies: and makes the latter reproach Apollo
with having ruined or destroyed (φθίσας) the antique
Fates by receiving Orestes at Delphi (1165), and again
with having persuaded the Fates to make mortals im-
mortal by the restoration to life of Alcestis (694). But,
in the *Agamemnon*, Fate (Μοῖρα or τὸ πεπρωμένον) is
spoken of only in the singular, except perhaps, in one
remarkable passage (947), which will be considered when
we reach it. In short, Aeschylus believes in predestina-
tion as strongly as the author of the Koran or the great
Genevese interpreter of the Bible.

3. But, as the Furies, avengers of Crime, are so near akin to the Fates, and co-operate with these, Aeschylus has a theory too on this subject, which acts an important part in this play, being often brought forward, especially in the choral ode which begins 640, and again in the scenes with Cassandra, and in the conclusion of the drama. The most pregnant word in Aeschylus on the subject is Ἄτη. We can cite no place in which ἄτη simply means *a crime* (this is rather ἁμαρτία) or even wickedness in the abstract (this is rather δυσσέβεια or ὕβρις): but it often means the madness attending crime, as in Homer (᾿Αλεξάνδρου ἕνεκ᾽ ἄτης) and, oftener, the woe and the curse consequent on crime, and propagating it. This sense we repeatedly see in the *Agamemnon*. Again, Ἄτη is deified as being, along with the Furies, an avenger of crime: that is, while the Erinyes torment the criminal by the horrors of conscience, Ate drives him on to add crime to crime, thus intensifying his guilt and his punishment. And so his πρώταρχος ἄτη (1117) entails upon him a ὑστερόποινος Ἄτη (*Choeph.* 377). See *Ag.* 1495.

4. And this Ἄτη attaches herself not only to the individual, but also to a family, to a house, which by the guilt of one progenitor may contract a clinging Woe, a Familiar Curse, pursuing it from generation to generation. Such is the Woe of Oedipus and his race, shown in the three plays of Sophocles, and finding its climax in the *Antigone*. Such, in the *Oresteia* of Aeschylus, is the Curse attaching to the Atreidan house, whether we are to derive it from the earliest sinner Tantalus (which may fairly be argued from *Agam.* 1398 &c.) or refer it only to the later deeds of Atreus and Thyestes, as

Aegisthus does in his speech, 1507 &c.[1]   See 1435 &c.,
where we read also of that demon or evil genius, the
ἀλάστωρ (unforgetting one), who dogs the guilty house
as the abettor and agent of Ἄτη.   To him corresponds
the Lemur of Roman mythology.

5.   But neither does Aeschylus represent Agamemnon as free from personal guilt.   He too has inherited
the Family Curse of criminal conduct, though in a less
heinous degree.   He has led a great host of Achaeans
to Troy, there to whiten with their bones the coast of
Asia, or leave them beneath the waters of Scamander
and Simois.   Nor was he permitted to sail on that great
expedition until he had expiated an affront to Artemis
by shedding at Aulis the blood of his daughter Iphigeneia.   Thus had he contracted the guilt of kindred
bloodshed : and this deed is made by Clytaemnestra the
apology for her own crime, as it might be, in part at
least, the motive.   See the choral ode, 640, and the anapaests following : also 1342 &c.

III.   We may here observe that the murder of Agamemnon is several times introduced in the Odyssey, and
in each place ascribed to the treachery of Aegisthus.   In
I. 33 &c. Zeus mentions it to Athene, and declares that
men impute their evils to the gods, but incur them really
by their own fault, as Aegisthus, whom he had warned
by the mouth of Hermes not to consort with Clytaemnestra and kill Agamemnon : yet he committed these
crimes and was slain in consequence by Orestes.   Again,
III. 253 &c., Nestor gives Telemachus a detailed account
of the murder, which Aegisthus accomplished by an am-

[1] The revolting legends on this subject vary considerably in their
details.   See Schliemann's *Mycenae and Tiryns*, ch. iii.

bush. And in IV. 512 &c. Proteus tells a similar story to
Menelaus. Neither of these narratives ascribes to Clytaemnestra a direct share in the deed, but her guilt is
implied in the fact that she marries Aegisthus, and so
conveys to him the throne of Argos. But in IV. 92,
Menelaus imputes the crime to her treachery:

> τείως μοι ἀδελφεὸν ἄλλος ἔπεφνεν
> λάθρῃ, ἀνωιστί, δόλῳ οὐλομένης ἀλόχοιο.

Virgil, a careful student of Greek dramatic poetry,
adopts the Aeschylean story:

> Ipse Mycenaeus magnorum ductor Achivom
> coniugis infandae prima inter limina dextra
> oppetiit : devictam Asiam subsedit adulter.
>
> *Aen.* XI. 266.

This version of the legend Aeschylus must have
drawn from post-Homeric poetry, probably from Stesi-
chorus.

IV. 1. In the earliest age of the Greek drama, the
Chorus was all in all. Thespis is said to have added
a monologue by a single actor ; which was improved
and dignified by Phrynichus. To Aeschylus is ascribed
the introduction of dialogue. But in his plays, as might
be expected, the Chorus continues to occupy a more
important place than in those of Sophocles and Euripides. In the *Supplices* and *Eumenides* it consists of
persons directly and prominently concerned in the story.
In the *Prometheus* and the *Septem contra Thebas*, as
in the *Choephoroe*, the choral maidens have the position
of sympathizers only, but the action of the two former
plays is so slight as hardly to deserve the name of a
dramatic plot. This is true of the *Persae* also : but in
that play the members of the Chorus hold the important

rank described by themselves in the opening lines: and
they have, consequently, a prominent interest in the
events that follow. Analogous to their position is that
of the aged men (πρέσβος Ἀργείων) who form the Chorus
of the *Agamemnon*. K. Ottfried Müller justly saw that
they (twelve in number) represent a council of state
appointed to cooperate with Clytaemnestra during the
absence of Agamemnon. Hence the patriotic solicitude
which they exhibit throughout; hence the anxious
doubts they hint to the herald and to Agamemnon;
hence their brief and hurried consultation at the
moment when they realize the assassination of the
king (a passage which almost seems meant to caricature
the 'strenuous inertness' of political assemblies): hence
the menacing indignation with which in the close of
the play they reproach the guilty queen, and defy the
regicide Aegisthus.

2. Outlines of the choral songs, and of the successive dialogues in which the plot is developed, will
be found in the Notes accompanying the English Translation.

3. As to the characters introduced :—

(1) The Watchman (Φύλαξ), who speaks the Prologue and then disappears, is a servant of the royal
household, a somewhat grumbling *spruchsprecher*, but
staunchly loyal to his absent lord.

(2) The herald Talthybius, in the second Epeisodion, after saluting his country and its deities, announces in a pompous tone the approaching arrival
of Agamemnon, then details with doleful emphasis the
sufferings of the army on its outward voyage, and at
Troy; and afterwards describes the violent tempest

by which the returning fleet was scattered. Aeschylus has assigned to this personage, in his two latter speeches, a tedious and disjointed style, for which it is not easy to discover a reason.

(3) Of Agamemnon's character, as it appears in the third Epeisodion, there is not much to be said. His tone and language are dignified; his sentiments religious, sage, and suitable to a constitutional βασιλεύς: he disapproves the oriental honours prepared for him, and declines to accept them: but a few sophistries of his treacherous wife prevail against his better judgment, and she leads him, walking on purple tapestries, to the chamber of death.

(4) Aegisthus is merely a contemptible and loathsome coward, gloating over the success of his stealthy vengeance.

(5) It is to the delineation of Clytaemnestra and Cassandra, and to the choral songs that Aeschylus has devoted the highest powers of his genius in this drama. The *Agamemnon* is often compared with the *Macbeth* of Shakespeare. But in any such comparison the *Choephoroe* must be taken with the *Agamemnon*; for *Macbeth* contains the retribution as well as the crime; and these are distributed by Aeschylus into the first two dramas of the Orestean trilogy. In these great works of Greek and English genius there are indeed several striking parallels. In each, the plot is founded on the murder of a king: but in the one, revenge and hatred prompt the crime; in the other, ambition only. In each, a woman is the principal agent: but in Aeschylus, Clytaemnestra both plans and perpetrates and exults in the perpetration; she has a dastard for

her accomplice; she is 'a lioness that cohabits with a wolf.' Shakespeare's heroine is a lioness who breathes her own spirit into a lion less resolute than herself: she instigates to the deed, she prepares, she would even have done it, had not Duncan looked like her father as he slept. In both plots, punishment follows crime, but, in the pagan poet, the criminals merely die by the hand of one avenger: in the modern drama, remorse is not omitted; the wife, more daring at first, breaks down first, and dies in phrensied anguish; the husband rushes to the battle-field, and falls despairing. Aeschylus has no parallel to Macbeth himself; and, were it for this cause only, he must yield the palm in the present comparison to our 'myriad-minded' poet. But his choral odes abound in maxims strikingly applicable to the story of Macbeth, to his crimes and his fate. Such are

βιᾶται δ' ἁ τάλαινα πειθὼ
πρόβουλος, παῖς ἄφερτος ἄτας·
ἄκος δὲ πᾶν μάταιον.   *Ag.* 360

βροτοὺς θρασύνει γὰρ αἰσχρόμητις
τάλαινα παρακοπὰ πρωτοπήμων.   201

τὸ δυσσεβὲς γὰρ ἔργον
μέτα μὲν πλείονα τίκτει σφετέρᾳ δ' εἰκότα γέννᾳ.   694

τῶν πολυκτόνων γὰρ οὐκ ἄσκοποι θεοί· κελαιναὶ δ' Ἐρινύες χρόνῳ
τυχηρὸν ὄντ' ἄνευ δίκας
παλιντυχεῖ τριβᾷ βίου
κτίζουσ' ἀμαυρόν, ἐν δ' ἀΐστοις
τελέθοντος οὔτις ἀλκά.   424

(6) A supernatural element enters into the Aeschylean and into the Shakesperian plot. Cassandra represents it in the former, the Witches in the latter; but

the representations are widely different in most respects. The Witches are creatures of mediæval credulity, satanic agents human and feminine, who tempt the innocent to sin, and lead them by fraudulent arts from crime to crime, ending in destruction. In Shakespeare's plot they are important characters, on account of the influence they exercise on the feelings and actions of Macbeth. Cassandra, the frantic prophetess, whose predictions find no belief, is a personage well known in the legend of Troy; and her interview with the Chorus, forming the fourth episode of the _Agamemnon_, is executed with a beauty and passionate power to which we know no parallel in the same kind. But, while she serves to heighten, we may almost say to constitute, the pathos of the play, she has no signal influence in the development of the plot. Her arrival at Argos as the prize, and, according to Greek custom, the assumed paramour of Agamemnon, supplies Clytaemnestra with a further excuse for her bloody deed, and enhances the luxury of its commission: but her motives were ample enough without it: they are, primarily, hatred and vengeance; secondarily, but, as we think, in a minor degree, ambition and guilty love. Lady Macbeth's crime is committed without hatred, without having a wrong to avenge, against a generous benefactor and a good sovereign. Ambition, high-soaring, all-grasping, is the one sole motive: ambition for a husband whom she loves, and, in that husband, for herself. Clytaemnestra is a mother robbed of her darling child and deserted by a husband whom she also knows to be unfaithful. As a wronged woman, she feels none of the repentant horror and anguish which kill Lady Macbeth: she is remorseless to her last moments. And so we recognise a just aesthesis in the delineation of both these women (so like in some respects, so different in others) by two great poets whom twenty centuries, with all the contrasts of ancient and modern thought, divide from one another.

V. The Scene of the *Agamemnon* is laid at Argos : see ll. 24, 462, 738. Yet the royal seat of Agamemnon, described as such throughout the Homeric poems, was not Argos itself, but Mycenae, which lay among the mountains in the north of the Argive plain, between five and six miles from Argos : and there its ruins have remained ever since its capture and destruction by the Argives B.C. 468, *Ol.* 78, 1, ten years before the *Oresteia* was produced. Yet Mycenae is not so much as mentioned in the *Agamemnon*. Dr Schliemann, the indefatigable explorer of its site, in his elaborate work entitled *Mycenae and Tiryns*, p. 36, says : "Strabo justly observes that, on account of the close vicinity of Argos and Mycenae, the tragic poets have made a confusion regarding their names, continually substituting the one for the other. But this is to be excused, because in antiquity travelling was both difficult and very unsafe. Besides, people were not archaeologists &c." Mr W. G. Clark writes more fully to the same effect in defence of Aeschylus for thus neglecting to distinguish the two neighbouring cities (*Peloponnesus*, p. 70). "Rigorous exactness," he says, "is quite alien from the spirit of Aeschylus and of all the old poets,...... The scene of the *Agamemnon* is before the palace of the Atreidae, and I question whether he wasted a second thought upon its site. There is not in all the play the faintest allusion to the scenery of the Argive plain, or the relative position of its cities. Aeschylus had evidently been a diligent reader or hearer of Homer—his characters, language, and

allusions prove this...He could not, therefore, have been
ignorant that Mycenae was constantly spoken of by
Homer as the city and abode of the Atreidae, and yet
throughout the play there is no mention of Mycenae...
No doubt the citizens of Argos, as they transported the
people of Mycenae and incorporated them with their
own body, were anxious also to appropriate their ancient legends and heroic fame. The *Agamemnon* was
represented ten years after this final destruction of the
ancient capital of the Atreidae. The fact that the poet
does not mention the city seems to indicate that its
fate excited little or no sympathy in contemporary
Greece. If the Argive topography of Aeschylus is thus
indefinite and negative, that of Sophocles is elaborately
wrong. In the opening scene of the *Electra*, the Paedagogue, addressing Orestes, says: ' Here is the ancient
Argos you were longing for, and this the Lycean agora
of the wolf-slaying god (to wit, the market-place of the
town of Argos), and this on the left is the renowned
temple of Hera ; and, at the place we are come to,
believe that you have before your eyes Mycenae rich in
gold, and here the blood-stained house of the Pelopidae.'
No one reading this description would infer that Argos
was between five and six miles distant, and the Heraeum
nearly two. The truth is, that neither Sophocles nor
his Paedagogue thought of administering a lecture on
topography under the guise of a dramatic entertainment,
as Milton or Ben Jonson might have done ; so far from
it, he held the entertainment to be all in all, and made
topography and everything else give way to it. He
wanted to produce an effect by bringing Argos, Mycenae,
and the Heraeum within the compass of a single *coup*

d'œil, and I warrant that not one of the spectators was pedantic enough to quarrel with him for it."

VI. The Translation which follows our Text was written to be read from time to time in lectures delivered at Cambridge during the months of February and March, 1878. It is not an attempt to poetise Aeschylus in English, but merely to supply students with a close rendering somewhat more agreeable than a prose version. Its dialogue metre is that of the Greek original, which in English is called Alexandrine[1]. The lyric lines do not imitate Greek rhythm, but the antistrophic verses correspond to those of the strophe[2]. At the close of the volume we have supplied a partial Index only, considering that our interpretation of particular words is indicated by our translation ; and also deeming it probable, that most students of the *Agamemnon* will have at hand the glossary of Linwood or that of Blomfield, or both, besides the Greek Lexicon of Liddell and Scott.

[1] This is the metre used in French epic and dramatic poetry, and by our own Drayton in his *Polyolbion*.

[2] Rhymeless lyric verse is adopted by Milton in his *Samson Agonistes*, by Southey in his *Thalaba*, and by Lord Lytton in his *Tales of Miletus*, and translation of Horace's Odes.

INTRODUCTION

TO THE SECOND EDITION.

I. As this Second Edition may possibly be the last word we shall have to speak respecting the Agamemnon, that word must be fully and distinctly spoken, with 'the courage of our opinions.' We first made acquaintance with this play sixty years ago, since which date we have read and lectured upon it more times than we can attempt to count, always finding some new light thrown on the text and interpretation. Our present views, therefore, whether right or wrong, have not been reached without long study and much reflection.

II. For the constitution of the text, we have to depend, of course, primarily and mainly on the extant manuscripts which contain it.

(1) The text of the Agamemnon is derived from the following manuscripts:

A. *a.* Codex Mediceus, in the Laurentian Library at Florence (cited as M.). This, the most valuable ms. of Aeschylus, is ascribed to the 10th century, and supposed by some to have been copied from an uncially written codex, though more probably it is a copy of such a copy. Of the Agamemnon, it exhibits only

ll. 1—286 (1—310, Dind. *Poet. Sc.*) and ll. 992—1087 (1067—1159), the remainder being unhappily lost.

β. Codex Guelpherbytanus (G.).

This is a 15th century copy of the Cod. Med. with the same lacunae.

γ. Codex Marcianus (Marc.) at Florence.

A similar 15th century copy, and of little value.

δ. Codex of Bessarion (B.), at Venice.

This, ascribed to the 13th cent., is supposed to have been copied from the Cod. Med. while entire. It contains about the first 330 lines of the play.

The foregoing codd. form the Medicean group, and are generally included in the citation M., except where any of them happens to bear a separate testimony.

B. Codex Florentinus (Fl.) of Cent. 14. This has the Agamemnon entire. Though some regard it as copied from the Medicean Cod., their opinion cannot be substantiated.

C. Codex Venetus (V.), of Cent. 13, contains the following fragments of the Agamemnon: ll. 1—45 and 1022 (1095) to the end.

D. Codex Farnesianus (F.) at Naples, written at the close of Cent. 14 by the grammarian Demetrius Triclinius, with his corrections, and with Scholia of his, and of Thomas Magister, contains the whole play.

When no codex differs from the rest, the reading first cited in the *Conspectus Lectionum* (a) must be taken as that of mss. generally.

The four earliest editions are those of (1) the Aldi, Venice, 1518, taken from G., cited A.: (2) Robortello,

Venice, 1552, from M., cited R. : (3) Turnèbe, Paris, 1552, cited T. : (4) Vettori, Paris, 1557, cited Vict. : this was taken from M. Fl. F., and is the first in which the Agamemnon appears entire. Canter's edition appeared at Antwerp in 1580, Stanley's in London 1663, Butler's (from Stanley's) at Cambridge in 1810.

The emendations of John Auratus and Joseph Scaliger were obtained by Hermann from a manuscript of Spanheim at Berlin, transcribed from Is. Voss's copies of the edition of Victorius. These are now at Leyden.

(2) Hence it appears that, of the Agamemnon, in our numeration,

vv. 1—45	appear in 7 Codd.
vv. 46—286	,, ,, 6 ,,
vv. 287—324	,, ,, 3 ,,
vv. 325—992	,, ,, 2 ,,
vv. 993—1022	,, ,, 5 ,,
vv. 1023—1087	,, ,, 6 ,,
vv. 1088—1603	,, ,, 3 ,,

Thus, in 667 lines, more than two-fifths of the play, we depend on two very corrupt copies (Fl. and F.) for our knowledge of the text. In the last 515 lines a third is added (V.), also very corrupt. Such is all the light we receive from mss. for 1182 out of 1603 lines.

(3) Mr Paley supplies no 'Conspectus Lectionum,' and his account of the codices is very cursory. But he evidently wishes them to be regarded as more trust-worthy than they really are. Thus in a note at p. vii of his general preface he gravely writes: 'A critical structure raised on the very arbitrary assumption that an original writing has been utterly corrupted, stands

on a very insecure basis.' Certainly any 'very arbitrary assumption' is a 'very insecure basis' for any 'critical structure.' But the degree of corruption—whether slight, or considerable, or great, or utter (whatever is meant by *utter*)—existing in ancient codices, ought never to be matter of 'arbitrary assumption.' It is a question to be determined by the sound judgment of good and upright scholars upon these codices, when carefully collated. A codex 'utterly corrupt' could hardly enable the most acute scholar to elicit from it a pure text. But Mr Paley shews, in his preface to the Choephoroe (p. 485), that one '*exceedingly corrupt* ms.' (M.) has preserved to us '*a very noble composition,*' owing to '*the pains and intellect* that have been devoted to its elucidation.'

We have tried to elicit a pure text of a nobler composition from several 'exceedingly corrupt' mss., devoting to the work great pains and such intellect as we possess. The result we submit to the judgment of all good Greek scholars who are candid as well as acute.

(4) All the copies we have noted (1) were written in a very dark period of human knowledge, from the eleventh to the fourteenth centuries—not so dark indeed as the three centuries which immediately preceded: but they inherited the codd. written during those barbarous ages: and how careless and unlearned their scribes and marginal annotators were, even Cod. M. affords ample proof by such readings as μῆκος δ' ἦν (2), ὅτ' ἂν (7), ἐπορθριάζειν (29), ἀγγέλων (30), ἐριδομένου (64), τιθιπεργήρως (80), ἡμερόφατον (84), ἄπλειστον (105), τὴν θυμοφθόρον λύπης φρένα (106), καταπνέει (108), τὰν γᾶν (112), παμπρέποις (117), πολίαδε (125), ἄτα (129), ἀέλπτοις—ὄντων (136), οὐδὲν λέξαι (159), κατέξενον (180), χειμαίρας (210),

ἐπιγένοιτ' (229), σύνορθον αὐταῖς (231), παιδίον ὡποῦ (274), and others, which may suffice without going on to the later fragment. Codd. Fl. F. and V. in subsequent parts afford still ampler specimens of similar error. Scribes of different capacities acquirements and temperaments seem to have transcribed different portions of the drama. We sometimes find a long stretch of verses continued with very little corruption; in other places corruption sets in and goes on through a series of passages. The choral and commatic parts are naturally more corrupt, in general, than the dialogues. The latter are comparatively pure, except the Exodos, of which many places are grossly corrupt. Thus it is evident that our 'critical structure' is not 'based on the very arbitrary assumption' that the Agamemnon 'has been *utterly* corrupted.' We said in the first edition, and now repeat, "The few extant mss. of the Agamemnon have come down to us laden with a heap of corruption: with miswritings, glosses intruded on the text, lacunae, dislocation of words and lines—errors of careless or ignorant transcribers and inadequate commentators accumulated from generation to generation. We may be thankful that the results affecting this magnificent work of a noble genius have not been more ruinous than we find them."

(5) The principles laid down by Karsten for the just use of these manuscripts in editing Aeschylus agree so closely with our own views, that we cite from the Preface to his edition of the Agamemnon several passages on this subject.

"Horum codicum ut antiquissimus ita optimus est Mediceus, non quod purior et limatior sit, sed ipsa quae habet vitia propius a

germana scriptura distant. Contra infimum locum tenet Farnesianus, non quod sordidior, sed quod lectio manifesto arguit
serioris grammatici manum, qui textum suo arbitratu ad gram-
matices et critices regulas refinxit, ut jam Victorius animadvertit et
hodie inter omnes convenit. Medium inter hos ambos locum tenet
Florentinus, qui, ut a veritate longius distat Mediceo, ita caret
sedula illa correctura quae Triclinianam officinam olet.

Hermannus censet Mediceum descriptum esse de libro quad-
ratis literis scripto, quod ad rectum ejus codicis usum non oblivis-
cendum esse. Sane, sive talis liber Medicei pater sive, quod
credibilius mihi videtur, avus fuerit, ingens est mendorum numerus,
qui ex unciali scriptura explicandus est, natus partim e perversa
syllabarum et vocum distinctione, partim e consimilium literarum
permutatione, partim e prava interpunctione aliisve ejus generis
causis. Horum vitiorum magnum numerum interpretes emenda-
runt, non pauca vero eaque turpissima adhuc relicta sunt, quae
criticorum aciem fugerunt. Quaesitum est autem, num Mediceus
habendus sit archetypus atque fons unde, ut Guelferbytanus, Marcianus et Bessarionis codex, ita ceteri quoque derivati sint. De
quo ut certum statuere difficile, nisi quis intentis ad id oculis et
mente codices ipse contulerit, ita illud certissimum, nullius trium
illorum librorum auxilio nos posse carere, quum nec pauca in
Mediceo peccata sint quae corrigat Florentinus, et hic aeque ac
Farnesianus interdum lectiones offerat, quae undecumque profectae
Mediceo sint anteponendae.

 * * * * * * * * *

Quodsi vitiorum genera quibus Orestea laborat attendimus
eorumque causas quaerimus, haec tam multiplicia sunt tamque
vetera, ut nusquam fere latior pateat critices exercendae palaestra.
Ne memorem menda, quae modo attigi, e syllabarum confusione
et literarum ac vocum permutatione orta, alia a scriptura compen-
diaria in verborum maxime terminationibus, aut a prava accentuum
notatione, e perversa interpunctione, e scribarum denique oscitantia
in literis vel omittendis vel iterandis profecta : haec ut omittam,
sunt alia minus in aperto posita eaque partim perantiqua, glosse-
mata dico, quae vel in obscurati verbi vacuum locum sunt illata
vel explicandi gratia annotata furtim in textum migrarunt. Nota-
bile ex hoc genere exemplum est, vs. 111, ubi germana lectio,
servata in Aristophanis Ranis vs. 1321, σὺν δορὶ καὶ χερὶ πράκτορι in

Mediceo ceterisque codicibus, cessit alteri huic σὺν δορὶ δίκας πράκτορι, quae aperte glossema olet.

*   *   *   *   *   *   *   *

Singula haec quae dixi vitiorum genera latius patent quam adhuc animadversum est ; quare non parca relicta est errorum messis, quae resecanda et evellenda est, ut pristinus poëtae nitor reddatur. Ad hoc autem, ut dixi, parum suppetit librorum auxilium ; in corruptissimis praesertim et obscurissimis locis hi plerumque ita vel concinunt inter se vel discrepant, ut parum inde lucri ad poëtae manum restituendam emergat. Nec Scholia vetera, ad Agamemnonem certe, quidquam, me judice, afferunt quod alicujus pretii sit.

Unde igitur auxilium petendum? Ubi libri deficiunt, confugiendum est ad ingenium, et conjectura resarciendum quod scriptura nobis negavit. Haec ratio si neque ita certa et firma est, ut codicum auctoritatem aequiparet, at neque ita est incerta et dubia ut vocabulum ipsum indicare videtur. Immo si quis ut prudens medicus, cognitis vitiorum causis perspectoque scriptoris ingenio, colore, habitu, procul a timida cunctatione aeque atque a temeraria festinatione operam adhibeat, plerumque eveniet ut sententia ipsa velut bona natura latentem sub ulcere sanam lectionem efferat et emendationem monstret tam verisimilem, ut scripturae testimonio paene par sit.

Principium autem et fundamentum critices est justa interpretatio, qua in re mirum est quam saepe Aeschyli interpretes a recta et simplici via deflexerint. Causa ejus rei partim posita est in ipsa lectionis depravatione, cujus emendandae difficultate fatigati qualicumque modo corrupta aeque ac sana explicare maluerunt quam vitiosa fateri ; accessit vero Aeschyleae audaciae et obscuritatis fama, unde nonnullis opinio nata, nihil tam insolite, tam licenter dictum esse, quin Aeschyleo cothurno dignum sit habendum ; nihil tam obscure et intricate, quin exquisita aliqua cogitatio aut abditum aliquod sapientiae effatum inde excudi posse videatur. Ita factum ut Aeschylum interpretari quibusdam, ut Paleius dicit, nihil aliud videretur quam grande aliquod et quasi continuum aenigma enucleare. Quodsi multi recentiorum interpretum ingenia tam acuissent ad verum inveniendum quam ad prava explicanda, jam pridem aliquanto puriorem, credo, et illustriorem hanc tragoediam haberemus."

(6)   To these wise and weighty words of Prof.
Karsten we desire to add the testimony, not less wise
and weighty, of a much-lamented scholar, a contemporary and friend of our own, learned and sagacious
beyond his years, who, if his valuable life had been
prolonged to a term far short of that which his distinguished brothers have reached, would in all probability
have occupied and adorned the Greek chair of Cambridge.   We allude to Mr John Wordsworth.   In his
Review of Prof. Scholefield's Aeschylus, which appears
in the *Philological Museum*, Vol. I. p. 209, he says,
"A scrupulous, we had almost said superstitious, reverence for the authority of the manuscripts, is the
principle to which Mr Wellauer has uniformly adhered
in his edition of Aeschylus; and this principle, which
under certain restrictions is an excellent and judicious
one, has been adopted by Professor Scholefield with
very slight modification or abatement.   Both of them
appear to us to have pushed it too far.   We are no
advocates for the licentious extravagance of those critics
who make a display of their own skill and ingenuity
at the expense of their author; but on the other hand
great caution is necessary, lest in our zeal for the
authority of the manuscripts we should assert it in
defiance of the laws of the language. *To the testimony
of manuscripts so corrupt as those of Aeschylus we must
not hastily surrender the established rules of syntax and
metre...* If every editor should adhere with the same
tenacity as Mr Wellauer to the readings of his manuscripts, and those readings, which are at variance with
rules, were to be added to the catalogue of exceptions,
there is no solecism or irregularity for which we might
not find a sanction; and the grammar of the language,

instead of being simplified and reduced to more general
principles as the language is more studied, would become almost a chaos of perplexity and confusion."
Then, after referring to several notes on the *Supplices*
in Prof. Scholefield's edition, Mr J. Wordsworth adds:
"In such instances he" (the Professor) "appears to us
to have been misled by an excess of caution, and to
have sacrificed the principles of the language to an
undue deference for the authority of the manuscripts."
Mr Paley, too, in the Preface to his 12mo edition of
1858 virtually recognises similar principles. He says:
"Tenenda semper est media quaedam via editori, qui
quidem studiosae iuventuti prodesse velit; ut nec vana
coniectandi libidine abripiatur neque nimia vulgatae
lectionis veneratione deceptus (id quod quïbusdam con-
tigisse videtur) inepte scripta aut male Graeca novis
anteponat, si modo quae nova feruntur multo proba-
biliora sint."

(7) To the principles thus laid down by these three
scholars (Karsten, J. Wordsworth, Paley) we declare
our cordial adherence; and we are willing to adopt as
our motto Karsten's words: 'Principium et fundamentum critices est iusta interpretatio.' We have, it is true,
emended largely: but no 'vana coniectandi libido,' no
wish to 'make a display of our own skill and ingenuity,'
has induced us to do so: the principles of just interpretation and just regard to the laws and requirements
of grammar and metre have determined and guided our
judgment everywhere.

III. The end we have set before us in this second
Edition is, to purify the text of the Agamemnon from
those errors of grammar sense and metre which in most

editions have been permitted to deface it : also to suggest reasonable modes of supplying the defect of sense
in many places where we cannot doubt that lines or
words of Aeschylus have been lost or spoilt by the
carelessness of scribes or the ignorance of marginal
annotators ; or (what we suppose to have often happened) by the combined influence of both these causes.

Such an enterprise we should deem presumptuous
and unjustifiable if it were not undertaken and executed
under the following conditions :

(1)   That we exhibit by signs in the text, and by
the *Conspectus Lectionum,* all readings which do not rest
on manuscript authority : excepting only such as merely
correct manifest blunders.   The meaning of our textual
signs is shown on p. 2.

(2)   That we give our reasons for adopting every
correction and interpretation open to dispute.

(3)   That we assign every such correction and interpretation to its original author, so far as possible.

To record all the opinions of every scholar on each
point is not possible; nor if possible would it be desirable.   But an editor of honourable feeling will always
strive to do full justice to meritorious learning.

As we have tried to fulfil these conditions, our
readers have before them all necessary facts in each
case, enabling them to form their own judgment, and,
if they see reason, to overrule ours.

IV.   The qualifications for just criticism of a Greek
drama are fairly summarised in the following line :

γραμματική, μετρική, νοῦς ῥήτορος ἠδὲ ποιητοῦ.

And, in considering any portions of its ms. text, we

may ask this question: is it worthy of the poet, and proper to be maintained in four respects: (*a*) grammatically; (*b*) metrically; (*c*) logically; (*d*) aesthetically? The answer should be carefully and maturely weighed, and full advantage given to the side of existing authority. But, if the great end in view is to place before students an incorrupt and intelligible text, which shall guide and improve their knowledge taste and judgment, then we think there is more responsibility incurred by leaving blots which cannot be what the poet wrote, than by supplying corrections which cannot be assailed on any of the grounds above named, even though we cannot be sure that they restore exactly what the poet did write. But we repeat that an editor thus freely correcting is bound to do what some have unjustly neglected, that is, to place the uncorrected text within the reach of students.

Every proposed emendation ought to be considered on its own merits: by these alone its reception or rejection ought to be determined. It is in the Notes on Lection principally that these questions have been discussed: and there, for the most part, the reasons for and against any proposed corrections will be found.

V. Most of the emendations, which we regard as necessary in the Agamemnon, occur in its lyric parts, and are required by the laws of correspondence in choral metre.

On antistrophic metre, and the corrections which it suggests, we repeat what was said in our first Edition.

The commentators, and perhaps most of the scribes, who dealt with the codices of Aeschylus before the invention of printing, had a fair knowledge of the laws of the iambic senarius in dialogue, and of those which govern anapaestic systems. But we believe them to have had very imperfect ideas of the metrical principles observed in the lyric strophe and antistrophe : and through this ignorance we are convinced that much corruption has been introduced into the choral portions of the Agamemnon, which has hitherto not been detected, at all events not removed.

A careful study of the lyric composition of Aeschylus leads us to think (1) that, in general, he made his strophic and antistrophic lines correspond exactly ; and this not only in the character of the metres, but, for the most part, in the number and quantity of the syllables also : (2) that he was unwilling to allow a short vowel at the close of a line to remain unelided before a vowel beginning the next ; or (3) a short syllable at the close of a line to count as a long one by virtue of that station ; except (a) when the vowel or syllable ends a strophe antistrophe or epode ; (β) when it precedes a speech ; προφῆται 380 : (γ) when the construction is interjectional. In most places where these laws are transgressed in the vulgate text, we believe that emendation is required, and that the fitness of such emendation will be found in every case to be supported by concurring reasons of great force. Moreover we think that the probability of corruption existing in such places is not a little strengthened by the facilities which they afford in almost every instance to emendation without impairing sense or construction, without obliterating or distorting what we may reasonably suppose to have been the true expression of the poet's mind : though we grant that a few passages occur, on which opinions may fairly differ. Laws (2) (3) apply, as is well known, to anapaestic as well as lyric rhythm in dramatic poetry, but not to the iambic senarius nor to the epic hexameter. Hence we find short syllables sometimes treated as long at the close of even those iambic senarii which occur in commatic passages mixed with lyric metres.

The apparent violation of these laws in the vulgate text of Aeschylus occurs chiefly in older plays, especially in Suppl. Pers. Sept.; in Prometheus hardly ever. In Agamemnon, corrupt as the mss. are, the instances are very few compared with the number of syllables in the strophic passages. We find that the syllables in the play subject to these rules, are 4566, that is, 2283 pairs. Mr Paley keeps in his text (if we have counted rightly) about 42 syllables, which violate this law of agreement. We have corrected all these at very slight cost: for among them we find only one change which makes any noticeable difference in the sense of the passage: namely, τοιάδε in 167 for βιαίως, which latter word seems to us an erroneous and mischievous gloss.

The subjoined table exhibits the metrical disagreements existing and the corrections we have supplied. After the numbers of the erring place (given according to the numeration in the two editions), the erring Greek is given in one column, and with it in a bracket the syllables to which it ought to correspond. Our correction appears in the last column; and its metrical agreement with the syllables within the bracket will be apparent. Where 'transposition' alone is expressed, this implies that correction is made by *merely* transposing the Greek words: and reference to such passages will prove that this change never hurts, but generally improves the expression of the Greek. In a few places (191, 356—8, 388—9, 711) correction accompanies transposition; and here too nothing is lost by changing the order, rather something is gained.

As regards 167, Mr Paley has adopted a correction of the antistrophe, suggested to obviate the disagreement with βιαίως, namely, παλιρρόχθοις (an invented word), in place of παλιρρόθοις. Also he has admitted τε καὶ λογχίμους for λογχίμους τε καὶ (376), on similar grounds: νῦν λελέξεται (159). Nor are these the only places in which he has allowed metrical disagreement as a ground for alteration. But if it can be passed over without correction in forty places, why not in fifty?

If it be said in respect of some lines (as in my numeration 357—9, 389, 427, 679) that, in certain metres, spondee or trochee, spondee or iambus, are equally admissible in certain places, and therefore he leaves one or the other as he finds it, we do not think this is an answer (except in the cases already allowed) to the exigency of correspondence between strophe and antistrophe, which will be found exceedingly strict: as the following specimens (taken from an immense variety) may suffice to prove,

1 *ἄναγνον ἀνίερον τόθεν*
2 *ἔθεντο φιλόμαχοι βραβῆς.*
1 *τὰ δὲ σῖγά τις βαΰζει,*
φθονερὸν δ' ὑπ' ἄλγος ἕρπε
προδίκοις 'Ατρείδαις.
2 *τὸ δ' ὑπερκόπως κλύειν εὖ*
βαρύ· βάλλεται γὰρ ὄσσοις
Διόθεν κεραυνός.

Hence, in emending the corrupt line *νεογνὸς ἀνθρώπων μάθοι*, Hermann, guided by the antistrophic *καί τις σε κακοφρονῶν τίθη*—writes *καὶ παῖς νεόγονος ἂν μάθοι*, which we follow, only preferring *τις* to *παῖς*.

121		*κεδνὸς δὲ στρ.* (*κύριος εἰ-*),	*τῶ δ' ἀγαθὸς στρ.*	
167	(176),	*βιαίως* (*παλίρρο-*),	*τοιάδε*	
180	(190),	*'Αργείων* (*-μοῦ πέλας*),	transposition	
189	(201),	*ἄγαλμα* (*ἀφειδεῖς*),	transposition	
191	(203),	*πατρῴους* (*-νον ἀνθ-*),	*πατρὸς χ.*	
216	(230),	*χέουσα* (*ἄκραντοι*),	*χέουσ' εἶτ'*	
346	(359),	*ἐξιχνεῦσαϊ* (*-φερτος ἄτας*),	*ἐξιχνεῦσαί τ'*	
356	(370),	*ἀπαρκεῖν* (*-στροφον τῶνδε*),	*ἀπαρκεῖν ἂν*	
„	„	*λαχόντι οὐ* (*καθαιρεῖ οἶ-*),	*λαχόντι πλού-*	transp.
357	(372),	*οὐ γάρ ἐστιν* (*οἶος καὶ Πα-*),	*πλούτου γὰρ τίς*	transp.
358	(373),	*πλούτου πρὸς* (*εἰς δόμον*),	*φωτὶ πρὸς*	transp.
„	„	*κόρον ἀνδρὶ* (*τὸν 'Ατρειδᾶν*),	*κόρον ἔξω*	
359	(374),	*λακτίσαιτι* (*ἤσχυνε ξε-*),	*λακτίζοντι*	

383	(402),	ἀλοίδορῦς (ξυνορμένοις),	ἀλοιδύρως
388	(407),	ἀνδρὶ (φωτῶν),	ἔρρει δ'
389	(408),	ὀμμάτων (τεύχῃ καὶ),	ὀφθαλμῶν
„	„	ἔρρει (-του δύ-),	ἀνδρὶ
397	(417),	ὑπερβατώτερα (στίβοι φιλά-νορἔς π.),	ὑπερβολὴν ἔχει
401	(421),	πρὸς ἧπἄρ οὖς (ἀνάσσειν),	πρὸς ἧπαρ· τοὶς
402	(422),	τις ἔπεμψἔν (δὲ κολοσσῶν),	ποτε πέμψας
427	(451),	τιθεῖσ' (τὸν δ' ἐν φ.),	κτίζουσ'
657	(686),	τίοντᾰς ὑμέναιον (πρεπόντως ἑλέναυς ἑ-),	τίοντας νέον ὑμέν'
658	(687),	ἐπέρρεπἔν γ. (ἐλέπτολις ἐκ),	ἐπέρρεπε
664	(694),	αἰῶν' ὦν ἀμφὶ (ἀκτὰς ἐπ' ἀεξ.),	αἰῶνα διαὶ
667	(698),	φιλόμαστὄν (-σιν ἀμείβων),	φιλόμαστον δ'
679	(715),	-ον ἐκ θεοῦ δ' (-αν φαιδρωπὺς),	-ον θείας ὧδ'
709	(744),	λιπυῦσ' (δαίμονά τ'),	ὄμμασιν (transp.)
913	(958),	ὑπ' Ἰλιὄν (ψύθῃ πεσεῖν),	transposition
923	(968),	-μενον κέἄρ (ξυνεμβυλαῖς),	transposition
942	(989),	πάλιν (γει-),	τοῦτ'
1012	(1058),	πολλὰ συνίστορα (τοῖσδ' ἐπι-πείθομαι),	πολλὰ συνίστορ' αὐ-
1013	(1059),	αὐτοφόνα κακὰ (κλαιόμενα βρε-),	-τοκτόνα κακὰ
1024	(1070),	νέον ἄχος μέγᾰ (-δέμνιον πό-σιν λ.),	νῦν ἄχος νέον μ.
1040	(1086),	φόνου (τύπτει),	λοιγοῦ
1051	(1097),	τεύχει (γένει),	κύτει
1066	(1112),	φρεσὶν Ἴτυν (νόμοις πυθεν),	Ἴτυν φρεσὶν
1101	(1147),	θανατύφορα (θρεομένας),	θανάσιμ' ὦν
1336	(1382),	ἀπέταμἔς (ἔτι σε χρή),	ἀπεταμές τ'
1382	(1428),	καὶ πολλὰ (μοι κόρακος),	καὶ πολύ γε
1407	(1457),	οἴκοις τοῖσδε (-αίτιος εἲ),	ἐν μελάθροις
1462	(1509),	μέριμνἄν (-τι κρῖναι φ.),	μεριμνᾶν
1492	(1540),	μίμνει δὲ (δέδοικα),	μένει δὲ

In only one of these places is the sense of the poet altered by the emendation (167): in many the very rendering is unchanged. At such slight expense are these metrical deformities removed.

VI. Having proposed to ourselves, as the object of our editorial labours, to place in the hands of readers a Greek text, which should be free from errors of grammar sense and metre, we found this could not be accomplished without venturing upon a novel step.

We ascertained, to our full conviction, that, in a certain number of places besides those which are manifestly and by admission defective, the text is corrupted by the hitherto undiscerned or unacknowledged loss of lines or parts of lines.   The step which in these places we have ventured to take is—to introduce, in connexion with the manuscript text, such Greek words (lines chiefly, but sometimes parts of lines), as seem competent to supply the defective sense of the place in a form not unworthy of the poet's mind.   These extraneous words we have so clearly distinguished (by signs explained on p. 2), both in Greek text and in English translation, from the ms. Greek handed down as Aeschylean, that no careful reader can suppose them to be other than what they are—i.e. matter suggested as capable of filling up gaps in the sense, which have arisen from the accidental omission of lines or parts of lines by careless transcribers.   As we make no pretension (except perhaps in 69) to ascribe any of these appended suggestions to the hand of Aeschylus, we have not included them in our numeration of lines.   They will be seen in the following places : 69, 101, 283, 377, 392, 530, 565, 722, 733, 736, 766, 977, 1367, 1526, 1579.

The reasons which prompt change, and the arguments in favour of each suggestion will be found in our *Notes on Lection.*

VII. As regards the general emendation of the ms. text (apart from changes made by all editors, such as the restitution of misspelt words, and the correction of other manifest blunders) its statistics in the present edition are as follows, approximately. Out of 1603 lines, 24 per cent. contain some emendation, by words being altered or substituted or transposed, or (in three or four places) removed from the text. Of these changes 8½ per cent. are due to the present editor, 15½ to other scholars. Of his own changes, the editor is disposed to regard (*a*) the following as approaching to certainty :

17, 61, 67, 69, 121, 123, 180, 190, 191, 265, 675, 704, 708, 742, 922—923, 1195—1197, 1249—1251 ;

(*b*) the following as highly probable:

7, 83, 91—2, 97, 154, 346, 388—389, 516, 564, 699, 712, 714, 716, 862, 871, 889, 893, 906, 913—914, 927—929, 933—934, 982, 1038, 1040, 1061, 1087, 1101 —1102, 1265, 1303, 1336, 1491, 1504—1505 ;

(*c*) the following as reasonably satisfactory :

139—140, 141, 157, 159, 167, 216, 232, 313, 355—359, 383—384, 397—398, 402, 419, 427, 565, 658, 667, 676, 679, 941—946, 1012—1014, 1024, 1065—1067, 1121, 1187, 1376, 1382, 1402—1404, 1411, 1454—1455, 1534, 1554—1556.

The corrections of other scholars are duly noted in the *Conspectus Lectionum*, and are capable of similar distinction, if it were desirable to attempt it.

ΥΠΟΘΕΣΙΣ

ΑΓΑΜΕΜΝΟΝΟΣ.

ΑΓΑΜΕΜΝΩΝ εἰς Ἴλιον ἀπιὼν τῇ Κλυταιμνήστρᾳ, εἰ πορθήσοι τὸ
Ἴλιον, ὑπέσχετο τῆς αὐτῆς ἡμέρας σημαίνειν διὰ πυρσοῦ. ὅθεν σκοπὸν
ἐκάθισεν ἐπὶ μισθῷ Κλυταιμνήστρα, ἵνα τηροίη τὸν πυρσόν. καὶ ὁ μὲν
ἰδὼν ἀπήγγειλεν· αὐτὴ δὲ τὸν τῶν πρεσβυτῶν ὄχλον μεταπέμπεται,
περὶ τοῦ πυρσοῦ ἐροῦσα· ἐξ ὧν καὶ ὁ χορὸς συνίσταται· οἵτινες ἀκού-
σαντες παιανίζουσι. μετ᾽ οὐ πολὺ δὲ καὶ Ταλθύβιος παραγίνεται, καὶ
τὰ κατὰ τὸν πλοῦν διηγεῖται. Ἀγαμέμνων δ᾽ ἐπὶ ἀπήνης ἔρχεται· εἵπετο
δ᾽ αὐτῷ ἑτέρα ἀπήνη, ἔνθ᾽ ἦν τὰ λάφυρα καὶ ἡ Κασάνδρα. αὐτὸς μὲν
οὖν προεισέρχεται εἰς τὸν οἶκον σὺν τῇ Κλυταιμνήστρᾳ. Κασάνδρα δὲ
προμαντεύεται, πρὶν εἰς τὰ βασίλεια εἰσελθεῖν, τὸν ἑαυτῆς καὶ τοῦ
Ἀγαμέμνονος θάνατον, καὶ τὴν ἐξ Ὀρέστου μητροκτονίαν, καὶ εἰσπηδᾷ
ὡς θανουμένη, ῥίψασα τὰ στέμματα. τοῦτο δὲ τὸ μέρος τοῦ δράματος
θαυμάζεται, ὡς ἔκπληξιν ἔχον καὶ οἶκτον ἱκανόν. ἰδίως δὲ Αἰσχύλος
τὸν Ἀγαμέμνονα ἐπὶ σκηνῆς[1] ἀναιρεῖσθαι ποιεῖ. τὸν δὲ Κασάνδρας
σιωπήσας θάνατον, νεκρὰν αὐτὴν ὑπέδειξε. πεποίηκέ τε Αἴγισθον καὶ
Κλυταιμνήστραν ἑκάτερον διϊσχυριζόμενον περὶ τῆς ἀναιρέσεως ἑνὶ κεφα-
λαίῳ· τὴν μέν, τῇ ἀναιρέσει Ἰφιγενείας· τὸν δέ, ταῖς τοῦ πατρὸς
Θυέστου ἐξ Ἀτρέως συμφοραῖς.

Ἐδιδάχθη τὸ δρᾶμα ἐπὶ ἄρχοντος Φιλοκλέους, Ὀλυμπιάδι ὀγδοηκοστῇ,
ἔτει δευτέρῳ. πρῶτος Αἰσχύλος Ἀγαμέμνονι, Χοηφόροις, Εὐμενίσι, Πρω-
τεῖ σατυρικῷ. ἐχορήγει Ξενοκλῆς Ἀφιδνεύς.

Προλογίζει δὲ ὁ φύλαξ, θεράπων Ἀγαμέμνονος.

---

[1] Ἐπὶ σκηνῆς. The writer of this argument may merely mean, that the cries of
Agamemnon from within are heard on the stage, but not those of Cassandra.

ΤΑ ΤΟΥ ΔΡΑΜΑΤΟΣ ΠΡΟΣΩΠΑ.

ΦΥΛΑΞ.

ΧΟΡΟΣ ΓΕΡΟΝΤΩΝ.

ΚΛΥΤΑΙΜΝΗΣΤΡΑ.

ΤΑΛΘΥΒΙΟΣ ΚΗΡΥΞ.

ΑΓΑΜΕΜΝΩΝ.

ΚΑΣΑΝΔΡΑ.

ΑΙΓΙΣΘΟΣ.

SIGNS USED.

* before a word, and in the line with it, implies that such word is an emendation of that which corresponds in mss.; *ἀλκᾷ 107.

* * above the line imply that the words between them are emendations of what corresponds in mss.; *ἐν τέμνων* 17.

† † inclose words added to complete the text where it is manifestly defective. Such additions cannot be warranted as the words of Aeschylus, but an editor printing them is responsible for their appropriateness in feeling and expression. The letters are spaced to manifest their distinction. See 69.

A point or points before or after words indicate the probable loss of a word or words which cannot be supplied for want of clue.

‖ stands before a line which contains transposition. See 67.

ΑΓΑΜΕΜΝΩΝ.

[Bracketed Numerals refer to Dindorf's Poetae Scenici.]

———•———

ΦΥΛΑΞ.

Θεοὺς μὲν αἰτῶ τῶνδ' ἀπαλλαγὴν πόνων
φρουρᾶς ἐτείας μῆκος, ἣν κοιμώμενος
στέγαις Ἀτρειδῶν ἄγκαθεν, κυνὸς δίκην,
ἄστρων κάτοιδα νυκτέρων ὁμήγυριν,
καὶ τοὺς φέροντας χεῖμα καὶ θέρος βροτοῖς   5
λαμπροὺς δυνάστας, ἐμπρέποντας αἰθέρι
*ἀθρῶν, ὅταν φθίνωσιν *ἀντέλλωσί τ' αὖ.*
καὶ νῦν φυλάσσω λαμπάδος τὸ σύμβολον,
αὐγὴν πυρός, φέρουσαν ἐκ Τροίας φάτιν
ἁλώσιμόν τε βάξιν· ὧδε γὰρ κρατεῖ   10
γυναικὸς ἀνδρόβουλον ἐλπίζον κέαρ.
εὖτ' ἂν δὲ νυκτίπλαγκτον ἔνδροσόν τ' ἔχω
εὐνὴν ὀνείροις οὐκ ἐπισκοπουμένην
ἐμήν· φόβος γὰρ ἀνθ' ὕπνου παραστατεῖ,
τὸ μὴ βεβαίως βλέφαρα συμβαλεῖν ὕπνῳ·   15
ὅταν δ' ἀείδειν ἢ μινύρεσθαι δοκῶ,
ὕπνου τόδ' ἀντίμολπον *ἐν τέμνων* ἄκος,
κλαίω τότ' οἴκου τοῦδε συμφορὰν στένων,
οὐχ ὡς τὰ πρόσθ' ἄριστα διαπονουμένου.
νῦν δ' εὐτυχὴς γένοιτ' ἀπαλλαγὴ πόνων,   20
εὐαγγέλου φανέντος ὀρφναίου πυρός.
ὦ χαῖρε λαμπτὴρ νυκτός, ἡμερήσιον

4 ΑΙΣΧΥΛΟΥ

φάος πιφαύσκων καὶ χορῶν κατάστασιν
πολλῶν ἐν Ἄργει τῆσδε συμφορᾶς χάριν.
ἰού, ἰού.   25
Ἀγαμέμνονος γυναικὶ σημαίνω τορῶς,
εὐνῆς ἐπαντείλασαν ὡς τάχος δόμοις
ὀλολυγμὸν εὐφημοῦντα τῇδε λαμπάδι
ἐπορθιάζειν, εἴπερ Ἰλίου πόλις
ἑάλωκεν, ὡς ὁ φρυκτὸς ἀγγέλλων πρέπει·   30
αὐτός τ' ἔγωγε φροίμιον χορεύσομαι·
τὰ δεσποτῶν γὰρ εὖ πεσόντα θήσομαι,
τρὶς ἓξ βαλούσης τῆσδέ μοι φρυκτωρίας.
γένοιτο δ' οὖν μολόντος εὐφιλῆ χέρα
ἄνακτος οἴκων τῇδε βαστάσαι χερί.   35
τὰ δ' ἄλλα σιγῶ· βοῦς ἐπὶ γλώσσῃ μέγας
βέβηκεν· οἶκος δ' αὐτός, εἰ φθογγὴν λάβοι,
σαφέστατ' ἂν λέξειεν· ὡς ἑκὼν ἐγὼ
μαθοῦσιν αὐδῶ κοὐ μαθοῦσι λήθομαι.

ΧΟΡΟΣ.

δέκατον μὲν ἔτος τόδ' ἐπεὶ Πριάμου   40
μέγας ἀντίδικος
Μενέλαος ἄναξ ἠδ' Ἀγαμέμνων,
διθρόνου Διόθεν καὶ δισκήπτρου
τιμῆς ὀχυρὸν ζεῦγος Ἀτρειδᾶν,
στόλον Ἀργείων χιλιοναύτην   45
τῆσδ' ἀπὸ χώρας
ἦραν στρατιῶτιν ἀρωγήν,
μέγαν ἐκ θυμοῦ κλάζοντες Ἄρη,
τρόπον αἰγυπιῶν,
οἵτ' ἐκπατίοις ἄλγεσι παίδων   50
ὕπατοι λεχέων στροφοδινοῦνται,
πτερύγων ἐρετμοῖσιν ἐρεσσόμενοι,

ΑΓΑΜΕΜΝΩΝ. 5

πόνον ὀρταλίχων ὀλέσαντες.
ὕπατος δ' ἀΐων ἤ τις Ἀπόλλων   55
ἢ Πὰν ἢ Ζεὺς οἰωνόθροον
γόον ὀξυβόαν τῶνδε μετοίκων
          ὑστερόποινον
πέμπει παραβᾶσιν Ἐρινύν.
οὕτω δ' Ἀτρέως παῖδας ὁ κρείσσων   60
          πέμπει ξένιος
Ζεύς, πολυάνορος ἀμφὶ γυναικὸς
πολλὰ παλαίσματα καὶ γυιοβαρῆ
γόνατος κονίαισιν ἐρειδομένου
διακναιομένης τ' ἐν προτελείοις   65
          κάμακος θήσων
Τρωσὶν Δαναοῖσι θ' ὁμοίως.
ἔστι δ' ὅπη νῦν ἔστι, τελεῖται δ'
ἐς τὸ πεπρωμένον· †οὐδέ τις ἀνδρῶν†
οὔθ' *ὑποκαίων οὔθ' ὑπολείβων   70
          ἀπύρων ἱερῶν
ὀργὰς ἀτενεῖς παραθέλξει.
ἡμεῖς δ' ἀτίται σαρκὶ παλαιᾷ
          τῆς τότ' ἀρωγῆς
ἱπολειφθέντες μίμνομεν, ἰσχὺν   75
ἰσόπαιδα νέμοντες ἐπὶ σκήπτροις.
          ὅ τε γὰρ νεαρὸς
μυελὸς στέρνων ἐντὸς *ἀνάσσων
ἰσόπρεσβυς, Ἄρης δ' οὐκ ἔνι χώρᾳ,
          τό θ' ὑπέργηρων,   80
φυλλάδος ἤδη κατακαρφομένης,
τρίποδας μὲν ὁδοὺς στείχει, παιδὸς δ'
          οὔ τις ἀρείων
ὄναρ ἡμερόφαντον ἀλαίνει.
          σὺ δέ, Τυνδάρεω   85

d. post v. 60 dant ἐπ' Ἀλεξάνδρῳ, p. v. 70 οὔτε δακρύων.

θύγατερ, βασίλεια Κλυταιμνήστρα,
τί χρέος; τί νέον; τί δ' ἐπαισθομένη,
τίνος ἀγγελίας
πειθοῖ περίπεμπτα θυοσκινεῖς;
πάντων δὲ θεῶν   90
τῶν *τ' ἀστυνόμων, ὑπάτων, χθονίων,
τῶν τ' ἀγοραίων,
βωμοὶ δώροισι φλέγονται·
ἄλλη δ' ἄλλοθεν οὐρανομήκης
λαμπὰς ἀνίσχει, χρίματος ἁγνοῦ   95
μαλακαῖς ἀδόλοισι παρηγορίαις
‖ φαρμασσομένη,
πελάνῳ μυχόθεν βασιλείῳ.
τούτων λέξασ' ὅ τι καὶ δυνατὸν
καὶ θέμις αἰνεῖν,   100
†δεῖξόν τι σαφές†, παιών τε γενοῦ
τῆσδε μερίμνης, ἢ νῦν τοτὲ μὲν   (100)
κακόφρων τελέθει, τοτὲ δ' ἐκ θυσιῶν
ἀγανὰ φαίνουσ' ἐλπὶς ἀμύνει
φροντίδ' ἄπληστον   105
λύπης, θυμοφθόρον *ἄτην.
κύριός εἰμι θροεῖν ὅδιον κράτος αἴσιον ἀνδρῶν   στρ.
*ἐντελέων· ἔτι γὰρ θεόθεν *καταπνείει
πειθὼ μολπᾶν
*ἀλκᾷ ξύμφυτος αἰών·   110
ὅπως Ἀχαιῶν δίθρονον κράτος, Ἑλλάδος *ἥβας
ξύμφρονα *τάγαν,
πέμπει ξὺν δορὶ *καὶ χερὶ* πράκτορι
θούριος ὄρνις Τευκρίδ' ἐπ' αἶαν,
οἰωνῶν βασιλεὺς βασιλεῦσι νεῶν, ὁ κελαινὸς ὅ τ' ἐξόπιν
*ἀργᾶς,   115
φανέντες ἴκταρ μελάθρων χερὸς ἐκ *δοριπάλτου
παμπρέποις ἐν ἕδραισι

Codd. post v. 91 dant τῶν τ' οὐρανίων.

βοσκόμενοι λαγίναν ἐρικύμονα φέρματι γένναν,
βλαβέντα λοισθίων δρόμων.
αἴλινον, αἴλινον εἰπέ, τὸ δ' εὖ νικάτω.   120
τὼ δ' ἀγαθὸς στρατόμαντις ἰδὼν δύο λήμασι *δισσοῖς
'Ατρεΐδας μαχίμους, ἐδάη λαγοδαίτας   [ἀντ.
    *πομπᾶς ἀρχούς,
    οὕτω δ' εἶπε τεράζων·
" Χρόνῳ μὲν *αἱρεῖ Πριάμου πόλιν ἅδε κέλευθος,   125
    πάντα δὲ πύργων
    κτήνη πρόσθε τὰ *δημιοπληθέα
    μοῖρα λαπάξει πρὸς τὸ βίαιον.
οἷον μή τις *ἄγα θεόθεν κνεφάσῃ προτυπὲν στόμιον μέγα
    Τροίας
στρατωθέν· οἴκῳ γὰρ ἐπίφθονος ᾽Αρτεμις ἀγνά,   130
    πτανοῖσιν κυσὶ πατρὸς
αὐτότοκον πρὸ λόχου μογερὰν πτάκα θυομένοισι·
    στυγεῖ δὲ δεῖπνον αἰετῶν.
    αἴλινον, αἴλινον εἰπέ, τὸ δ' εὖ νικάτω.
    τόσσον περ εὔφρων ἁ καλὰ   ἐπῳδ.
    δρόσαις ἀέπτοις μαλερῶν*λεόντων,   136
    πάντων τ' ἀγρονόμων φιλομάστοις
    θηρῶν ὀβρικάλοισι, τερπνὰ
‖στρουθῶν αἰτεῖ ξύμβολα τούτων,
‖δεξιὰ μὲν κατάμομφα δὲ φάσματα, κρᾶναι.   140
    'Ιήιον *δ' ἐκκαλέω* Παιᾶνα,
μή τινας ἀντιπνόους Δαναοῖς χρονίας ἐχενῇδας ἀπλοίας (150)
τεύξῃ, σπευδομένα θυσίαν ἑτέραν, ἄνομόν τιν', ἄδαιτον,
νεικέων τέκτονα σύμφυτον, οὐ δεισήνορα· μίμνει
    γὰρ φοβερὰ παλίνορτος   145
οἰκονόμος δολία μνάμων μῆνις τεκνόποινος."—
τοιάδε Κάλχας ξὺν μεγάλοις ἀγαθοῖς ἀπέκλαγξεν
μόρσιμ' ἀπ' ὀρνίθων ὁδίων οἴκοις βασιλείοις·
    τοῖς δ' ὁμόφωνον
    αἴλινον, αἴλινον εἰπέ, τὸ δ' εὖ νικάτω.   150

Ζεύς, ὅστις ποτ᾽ ἐστίν, εἰ τόδ᾽ αὐ-   στρ. α΄.
    τῷ φίλον κεκλημένῳ,
    τοῦτό νιν προσεννέπω
τοὔνομ᾽· ἄλλο δ᾽ οὐκ ἔχω, πάντ᾽ ἐπισταθμώμενος,
    πλὴν Διός, εἰ τὸ μάταν ἀπὸ φροντίδος ἄχθος
    χρὴ βαλεῖν ἐτητύμως.   156
εἰ δ᾽ εἷς τις πάροιθεν ἦν μέγας,   ἀντ. α΄.
    παμμάχῳ θράσει βρύων,
    οὐδ᾽ ἐλέγξεται πρὶν ὤν,
    ὅς δ᾽ ἔπειτ᾽ ἔφυ, τριακτῆρος οἴχεται τυχών.   160
    Ζῆνα δέ τις προφρόνως ἐπινίκια κλάζων
    τεύξεται φρενῶν τὸ πᾶν·
    τὸν φρονεῖν βροτοὺς ὁδώσαντα, *τὸν πάθει μάθος*   στρ. β΄.
    θέντα κυρίως ἔχειν.
    στάζει δ᾽ ἔν θ᾽ ὕπνῳ πρὸ καρδίας   165
    μνησιπήμων πόνος, καὶ παρ᾽ ἄκοντας ἦλθε σωφρονεῖν·
    δαιμόνων δέ που χάρις *τοιάδε*
    σέλμα σεμνὸν ἡμένων.
    καὶ τόθ᾽ ἡγεμὼν ὁ πρέσβυς νεῶν Ἀχαιϊκῶν,   ἀντ. β΄.
    μάντιν οὔτινα ψέγων,   170
    ἐμπαίοις τύχαισι συμπνέων,—
    εὖτ᾽ ἀπλοίᾳ κεναγγεῖ βαρύνοντ᾽ Ἀχαιϊκὸς λεὼς
    Χαλκίδος πέραν ἔχων παλιρρό-
    θοις ἐν Αὐλίδος τόποις,
    πνοαὶ δ᾽ ἀπὸ Στρύμονος μολοῦσαι   στρ. γ΄.
    κακόσχολοι, νήστιδες, δύσορμοι   176
    βροτῶν ἄλαι,
    νεῶν τε καὶ πεισμάτων ἀφειδεῖς,
    παλιμμήκη χρόνον τιθεῖσαι
    ‖κατέξαινον ἄνθος Ἀργείων τρίβῳ·   180
    ἐπεὶ δὲ καὶ πικροῦ
    χείματος ἄλλο μῆχαρ
    βριθύτερον πρόμοισιν   (200)

ΑΓΑΜΕΜΝΩΝ. 9

μάντις ἔκλαγξεν, προφέρων
Ἄρτεμιν, ὥστε χθόνα βάκτροις ἐπικρούσαντας Ἀτρείδας
    δάκρυ μὴ κατασχεῖν—   185
    ἄναξ δ᾽ ὁ πρέσβυς τόδ᾽ εἶπε φωνῶν·   ἀντ. γ᾽.
    "Βαρεῖα μὲν κὴρ τὸ μὴ πιθέσθαι·
        βαρεῖα δ᾽, εἰ
    τέκνον δαΐξω, δόμων ἄγαλμα,
    ‖ ῥεέθροις παρθενοσφάγοισιν   190
‖ μιαίνων *πατρὸς χέρας βωμοῦ πέλας.
        τί τῶνδ᾽ ἄνευ κακῶν;
    πῶς λιπόναυς γένωμαι,
    ξυμμαχίας ἁμαρτών;   194
    παυσανέμου γὰρ θυσίας   [γὰρ εἴη."
παρθενίου θ᾽ αἵματος ὀργᾷ περιόργως ἐπιθυμεῖν θέμις· εὖ
    ἐπεὶ δ᾽ ἀνάγκας ἔδυ λέπαδνον,   στρ. δ᾽.
    φρενὸς πνέων δυσσεβῆ τροπαίαν
        ἄναγνον, ἀνίερον, τόθεν
    τὸ παντότολμον φρονεῖν μετέγνω·   200
    *βροτοὺς θρασύνει γὰρ αἰσχρόμητις
    τάλαινα παρακοπὰ πρωτοπήμων·
        ἔτλα δ᾽ οὖν θυτὴρ γενέ-
    σθαι θυγατρός, γυναικοποίνων πολέμων ἀρωγὰν
        καὶ προτέλεια ναῶν.   205
    λιτὰς δὲ καὶ κληδόνας πατρῴους   ἀντ. δ᾽.
    παρ᾽ οὐδὲν αἰῶνα παρθένειόν *τ᾽
        ἔθεντο φιλόμαχοι βραβῆς.
    φράσεν δ᾽ ἀόζοις πατὴρ μετ᾽ εὐχὰν
    δίκαν χιμαίρας ὕπερθε βωμοῦ   210
    πέπλοισι περιπετῆ παντὶ θυμῷ
        προνωπῆ λαβεῖν ἀέρ-
δην, στόματός τε καλλιπρῴρου φυλακὰν κατασχεῖν
    φθόγγον ἀραῖον οἴκοις

βία χαλίνων τ' ἀναύδῳ μένει.　　　στρ. έ.
κρόκου βαφὰς δ' ἐς πέδον χέουσ' †εἶτ'†　216
ἔβαλλ' ἕκαστον θυτήρων
ἀπ' ὄμματος βέλει φιλοίκτῳ,
πρέπουσά θ' ὡς ἐν γραφαῖς, προσεννέπειν
θέλουσ'· ἐπεὶ πολλάκις　　　　　220
πατρὸς κατ' ἀνδρῶνας εὐτραπέζους
ἔμελψεν, ἀγνᾷ δ' ἀταύρωτος αὐδᾷ πατρὸς
φίλου τριτόσπονδον εὔποτμον *παιᾶνα φίλως ἐτίμα.
τὰ δ' ἔνθεν οὔτ' εἶδον οὔτ' ἐννέπω·　ἀντ. έ.
τέχναι δὲ Κάλχαντος οὐκ ἄκραντοι.　226
Δίκα δὲ τοῖς μὲν παθοῦσιν　　　(250)
μαθεῖν ἐπιρρέπει· τὸ μέλλον *δ',
ἐπεὶ γένοιτ', ἂν κλύοις· προχαιρέτω·
ἴσον δὲ τῷ προστένειν·　　　　230
τορὸν γὰρ ἥξει *ξύνορθρον αὐγαῖς.*
πέλοιτο δ' οὖν *ἡ 'πὶ* τούτοισιν *εὖ πρᾶξις,* ὡς
θέλει τόδ' ἄγχιστον Ἀπίας γαί-
ας μονόφρουρον ἕρκος.
ἥκω σεβίζων σόν, Κλυταιμνήστρα, κράτος· 235
δίκη γάρ ἐστι φωτὸς ἀρχηγοῦ τίειν
γυναῖκ', ἐρημωθέντος ἄρσενος θρόνου.
σὺ δ' *εἴ τι* κεδνὸν εἴτε μὴ πεπυσμένη
εὐαγγέλοισιν ἐλπίσιν θυηπολεῖς
κλύοιμ' ἂν εὔφρων· οὐδὲ σιγώσῃ φθόνος.　240

ΚΛΥΤΑΙΜΝΗΣΤΡΑ.

εὐάγγελος μέν, ὥσπερ ἡ παροιμία,
Ἕως γένοιτο μητρὸς Εὐφρόνης πάρα.
πεύσει δὲ χάρμα μεῖζον ἐλπίδος κλύειν·
Πριάμου γὰρ ᾑρήκασιν Ἀργεῖοι πόλιν.

ΧΟ. πῶς φής; πέφευγε τοὔπος ἐξ ἀπιστίας.   245
ΚΛ. Τροίαν Ἀχαιῶν οὖσαν· ἦ τορῶς λέγω;
ΧΟ. χαρά μ' ὑφέρπει δάκρυον ἐκκαλουμένη.
ΚΛ. εὖ γὰρ φρονοῦντος ὄμμα σοῦ κατηγορεῖ.
ΧΟ. τί γὰρ τὸ πιστόν; *ἔστι τῶνδέ σοι τέκμαρ;
ΚΛ. ἔστιν· τί δ' οὐχί, μὴ δολώσαντος θεοῦ;   250
ΧΟ. πότερα δ' ὀνείρων φάσματ' εὐπειθῆ σέβεις;
ΚΛ. οὐ δόξαν ἂν λάβοιμι βριζούσης φρενός.
ΧΟ. ἀλλ' ἦ σ' ἐπίανέν τις ἄπτερος φάτις;
ΚΛ. παιδὸς νέας ὣς κάρτ' ἐμωμήσω φρένας.
ΧΟ. ποίου χρόνου δὲ καὶ πεπόρθηται πόλις;   255
ΚΛ. τῆς νῦν τεκούσης φῶς τόδ' εὐφρόνης λέγω.
ΧΟ. καὶ τίς τόδ' ἐξίκοιτ' ἂν ἀγγέλων τάχος;
ΚΛ. Ἥφαιστος, Ἴδης λαμπρὸν ἐκπέμπων σέλας.
      φρυκτὸς δὲ φρυκτὸν δεῦρ' ἀπ'*ἀγγάρου πυρὸς
      ἔπεμπεν· Ἴδη μὲν πρὸς Ἑρμαῖον λέπας   260
      Λήμνου· μέγαν δὲ*πανὸν ἐκ νήσου τρίτον
      Ἄθῳον αἶπος Ζηνὸς ἐξεδέξατο,
      ὑπερτελής τε πόντον ὥστε νωτίσαι
      ἰσχὺς πορευτοῦ λαμπάδος ·πρὸς ἡδονὴν
      *προὔκειτο χρυσοφεγγές, ὥς τις ἥλιος,   265
      σέλας παραγγείλασα Μακίστου*σκοπαῖς·
      ὁ δ' οὔ τι μέλλων οὐδ' ἀφρασμόνως ὕπνῳ
      νικώμενος παρῆκεν ἀγγέλου μέρος·
      ἑκὰς δὲ φρυκτοῦ φῶς ἐπ' Εὐρίπου ῥοὰς
      Μεσσαπίου φύλαξι σημαίνει μολόν.   270
      οἱ δ' ἀντέλαμψαν καὶ παρήγγειλαν πρόσω,
      γραίας ἐρείκης θωμὸν ἅψαντες πυρί.
      σθένουσα λαμπὰς δ' οὐδέπω μαυρουμένη,
      ὑπερθοροῦσα πεδίον Ἀσωποῦ, δίκην
      φαιδρᾶς σελήνης, πρὸς Κιθαιρῶνος λέπας,   275
      ἤγειρεν ἄλλην ἐκδοχὴν πομποῦ πυρός.
      φάος δὲ τηλέπομπον οὐκ ἠναίνετο   (300)

12 ΑΙΣΧΥΛΟΥ

φρουρά, πλέον καίουσα τῶν εἰρημένων·
λίμνην δ' ὑπὲρ Γοργῶπιν ἔσκηψεν φάος·
ὄρος τ' ἐπ' Αἰγίπλαγκτον ἐξικνούμενον   280
ὤτρυνε θεσμὸν *μηχαρίζεσθαι πυρός.
πέμπουσι δ', ἀνδαίοντες ἀφθόνῳ μένει,
φλογὸς μέγαν πώγωνα, †καὶ κεκτημένον
ἰσχὺν τοσαύτην ὥστε† καὶ Σαρωνικοῦ
πορθμοῦ *κάτοπτον πρῶν' ὑπερβάλλειν πρόσω
φλέγουσαν· εἶτ' ἔσκηψεν, *ἔς τ' ἀφίκετο   285
'Αραχναῖον αἶπος, ἀστυγείτονας σκοπάς·
κἄπειτ' 'Ατρειδῶν εἰς τόδε σκήπτει στέγος
φάος τόδ', οὐκ ἄπαππον 'Ιδαίου πυρός.
τοιοίδ' ἔτοιμοι λαμπαδηφόρων νόμοι,
ἄλλος παρ' ἄλλου διαδοχαῖς πληρούμενοι·   290
νικᾷ δ' ὁ πρῶτος καὶ τελευταῖος δραμών.
τέκμαρ τοιοῦτον ξύμβολόν τε σοὶ λέγω,
ἀνδρὸς παραγγείλαντος ἐκ Τροίας ἐμοί.

ΧΟ.   θεοῖς μὲν αὖθις, ὦ γύναι, προσεύξομαι·
λόγους δ' ἀκοῦσαι τούσδε κἀποθαυμάσαι   295
διηνεκῶς θέλοιμ' ἂν ὡς λέγοις πάλιν.

ΚΛ.   Τροίαν 'Αχαιοὶ τῇδ' ἔχουσ' ἐν ἡμέρᾳ.
οἶμαι βοὴν ἄμικτον ἐν πόλει πρέπειν.
ὄξος τ' ἄλειφά τ'*ἐγχέας ταὐτῷ κύτει
διχοστατοῦντ' ἂν οὐ *φίλω προσεννέποις·   300
καὶ τῶν ἁλόντων καὶ κρατησάντων δίχα
φθογγὰς ἀκούειν ἔστι συμφορᾶς διπλῆς.
οἱ μὲν γὰρ ἀμφὶ σώμασιν πεπτωκότες
ἀνδρῶν κασιγνήτων τε, καὶ φυταλμίων
παῖδες γερόντων, οὐκέτ' ἐξ ἐλευθέρου   305
δέρης ἀποιμώζουσι φιλτάτων μόρον·
τοὺς δ' αὖτε νυκτίπλαγκτος ἐκ μάχης πόνος
νήστεις πρὸς ἀρίστοισιν ὧν ἔχει πόλις
τάσσει, πρὸς οὐδὲν ἐν μέρει τεκμήριον,
ἀλλ' ὡς ἕκαστος ἔσπασεν τύχης πάλον.   310

ἐν αἰχμαλώτοις Τρωϊκοῖς οἰκήμασι
ναίουσιν ἤδη τῶν ὑπαιθρίων πάγων
δρόσων τ' ἀπαλλαγέντες, *ὡς δ' εὐδαίμονες*
ἀφύλακτον εὐδήσουσι πᾶσαν εὐφρόνην.
εἰ δ' εὐσεβοῦσι τοὺς πολισσούχους θεοὺς   315
τοὺς τῆς ἁλούσης γῆς θεῶν θ' ἱδρύματα,
*οὐτᾶν ἑλόντες αὖθις *ἀνθαλοῖεν ἄν.
ἔρως δὲ μή τις πρότερον ἐμπίπτῃ στρατῷ
πορθεῖν ἃ μὴ χρή, κέρδεσιν νικωμένους.
δεῖ γὰρ πρὸς οἴκους νοστίμου σωτηρίας   320
κάμψαι διαύλου θάτερον κῶλον πάλιν.
θεοῖς δ' ἂν ἀμπλάκητος εἰ μόλοι στρατός,
*ἐγρηγορὸς τὸ πῆμα τῶν ὀλωλότων
γένοιτ' ἄν, εἰ πρόσπαια μὴ τύχοι κακά.
τοιαῦτά τοι γυναικὸς ἐξ ἐμοῦ *κλύεις·   325
τὸ δ' εὖ κρατοίη, μὴ διχορρόπως ἰδεῖν·
πολλῶν γὰρ ἐσθλῶν τὴν ὄνησιν εἱλόμην.   (350)
ΧΟ. γύναι, κατ' ἄνδρα σώφρον' εὐφρόνως λέγεις.
ἐγὼ δ', ἀκούσας πιστά σου τεκμήρια,
θεοὺς προσειπεῖν εὖ παρασκευάζομαι·   330
χάρις γὰρ οὐκ ἄτιμος εἴργασται πόνων.
    ὦ Ζεῦ βασιλεῦ καὶ νὺξ φιλία
      μεγάλων κόσμων κτεάτειρα,
    ἥτ' ἐπὶ Τροίας πύργοις ἔβαλες
    στεγανὸν δίκτυον, ὡς μήτε μέγαν   335
    μήτ' οὖν νεαρῶν τιν' ὑπερτελέσαι
        μέγα δουλείας
      γάγγαμον, ἄτης παναλώτου.
    Δία τοι ξένιον· μέγαν αἰδοῦμαι
        τὸν τάδε πράξαντ',   340
    ἐπ' Ἀλεξάνδρῳ τείνοντα πάλαι
    τόξον, ὅπως ἂν μήτε πρὸ καιροῦ
        μήθ' ὑπὲρ ἄστρων
      βέλος ἠλίθιον σκήψειεν.

Διὸς πλαγὰν ἔχουσιν· εἰπεῖν   στρ. α'.
πάρεστιν τοῦτό γ' ἐξιχνεῦσαί *τ'·   346
*ἔπραξαν ὡς ἔκρανεν. οὐκ ἔφα τις
θεοὺς βροτῶν ἀξιοῦσθαι μέλειν,
    ὅσοις ἀθίκτων χάρις
    πατοῖθ'· ὁ δ' οὐκ εὐσεβής.   350
πέφανται δ' *ἐκγόνοις
ἀτολμήτως* Ἄρη
πνεόντων μεῖζον ἢ δικαίως,
φλεόντων δωμάτων ὑπέρφευ.
τὸ δ' οὖ τι βέλτιστόν *ἐστ' οὐδ'* ἀπή- 355
μαντον, ὥστ' ἀπαρκεῖν *ἂν εὖ πραπίδων *λαχόντι·
‖πλούτου γὰρ *τίς ἔπαλξις
‖*φωτὶ πρὸς κόρον *ἔξω
λακτίζοντι μέγαν* δίκας βωμὸν εἰς ἀφάνειαν ;
βιᾶται δ' ἁ τάλαινα πειθὼ   ἀντ. α'.
πρόβουλος, παῖς ἄφερτος ἄτας·   361
ἄκος δὲ *πᾶν μάταιον.* οὐκ ἐκρύφθη,
πρέπει δὲ φῶς αἰνολαμπές, σίνος·
    κακοῦ δὲ χαλκοῦ τρόπον,
    τρίβῳ τε καὶ προσβολαῖς   365
    μελαμπαγὴς πέλει
    δικαιωθείς, ἐπεὶ
διώκει παῖς *ποτανὸν ὄρνιν,
πόλει πρόστριμμ' ἄφερτον ἐνθείς.
λιτᾶν δ' ἀκούει μὲν οὖτις θεῶν·   370
τὸν δ' ἐπίστροφον τῶνδε φῶτ' ἄδικον καθαιρεῖ.
    οἷος καὶ Πάρις, ἐλθὼν
    εἰς δόμον τὸν Ἀτρειδᾶν,   (400)
ᾔσχυνε ξενίαν τράπεζαν κλοπαῖσι γυναικός.   374
    λιποῦσα δ' ἀστοῖσιν ἀσπίστορας   στρ. β'.
‖κλόνους τε καὶ λογχίμους ναυβάτας ὁπλισμούς,
ἄγουσά τ' ἀντίφερνον Ἰλίῳ φθοράν,

†δυοῖν μί' Ἄτα πολέοιν μέτοικος†,
  βέβακε ῥίμφα διὰ πυλᾶν,
 ἄτλητα τλᾶσα· πολλὰ δ' ἔστενον
τόδ' ἐννέποντες δόμων προφῆται·   380
"Ἰὼ ἰὼ δῶμα, δῶμα καὶ πρόμοι·
ἰὼ λέχος καὶ στίβοι φιλάνορες.
πάρεστι *σῖγ' ἀτίμως ἀλοιδόρως
  ἄδισθ' ὅσ' ἦν ἀφειμένων.*
    πόθῳ δ' ὑπερποντίας   385
  φάσμα δόξει δόμων ἀνάσσειν·
   εὐμόρφων δὲ κολοσσῶν
  ‖ἔχθεται χάρις, ἔρρει δ'
‖ὀφθαλμῶν ἐν ἀχηνίαις ἀνδρὶ πᾶσ' Ἀφροδίτα.
   ὀνειρόφαντοι δὲ πενθήμονες   ἀντ. β'.
πάρεισι δόξαι φέρουσαι χάριν ματαίαν.   391
 μάταν γάρ, εὖτ' ἂν ἐσθλά τις δοκῶν ὁρᾶν
  †φίλοισιν εὕδῃ ξυνὼν ὀνείροις,†
    παραλλάξασα διὰ χερῶν
  βέβακεν ὄψις, οὐ μεθύστερον
πτεροῖς *ὀπαδοῦσ' ὕπνου κελεύθοις."   395
τὰ μὲν κατ' οἴκους *ἐφεστίους ἄχη
τάδ' ἐστί, καὶ τῶνδ' *ὑπερβολὴν ἔχει.*
τὸ πᾶν δ' ἀφ' Ἑλλάδος *γᾶς ξυνορμένοις
    πένθεια τλησικάρδιος
    δόμων ἑκάστου πρέπει.   400
  πολλὰ γοῦν θιγγάνει πρὸς ἧπαρ·
    τοὺς μὲν γάρ ποτε πέμψας
    οἶδεν, ἀντὶ δὲ φωτῶν
τεύχη καὶ σποδὸς εἰς ἑκάστου δόμους ἀφικνεῖται.
   ὁ χρυσαμοιβὸς δ' Ἄρης σωμάτων, στρ. γ'.
   καὶ ταλαντοῦχος ἐν μάχῃ δορός,   406
    πυρωθὲν ἐξ Ἰλίου
    φίλοισι πέμπει βαρὺ

ψῆγμα δυσδάκρυτον, ἀντήνορος σποδοῦ γεμίζων λέβητας
εὐθέτου.

στένουσι δ' εὖ λέγοντες ἄν-   410
δρα τὸν μὲν ὡς μάχης ἴδρις·
τὸν δ' ἐν φοναῖς καλῶς πεσόντ' ἀλ-
λοτρίας*διαὶ γυναικός·
τὰ δὲ σῖγά τις βαΰζει·
φθονερὸν δ' ὑπ' ἄλγος ἕρπει   415 (450)
προδίκοις Ἀτρείδαις.
οἱ δ' αὐτοῦ περὶ τεῖχος
θήκας Ἰλιάδος γᾶς
*ἔμμορφοι κατέχουσιν· ἐχθρὰ δ' ἔχοντας ἔκρυψεν.
βαρεῖα δ' ἀστῶν φάτις ξὺν κότῳ,   ἀντ. γ'.
δημοκράντου δ' ἀρᾶς τίνει χρέος.   421
μένει δ' ἀκοῦσαί τί μου
μέριμνα νυκτηρεφές.
τῶν πολυκτόνων γὰρ οὐκ ἄσκοποι θεοί· κελαιναὶ δ' Ἐρινύες
χρόνῳ
τυχηρὸν ὄντ' ἄνευ δίκας   425
*παλιντυχεῖ τριβᾷ βίου
*κτίζουσ' ἀμαυρόν, ἐν δ' ἀΐστοις
τελέθοντος οὔτις ἀλκά.
τὸ δ' *ὑπερκόπως κλύειν εὖ
βαρύ· βάλλεται γὰρ ὄσσοις   430
Διόθεν κεραυνός.
κρίνω δ' ἄφθονον ὄλβον.
μήτ' εἴην πτολιπόρθης,
μήτ' οὖν αὐτὸς ἁλοὺς ὑπ' ἄλλων βίον κατίδοιμι.
πυρὸς δ' ὑπ' εὐαγγέλου   ἐπῳδ.
πόλιν διήκει θοὰ   436
βάξις· εἰ δ' ἐτητύμως,
τίς οἶδεν, *εἴτε θεῖόν ἐστί *τι ψύθος;
τίς ὧδε παιδνὸς ἢ φρενῶν κεκομμένος,

φλογὸς παραγγέλμασιν   440
νέοις πυρωθέντα καρδίαν ἔπειτ'
ἀλλαγᾷ λόγου καμεῖν;
γυναικὸς αἰχμᾷ πρέπει
πρὸ τοῦ φανέντος χάριν ξυναινέσαι.
πιθανὸς ἄγαν ὁ θῆλυς ὅρος ἐπινέμεται   445
ταχύπορος· ἀλλὰ ταχύμορον
γυναικογήρυτον ὄλλυται κλέος.
τάχ' εἰσόμεσθα λαμπάδων φαεσφόρων
φρυκτωριῶν τε καὶ πυρὸς παραλλαγάς,
εἴτ' οὖν ἀληθεῖς, εἴτ' ὀνειράτων δίκην   450
τερπνὸν τόδ' ἐλθὸν φῶς ἐφήλωσεν φρένας.
κήρυκ' ἀπ' ἀκτῆς τόνδ' ὁρῶ κατάσκιον
κλάδοις ἐλαίας· μαρτυρεῖ δέ μοι κάσις
πηλοῦ ξύνουρος, διψία κόνις, τάδε,
ὡς οὔτ' ἄναυδος οὔτε σοι δαίων φλόγα   455
ὕλης ὀρείας σημανεῖ καπνῷ πυρός,
ἀλλ' ἢ τὸ χαίρειν μᾶλλον ἐκβάξει λέγων—
τὸν ἀντίον δὲ τοῖσδ' ἀποστέργω λόγον·
εὖ γὰρ πρὸς εὖ φανεῖσι προσθήκη πέλοι.   (500)
ὅστις τάδ' ἄλλως τῇδ' ἐπεύχεται πόλει,   460
αὐτὸς φρενῶν καρποῖτο τὴν ἁμαρτίαν.

ΚΗΡΥΞ.

ἰὼ πατρῷον οὖδας Ἀργείας χθονός·
δεκάτῳ σε φέγγει τῷδ' ἀφικόμην ἔτους,
πολλῶν ῥαγεισῶν ἐλπίδων, μιᾶς τυχών.
οὐ γάρ ποτ' ηὔχουν τῇδ' ἐν Ἀργείᾳ χθονὶ   465
θανὼν μεθέξειν φιλτάτου τάφου μέρος.
νῦν χαῖρε μὲν χθών, χαῖρε δ' ἡλίου φάος,
ὕπατός τε χώρας Ζεύς, ὁ Πύθιός τ' ἄναξ,
τόξοις ἰάπτων μηκέτ' εἰς ἡμᾶς βέλη.

18   ΑΙΣΧΥΛΟΥ

ἅλις παρὰ Σκάμανδρον *ἦσθ' ἀνάρσιος·   470
νῦν δ' αὖτε σωτὴρ ἴσθι *καὶ παιώνιος,*
ἄναξ Ἄπολλον. τούς τ' ἀγωνίους θεοὺς
πάντας προσαυδῶ, τόν τ' ἐμὸν τιμάορον
Ἑρμῆν, φίλον κήρυκα, κηρύκων σέβας,
ἥρως τε τοὺς πέμψαντας, εὐμενεῖς πάλιν   475
στρατὸν δέχεσθαι τὸν λελειμμένον δορός.
ἰὼ μέλαθρα βασιλέων, φίλαι στέγαι,
σεμνοί τε θᾶκοι, δαίμονές τ' ἀντήλιοι·
*εἴ που πάλαι, φαιδροῖσι τοισίδ' ὄμμασι
δέξασθε κόσμῳ βασιλέα πολλῷ χρόνῳ.   480
ἥκει γὰρ ὑμῖν φῶς ἐν εὐφρόνῃ φέρων
καὶ τοῖσδ' ἅπασι κοινὸν Ἀγαμέμνων ἄναξ.
ἀλλ' εὖ νιν ἀσπάσασθε, καὶ γὰρ οὖν πρέπει,
Τροίαν κατασκάψαντα τοῦ δικηφόρου
Διὸς μακέλλῃ, τῇ κατείργασται πέδον.   485
βωμοὶ δ' ἄϊστοι καὶ θεῶν ἱδρύματα,
καὶ σπέρμα πάσης ἐξαπόλλυται χθονός.
τοιόνδε Τροίᾳ περιβαλὼν ζευκτήριον
ἄναξ Ἀτρείδης πρέσβυς εὐδαίμων ἀνὴρ
ἥκει, τίεσθαι δ' ἀξιώτατος βροτῶν   490
τῶν νῦν· Πάρις γὰρ οὔτε συντελὴς πόλις
ἐξεύχεται τὸ δρᾶμα τοῦ πάθους πλέον·
ὀφλὼν γὰρ ἁρπαγῆς τε καὶ κλοπῆς δίκην
τοῦ ῥυσίου θ' ἥμαρτε, καὶ πανώλεθρον
αὐτόχθονον πατρῷον ἔθρισεν δόμον·   495
διπλᾶ δ' ἔτισαν Πριαμίδαι θάμάρτια.
ΧΟ.   κῆρυξ Ἀχαιῶν, χαῖρε, τῶν ἀπὸ στρατοῦ.
ΚΗ.   χαίρω· τεθνάναι δ' οὐκ ἔτ' ἀντερῶ θεοῖς.
ΧΟ.   ἔρως πατρῴας τῆσδε γῆς σ' ἐγύμνασεν;
ΚΗ.   ὥστ' ἐνδακρύειν γ' ὄμμασιν χαρᾶς ὕπο.   500
ΧΟ.   τερπνῆς ἄρ' ἦτε τῆσδ' ἐπήβολοι νόσου.
ΚΗ.   πῶς δή; διδαχθεὶς τοῦδε δεσπόσω λόγου.

ΑΓΑΜΕΜΝΩΝ. 19

ΧΟ. τῶν ἀντερώντων ἱμέρῳ *πεπληγμένοι.
ΚΗ. ποθεῖν ποθοῦντα τήνδε γῆν στρατὸν λέγεις;
ΧΟ. ὡς πόλλ' ἀμαυρᾶς ἐκ φρενός*μ' ἀναστενειν. 505
ΚΗ. πόθεν τὸ δύσφρον τοῦτ' ἐπῆν στύγος *πόλει;
ΧΟ. πάλαι τὸ σιγᾶν φάρμακον βλάβης ἔχω.
ΚΗ. καὶ πῶς; ἀπόντων κοιράνων ἔτρεις τινάς;
ΧΟ. ὡς νῦν τὸ σὸν δή, καὶ θανεῖν πολλὴ χάρις. (550)
ΚΗ. εὖ γὰρ πέπρακται. ταῦτα δ' ἐν πολλῷ χρόνῳ
τὰ μέν τις *ἂν λέξειεν εὐπετῶς ἔχειν, 511
τὰ δ' αὖτε κἀπίμομφα. τίς δέ, πλὴν θεῶν,
ἅπαντ' ἀπήμων τὸν δι' αἰῶνος χρόνον;
μόχθους γὰρ εἰ λέγοιμι καὶ δυσαυλίας,
σπαρνὰς παρήξεις καὶ κακοστρώτους,—τί δ' οὐ
στένοντες, οὐ *λάσκοντες ἤματος μέρος; 516
τὰ δ' αὖτε χέρσῳ, καὶ προσῆν πλέον στύγος·
εὐναὶ γὰρ ἦσαν δηΐων πρὸς τείχεσιν·
ἐξ οὐρανοῦ γὰρ κἀπὸ γῆς λειμώνιαι
δρόσοι κατεψάκαζον, ἔμπεδον σίνος 520
ἐσθημάτων, τιθέντες ἔνθηρον τρίχα.
χειμῶνα δ' εἰ λέγοι τις οἰωνοκτόνον,
οἷον παρεῖχ' ἄφερτον Ἰδαία χιών,
ἢ θάλπος, εὖτε πόντος ἐν μεσημβριναῖς
κοίταις ἀκύμων νηνέμοις εὕδοι πεσών— 525
τί ταῦτα πενθεῖν δεῖ; παροίχεται πόνος·
παροίχεται δὲ τοῖσι μὲν τεθνηκόσιν
τὸ μήποτ' αὖθις μηδ' ἀναστῆναι μέλειν.
τί τοὺς ἀναλωθέντας ἐν ψήφῳ λέγειν,
τὸν ζῶντα δ' ἀλγεῖν χρὴ τύχης παλιγκότου; 530
†τούτων ἐπαινῶ μηδὲ φροντίζειν ἔτι,†
καὶ πολλὰ χαίρειν ξυμφοραῖς καταξιῶ.
ἡμῖν δὲ τοῖς λοιποῖσιν Ἀργείων στρατοῦ
νικᾷ τὸ κέρδος, πῆμα δ' οὐκ ἀντιρρέπει·
ὡς κομπάσαι τῷδ' εἰκὸς ἡλίου φάει,
ὑπὲρ θαλάσσης καὶ χθονὸς ποτωμένοις· 535

2—2

20   ΑΙΣΧΥΛΟΥ

" Τροίαν ἑλόντες δήποτ' Ἀργείων στόλος
θεοῖς λάφυρα ταῦτα τοῖς καθ' Ἑλλάδα
δόμοις ἐπασσάλευσαν ἀρχαῖον γάνος."
τοιαῦτα χρὴ κλύοντας εὐλογεῖν πόλιν
καὶ τοὺς στρατηγούς· καὶ χάρις τιμήσεται   540
Διὸς τάδ' ἐκπράξασα. πάντ' ἔχεις λόγον.

ΧΟ. νικώμενος λόγοισιν οὐκ ἀναίνομαι·
ἀεὶ γὰρ ἡβᾷ τοῖς γέρουσιν εὖ μαθεῖν.
δόμοις δὲ ταῦτα καὶ Κλυταιμνήστρᾳ μέλειν
εἰκὸς μάλιστα, ξὺν δὲ πλουτίζειν ἐμέ.   545

ΚΛ. ἀνωλόλυξα μὲν πάλαι χαρᾶς ὕπο,
ὅτ' ἦλθ' ὁ πρῶτος νύχιος ἄγγελος πυρὸς
φράζων ἅλωσιν Ἰλίου τ' ἀνάστασιν·
καί τίς μ' ἐνίπτων εἶπε, Φρυκτωρῶν διὰ
πεισθεῖσα Τροίαν νῦν πεπορθῆσθαι δοκεῖς;   550
ἦ κάρτα πρὸς γυναικὸς αἴρεσθαι κέαρ.
λόγοις τοιούτοις πλαγκτὸς οὖσ' ἐφαινόμην·
ὅμως δ' ἔθυον· καὶ γυναικείῳ νόμῳ
ὀλολυγμὸν ἄλλος ἄλλοθεν κατὰ πτόλιν
ἔλασκον εὐφημοῦντες ἐν θεῶν ἕδραις   555
θυηφάγον κοιμῶντες εὐώδη φλόγα.
καὶ νῦν τὰ μάσσω μὲν τί δεῖ σ' ἐμοὶ λέγειν;
ἄνακτος αὐτοῦ πάντα πεύσομαι λόγον.
ὅπως δ' ἄριστα τὸν ἐμὸν αἰδοῖον πόσιν   (600)
σπεύσω πάλιν μολόντα δέξασθαι· τί γὰρ   560
γυναικὶ τούτου φέγγος ἥδιον δρακεῖν,
ἀπὸ στρατείας ἄνδρα σώσαντος θεοῦ,
πύλας ἀνοῖξαι;—ταῦτ' ἀπάγγειλον πόσει·
ἥκειν ὅπως *μάλιστ' ἐράσμιον πόλει,
†ὅστις κατ' Ἄργος πρῶτα μὲν μέλλοι λεὼν†
‖ *πιστόν, γυναῖκα δ' ἐν δόμοις *εὑρεῖν μολὼν   565
οἵανπερ οὖν ἔλειπε, δωμάτων κύνα
ἐσθλὴν ἐκείνῳ, πολεμίαν τοῖς δύσφροσιν,
καὶ τἄλλ' ὁμοίαν πάντα, σημαντήριον

ΑΓΑΜΕΜΝΩΝ. 21

οὐδὲν διαφθείρασαν ἐν μήκει χρόνου.
*οὐκ οἶδα τέρψιν οὐδ' ἐπίψογον φάτιν   570
ἄλλου πρὸς ἀνδρὸς μᾶλλον ἢ χαλκοῦ βαφάς.
τοιόσδ' ὁ κόμπος, τῆς ἀληθείας γέμων,
οὐκ αἰσχρὸς ὡς γυναικὶ γενναίᾳ λακεῖν.

ΧΟ. αὕτη μὲν οὕτως εἶπε μανθάνοντί σοι,
τοροῖσιν ἑρμηνεῦσιν εὐπρεπῶς λόγον.   575
σὺ δ' εἰπέ, κῆρυξ, Μενέλεων δὲ πεύθομαι,
εἰ νόστιμός *τε καὶ σεσωσμένος πάλιν
ἥξει ξὺν ὑμῖν, τῆσδε γῆς φίλον κράτος.

ΚΗ. οὐκ ἔσθ' ὅπως λέξαιμι τὰ ψευδῆ καλὰ
ἐς τὸν πολὺν φίλοισι καρποῦσθαι χρόνον.   580

ΧΟ. πῶς δῆτ' ἂν εἰπὼν κεδνὰ τἀληθῆ *τύχοις;
σχισθέντα δ' οὐκ εὔκρυπτα γίγνεται τάδε.

ΚΗ. *ἀνὴρ ἄφαντος ἐξ Ἀχαιϊκοῦ στρατοῦ,
αὐτός τε καὶ τὸ πλοῖον. οὐ ψευδῆ λέγω.

ΧΟ. πότερον ἀναχθεὶς ἐμφανῶς ἐξ Ἰλίου,   585
ἢ χεῖμα, κοινὸν ἄχθος, ἥρπασε στρατοῦ;

ΚΗ. ἔκυρσας ὥστε τοξότης ἄκρος σκοποῦ,
μακρὸν δὲ πῆμα συντόμως ἐφημίσω.

ΧΟ. πότερα γὰρ αὐτοῦ ζῶντος ἢ τεθνηκότος
φάτις πρὸς ἄλλων ναυτίλων ἐκλῄζετο;   590

ΚΗ. οὐκ οἶδεν οὐδεὶς ὥστ' ἀπαγγεῖλαι τορῶς
πλὴν τοῦ τρέφοντος Ἡλίου χθονὸς φύσιν.

ΧΟ. πῶς γὰρ λέγεις χειμῶνα ναυτικῷ στρατῷ
ἐλθεῖν τελευτῆσαί τε δαιμόνων κότῳ;

ΚΗ. εὔφημον ἦμαρ οὐ πρέπει κακαγγέλῳ   595
γλώσσῃ μιαίνειν· χωρὶς ἡ τιμὴ θεῶν.
ὅταν δ' ἀπευκτὰ πήματ' ἄγγελος πόλει
στυγνῷ προσώπῳ πτωσίμου στρατοῦ φέρῃ,—
πόλει μὲν ἕλκος ἓν τὸ δήμιον τυχεῖν,
πολλοὺς δὲ πολλῶν ἐξαγισθέντας δόμων   600
ἄνδρας διπλῇ μάστιγι, τὴν Ἄρης φιλεῖ,

δίλογχον ἄτην, φοινίαν ξυνωρίδα,—
τοιῶνδε μέντοι πημάτων*σεσαγμένον
πρέπει λέγειν παιᾶνα τόνδ' Ἐρινύων·
σωτηρίων δὲ πραγμάτων εὐάγγελον   605
ἥκοντα πρὸς χαίρουσαν εὐεστοῖ πόλιν—
πῶς κεδνὰ τοῖς κακοῖσι συμμίξω, λέγων
χειμῶν'*'Αχαιοῖς οὐκ ἀμήνιτον*θεῶν;
ξυνώμοσαν γάρ, ὄντες ἔχθιστοι τὸ πρίν,   (650)
Πῦρ καὶ Θάλασσα, καὶ τὰ πίστ' ἐδειξάτην   610
φθείροντε τὸν δύστηνον 'Αργείων στρατόν.
ἐν νυκτὶ δυσκύμαντα δ' ὠρώρει κακά·
ναῦς γὰρ πρὸς ἀλλήλαισι Θρήκιαι πνοαὶ
ἤρεικον· αἱ δὲ κεροτυπούμεναι βίᾳ
χειμῶνι, *τυφῷ ξὺν ζάλῃ τ' ὀμβροκτύπῳ,   615
ᾤχοντ' ἄφαντοι ποιμένος κακοῦ στρόβῳ.
ἐπεὶ δ' ἀνῆλθε λαμπρὸν ἡλίου φάος,
ὁρῶμεν ἀνθοῦν πέλαγος Αἰγαῖον νεκροῖς
ἀνδρῶν 'Αχαιῶν ναυτικῶν τ' ἐρειπίων.
ἡμᾶς γε μὲν δὴ ναῦν τ', ἀκήρατον σκάφος,   620
ἤτοι τις ἐξέκλεψεν ἢ 'ξῃτήσατο,
θεός τις, οὐκ ἄνθρωπος, οἴακος θιγών.
Τύχη δὲ σωτὴρ ναῦν θέλουσ' ἐφέζετο,
ὡς μήτ' ἐν ὅρμῳ κύματος ζάλην ἔχειν,
μήτ' ἐξοκεῖλαι πρὸς κραταίλεων χθόνα.   625
ἔπειτα δ' ἅδην πόντιον πεφευγότες,
λευκὸν κατ' ἦμαρ, οὐ πεποιθότες τύχῃ,
ἐβουκολοῦμεν φροντίσιν νέον πάθος
στρατοῦ καμόντος καὶ κακῶς σποδουμένου.
καὶ νῦν ἐκείνων εἴ τις ἐστὶν ἐμπνέων,   630
λέγουσιν ἡμᾶς ὡς ὀλωλότας· τί μήν;
ἡμεῖς τ' ἐκείνους ταῦτ' ἔχειν δοξάζομεν.
γένοιτο δ' ὡς ἄριστα· Μενέλεων γὰρ οὖν
πρῶτόν τε καὶ μάλιστα προσδόκα μολεῖν·

εἰ δ' οὖν τις ἀκτὶς ἡλίου νιν ἱστορεῖ		635
καὶ ζῶντα καὶ βλέποντα, μηχαναῖς Διὸς
οὔπω θέλοντος ἐξαναλῶσαι γένος,
ἐλπίς τις αὐτὸν πρὸς δόμους ἥξειν πάλιν.
τοσαῦτ' ἀκούσας ἴσθι τἀληθῆ κλύων.		639

ΧΟ.	τίς ποτ' ὠνόμαζεν ὧδ' ἐς τὸ πᾶν ἐτητύμως— στρ. α'.
μή τις, ὅντιν' οὐχ ὁρῶμεν,*προνοίαισι τοῦ πεπρωμένου
		γλῶσσαν ἐν τύχᾳ νέμων;—
		τὰν δορίγαμβρον ἀμφινεικῆ θ'
		Ἑλέναν; ἐπεὶ πρεπόντως
		ἑλέναυς, ἕλανδρος, ἑλέπτολις,		645
		ἐκ τῶν ἀβροτίμων
		προκαλυμμάτων ἔπλευσε
		Ζεφύρου γίγαντος αὔρᾳ,
		πολύανδροί τε φεράσπιδες κυναγοὶ
			κατ' ἴχνος πλάταν ἄφαντον		650
		κελσάντων Σιμόεντος ἀκτὰς ἐπ' ἀεξιφύλλους
			δι' ἔριν αἱματόεσσαν.		[(700)
Ἰλίῳ δὲ κῆδος ὀρθώνυμον τελεσσίφρων		ἀντ. α'.
μῆνις ἤλασεν, τραπέζας*ἀτίμωσιν ὑστέρῳ χρόνῳ
		καὶ ξυνεστίου Διὸς		655
		πρασσομένα τὸ νυμφότιμον
		μέλος ἐκφάτως τίοντας,
		νέον ὑμέν', ὃς τότ' ἐπέρρεπε
		γαμβροῖσιν ἀείδειν.
		μεταμανθάνουσα δ' ὕμνον		660
		Πριάμου πόλις γεραιὰ
		πολύθρηνον μέγα που στένει, κικλησκου-
			σα Πάριν τὸν αἰνόλεκτρον,
		πάμπροσθ' ἢ πολύθρηνον αἰῶνα *διαὶ πολιτᾶν
			μέλεον αἷμ' ἀνατλᾶσα.		665
			ἔθρεψεν δὲ *λέοντος ἶν-		στρ. β'.

ιν* δόμοις ἀγάλακτον οὕτως ἀνὴρ φιλόμαστον *δ᾽,
 ἐν βιότου προτελείοις
 ἅμερον, εὐφιλόπαιδά *τε καὶ γεραροῖς ἐπίχαρτον.
 πολέα δ᾽ ἔσχ᾽ ἐν ἀγκάλαις   670
 νεοτρόφου τέκνου δίκαν,
φαιδρωπὸς ποτὶ χεῖρα, σαίνων τε γαστρὸς ἀνάγκαις.
 χρονισθεὶς δ᾽ ἀπέδειξεν *ἦ-   ἀντ. β᾽.
θος τὸ πρὸς τοκέων· χάριν γὰρ τροφεῦσιν ἀμείβων
 μηλοφόνοις *θανάτοισιν   675
δαῖτ᾽ ἀκέλευστος ἔτευξεν, *ἐν αἵμασι* δ᾽ οἶκος ἐφύρθη,
 ἄμαχον ἄλγος οἰκέταις,
 μέγα σίνος πολυκτόνον·
θείας ὧδ᾽ ἱερεύς τις ἄτας δόμοις *προσεθρέφθη.
πάραυτα δ᾽ ἐλθεῖν ἐς Ἰλίου πόλιν λέγοιμ᾽ ἂν στρ. γ᾽.
φρόνημα μὲν νηνέμου γαλάνας,   681
 ἀκασκαῖον δ᾽ ἄγαλμα πλούτου,
 μαλθακὸν ὀμμάτων βέλος,
 δηξίθυμον ἔρωτος ἄνθος·   684
παρακλίνασ᾽ ἐπέκρανεν δὲ γάμου πικρὰς τελευτάς,
δύσεδρος καὶ δυσόμιλος συμένα Πριαμίδαισιν
 πομπᾷ Διὸς ξενίου
 νυμφόκλαυτος Ἐρινύς.
παλαίφατος δ᾽ ἐν βροτοῖς γέρων λόγος τέτυκται, ἀντ.γ᾽.
μέγαν τελεσθέντα φωτὸς ὄλβον   [(750)
 τεκνοῦσθαι, μηδ᾽ ἄπαιδα θνήσκειν·   691
 ἐκ δ᾽ ἀγαθᾶς τύχας γένει
 βλαστάνειν ἀκόρεστον οἰζύν.
δίχα δ᾽ ἄλλων μονόφρων εἰμί· τὸ δυσσεβὲς γὰρ ἔργον
μέτα μὲν πλείονα τίκτει, σφετέρᾳ δ᾽ εἰκότα γέννᾳ. 695
 οἴκων γὰρ εὐθυδίκων
 καλλίπαις πότμος αἰεί.
φιλεῖ δὲ τίκτειν Ὕβρις μὲν παλαιὰ νεά- στρ. δ᾽.
ζουσαν *ἔν γε τοῖς* κακοῖς βροτῶν

Ὕβριν τότ᾽ ἢ τόθ᾽, *ὅτε τὸ κύριον μόλῃ·　700
　νέα δ᾽ ἔφυσεν Κόρον,
δαίμονά *τ᾽ ἄμαχον,* ἀπόλεμον,
ἀνίερον Θράσος, μελαίνας μελάθροισιν Ἄτας
　*εἰδομένας τοκεῦσιν.
Δίκα δὲ λάμπει μὲν ἐν δυσκάπνοις δώμασιν,　ἀντ. δ΄.
　τὸν δ᾽ ἐναίσιμον τίει βίον.　706
τὰ χρυσόπαστα δ᾽ *ἔδεθλα σὺν πίνῳ χερῶν
　‖ *παλιντρόποισιν λιποῦσ᾽
　‖ ὄμμασιν ὅσια *προσέμολε,
δύναμιν οὐ σέβουσα πλούτου παράσημον αἴνῳ.　710
　πᾶν δ᾽ ἐπὶ τέρμα νωμᾷ.
*λέγε δή, βασιλεῦ, Τροίας πτολίπορθ᾽,
᾽Ατρέως γένεθλον, πῶς σε προσείπω,
πῶς *δὲ σεβίζω μήθ᾽ ὑπεράρας
μήθ᾽ ὑποκάμψας καιρὸν χάριτος·　715
‖ *τοῦ τε γὰρ* εἶναι πολλοὶ τὸ δοκεῖν
　προτίουσι δίκην παραβάντες,
τῷ δυσπραγοῦντί τ᾽ ἐπιστενάχειν
πᾶς τις ἕτοιμος· δῆγμα δὲ λύπης
　οὐδὲν ἐφ᾽ ἧπαρ προσικνεῖται·　720
καὶ ξυγχαίρουσιν ὁμοιοπρεπεῖς
ἀγέλαστα πρόσωπα βιαζόμενοι
†τὸν μὴ καθορῶντ᾽ ἀπατῶσιν.†
ὅστις δ᾽ ἀγαθὸς προβατογνώμων,
οὐκ ἔστι λαθεῖν ὄμματα φωτὸς
τὰ δοκοῦντ᾽ εὔφρονος ἐκ διανοίας　725
　ὑδαρεῖ σαίνειν φιλότητι.
σὺ δέ μοι τότε μέν, στέλλων στρατιὰν
῾Ελένης ἕνεκ᾽, οὐ γάρ *σ᾽ ἐπικεύσω,　(800)
κάρτ᾽ ἀπομούσως ἦσθα γεγραμμένος
οὐδ᾽ εὖ πραπίδων οἴακα νέμων,　730

26 ΑΙΣΧΥΛΟΥ

θράσος *ἐκ θυσιῶν*
ἀνδράσι θνήσκουσι κομίζων·
νῦν δ᾽ οὐκ ἀπ᾽ ἄκρας φρενὸς οὐδ᾽ ἀφίλως
†αἰνῶ σε λέγων,†
εὔφρων πόνος εὖ τελέσασιν.
γνώσει δὲ χρόνῳ διαπευθόμενος   735
τόν τε δικαίως καὶ τὸν ἀκαίρως
†σέθεν οἰχομένου†
πόλιν οἰκουροῦντα πολιτῶν.

ΑΓΑΜΕΜΝΩΝ.

πρῶτον μὲν Ἄργος καὶ θεοὺς ἐγχωρίους
δίκη προσειπεῖν, τοὺς ἐμοὶ μεταιτίους
νόστου, δικαίων θ᾽ ὧν ἐπραξάμην πόλιν   740
Πριάμου· δίκας γὰρ οὐκ ἀπὸ γλώσσης θεοὶ
*κρίνοντες, ἀνδροθνῆτας Ἰλίου φθοράς,
εἰς αἱματηρὸν τεῦχος οὐ διχορρόπως
ψήφους ἔθεντο· τῷ δ᾽ ἐναντίῳ κύτει
ἐλπὶς προσῄει χειρὸς οὐ πληρουμένῳ.   745
καπνῷ δ᾽ ἀλοῦσα νῦν ἔτ᾽ εὔσημος πόλις.
ἄτης *θυηλαὶ ζῶσι· συνθνήσκουσα δὲ
σποδὸς προπέμπει πίονας πλούτου πνοάς.
τούτων θεοῖσι χρὴ πολύμνηστον χάριν
τίνειν· ἐπείπερ καὶ πάγας ὑπερκότους   750
*ἐφραξάμεσθα, καὶ γυναικὸς εἵνεκα
πόλιν διημάθυνεν Ἀργεῖον δάκος,
ἵππου νεοσσός, ἀσπιδοστρόφος λεώς,
πήδημ᾽ ὀρούσας ἀμφὶ Πλειάδων δύσιν·
ὑπερθορὼν δὲ πύργον ὠμηστὴς λέων   755
ἄδην ἔλειξεν αἵματος τυραννικοῦ.
θεοῖς μὲν ἐξέτεινα φροίμιον τόδε·
τὰ δ᾽ ἐς τὸ σὸν φρόνημα, μέμνημαι κλύων,

καὶ φημὶ ταὐτὰ καὶ ξυνήγορόν μ' ἔχεις.
παύροις γὰρ ἀνδρῶν ἐστι συγγενὲς τόδε,　760
φίλον τὸν εὐτυχοῦντ' ἄνευ φθόνου σέβειν.
δύσφρων γὰρ ἰὸς *καρδίᾳ προσήμενος
ἄχθος διπλοΐζει τῷ πεπαμένῳ νόσον·
τοῖς τ' αὐτὸς αὐτοῦ πήμασιν βαρύνεται,
καὶ τὸν θυραῖον ὄλβον εἰσορῶν στένει.　765
εἰδὼς λέγοιμ' ἄν· εὖ γὰρ ἐξεπίσταμαι
ὁμιλίας κάτοπτρον, εἴδωλον σκιᾶς
†ἀνδρῶν φανέντας τῶν ξυνορμένων τινὰς†
δοκοῦντας εἶναι κάρτα πρευμενεῖς ἐμοί.
μόνος δ' Ὀδυσσεύς, ὅσπερ οὐχ ἑκὼν ἔπλει,
ζευχθεὶς ἕτοιμος ἦν ἐμοὶ σειραφόρος·　770
εἴτ' οὖν θανόντος εἴτε καὶ ζῶντος πέρι
λέγω. τὰ δ' ἄλλα πρὸς πόλιν τε καὶ θεούς,
κοινοὺς ἀγῶνας θέντες, ἐν πανηγύρει
βουλευσόμεσθα. καὶ τὸ μὲν καλῶς ἔχον
ὅπως χρονίζον εὖ μενεῖ βουλευτέον·　775
ὅτῳ δὲ καὶ δεῖ φαρμάκων παιωνίων,
ἤτοι κέαντες ἢ τεμόντες εὐφρόνως
πειρασόμεσθα *πῆμ' ἀποστρέψαι νόσου.*　(850)
νῦν δ' ἐς μέλαθρα καὶ δόμους ἐφεστίους
ἐλθὼν θεοῖσι πρῶτα δεξιώσομαι,　780
οἵπερ πρόσω πέμψαντες ἤγαγον πάλιν.
νίκη δ' ἐπείπερ ἕσπετ', ἐμπέδως μένοι.

ΚΛ.　Ἄνδρες πολῖται, πρέσβος Ἀργείων τόδε,
οὐκ αἰσχυνοῦμαι τοὺς φιλάνορας τρόπους
λέξαι πρὸς ὑμᾶς· ἐν χρόνῳ δ' ἀποφθίνει　785
τὸ τάρβος ἀνθρώποισιν. οὐκ ἄλλων πάρα
μαθοῦσ' ἐμαυτῆς δύσφορον λέξω βίον
τοσόνδ', ὅσονπερ οὗτος ἦν ὑπ' Ἰλίῳ.
τὸ μὲν γυναῖκα πρῶτον ἄρσενος δίχα
ἧσθαι δόμοις ἔρημον, ἔκπαγλον κακόν,　790
πολλὰς κλύουσαν *κληδόνας παλιγκότους·

καὶ τὸν μὲν ἥκειν, τὸν δ᾽ ἐπεισφέρειν κακοῦ
κάκιον ἄλλο πῆμα, λάσκοντας δόμοις.
καὶ τραυμάτων μὲν εἰ τόσων ἐτύγχανεν
ἀνὴρ ὅδ᾽, ὡς πρὸς οἶκον ὠχετεύετο
φάτις, τέτρωται δικτύου πλέω λέγειν.   795
εἰ δ᾽ ἦν τεθνηκώς, ὡς *ἐπλήθυον λόγοι,
τρισώματος τὰν Γηρυὼν ὁ δεύτερος
χθονὸς τρίμοιρον χλαῖναν ἐξηύχει *λαβεῖν,   800
ἅπαξ ἑκάστῳ κατθανὼν μορφώματι.
τοιῶνδ᾽ ἕκατι κληδόνων παλιγκότων
πολλὰς ἄνωθεν ἀρτάνας ἐμῆς δέρης
ἔλυσαν ἄλλοι πρὸς βίαν λελημμένης.
ἐκ τῶνδέ τοι παῖς ἐνθάδ᾽ οὐ παραστατεῖ,   805
ἐμῶν τε καὶ σῶν κύριος πιστευμάτων,
ὡς χρῆν, Ὀρέστης· μηδὲ θαυμάσῃς τόδε·
τρέφει γὰρ αὐτὸν εὐμενὴς δορύξενος
Στρόφιος ὁ Φωκεύς, ἀμφίλεκτα πήματα
ἐμοὶ προφωνῶν, τόν θ᾽ ὑπ᾽ Ἰλίῳ σέθεν   810
κίνδυνον, εἴ τε δημόθρους ἀναρχία
βουλὴν καταρρίψειεν, ὥστε σύγγονον
βροτοῖσι τὸν πεσόντα λακτίσαι πλέον.
τοιάδε μέν τοι σκῆψις οὐ δόλον φέρει.
ἔμοιγε μὲν δὴ κλαυμάτων ἐπίσσυτοι   815
πηγαὶ κατεσβήκασιν, οὐδ᾽ ἔνι σταγών.
ἐν ὀψικοίτοις δ᾽ ὄμμασιν βλάβας ἔχω,
τὰς ἀμφί σοι κλαίουσα λαμπτηρουχίας
ἀτημελήτους αἰέν. ἐν δ᾽ ὀνείρασιν
λεπταῖς ὑπαὶ κώνωπος ἐξηγειρόμην   820
ῥιπαῖσι θωΰσσοντος, ἀμφί σοι πάθη
ὁρῶσα πλείω τοῦ ξυνεύδοντος χρόνου.
νῦν, ταῦτα πάντα τλᾶσ᾽, ἀπενθήτῳ φρενὶ
λέγοιμ᾽ ἂν ἄνδρα τόνδε τῶν σταθμῶν κύνα,

799 Codd. dant : πολλὴν ἄνωθεν, τὴν κάτω γὰρ οὐ λέγω,

σωτῆρα ναὸς πρότονον, ὑψηλῆς στέγης   825
στῦλον ποδήρη, μονογενὲς τέκνον πατρί,
καὶ γῆν φανεῖσαν ναυτίλοις παρ' ἐλπίδα,
κάλλιστον ἦμαρ εἰσιδεῖν ἐκ χείματος,   (900)
ὁδοιπόρῳ διψῶντι πηγαῖον ῥέος.
τερπνὸν δὲ τἀναγκαῖον ἐκφυγεῖν ἅπαν.   830
τοιοῖσδέ *τοί νιν* ἀξιῶ προσφθέγμασιν.
φθόνος δ' ἀπέστω· πολλὰ γὰρ τὰ πρὶν κακὰ
ἠνειχόμεσθα· νῦν δέ μοι, φίλον κάρα,
ἔκβαιν' ἀπήνης τῆσδε, μὴ χαμαὶ τιθεὶς
τὸν σὸν πόδ', ὦ 'ναξ, Ἰλίου πορθήτορα.   835
δμωαί, τί μέλλεθ', αἷς ἐπέσταλται τέλος
πέδον κελεύθου στρωννύναι πετάσμασιν;
εὐθὺς γενέσθω πορφυρόστρωτος πόρος,
ἐς δῶμ' ἄελπτον ὡς ἂν ἡγῆται Δίκη.
τὰ δ' ἄλλα φροντὶς οὐχ ὕπνῳ νικωμένη   840
θήσει δικαίως ξὺν θεοῖς εἱμαρμένα.

ΑΓ. Λήδας γένεθλον, δωμάτων ἐμῶν φύλαξ,
ἀπουσίᾳ μὲν εἶπας εἰκότως ἐμῇ·
μακρὰν γὰρ ἐξέτεινας· ἀλλ' ἐναισίμως
αἰνεῖν, παρ' ἄλλων χρὴ τόδ' ἔρχεσθαι γέρας.   845
καὶ τἆλλα, μὴ γυναικὸς ἐν τρόποις ἐμὲ
ἅβρυνε, μηδὲ βαρβάρου φωτὸς δίκην
χαμαιπετὲς βόαμα προσχάνῃς ἐμοί·
μηδ' εἵμασι στρώσασ' ἐπίφθονον πόρον
τίθει. θεούς τοι τοῖσδε τιμαλφεῖν χρεών·   850
ἐν ποικίλοις δὲ θνητὸν ὄντα κάλλεσιν
βαίνειν, ἐμοὶ μὲν οὐδαμῶς ἄνευ φόβου.
λέγω κατ' ἄνδρα, μὴ θεόν, σέβειν ἐμέ.
χωρὶς ποδοψήστρων τε καὶ τῶν ποικίλων
κληδὼν ἀϋτεῖ· καὶ τὸ μὴ κακῶς φρονεῖν   855
θεοῦ μέγιστον δῶρον. ὀλβίσαι δὲ χρὴ
βίον τελευτήσαντ' ἐν εὐεστοῖ φίλῃ.

εἰ πάντα δ᾽ ὡς *πράσσοιμεν, εὐθαρσὴς ἐγώ.
ΚΛ. καὶ μὴν τόδ᾽ εἰπὲ μὴ παρὰ γνώμην ἐμοί.
ΑΓ. γνώμην μὲν ἴσθι μὴ διαφθεροῦντ᾽ ἐμέ.   860
ΚΛ. ηὔξω θεοῖς δείσας ἂν ὧδ᾽ ἔρδειν τάδε;
ΑΓ. εἴπερ τις εἰδώς γ᾽ εὖ τόδ᾽ *ἐξειπεῖν τέλος.
ΚΛ. τί δ᾽ ἂν δοκεῖ σοι Πρίαμος, εἰ τάδ᾽ ἤνυσεν;
ΑΓ. ἐν ποικίλοις ἂν κάρτα μοι βῆναι δοκεῖ.
ΚΛ. μή νυν τὸν ἀνθρώπειον αἰδεσθῇς ψόγον.   865
ΑΓ. φήμη γε μέντοι δημόθρους μέγα σθένει.
ΚΛ. ὁ δ᾽ ἀφθόνητός γ᾽ οὐκ ἐπίζηλος πέλει.
ΑΓ. οὔ τοι γυναικός ἐστιν ἱμείρειν μάχης.
ΚΛ. τοῖς δ᾽ ὀλβίοις γε καὶ τὸ νικᾶσθαι πρέπει.
ΑΓ. ἦ καὶ σὺ νίκην τήνδε δήριος τίεις;   870
ΚΛ. πιθοῦ· κράτος πάρες γε *μὴν ἑκὼν ἐμοί.
ΑΓ. ἀλλ᾽ εἰ δοκεῖ σοι ταῦθ᾽, ὑπαί τις ἀρβύλας
λύοι τάχος, πρόδουλον ἔμβασιν ποδός,
καὶ τοῖσδέ μ᾽ ἐμβαίνονθ᾽ ἁλουργέσιν θεῶν
μή τις πρόσωθεν ὄμματος βάλοι φθόνος.   875
πολλὴ γὰρ αἰδὼς *δωματοφθορεῖν ποσὶν
φθείροντα πλοῦτον ἀργυρωνήτους θ᾽ ὑφάς.
τούτων μὲν οὕτω· τὴν ξένην δὲ πρευμενῶς   (950)
τήνδ᾽ ἐσκόμιζε. τὸν κρατοῦντα μαλθακῶς
θεὸς πρόσωθεν εὐμενῶς προσδέρκεται.   880
ἑκὼν γὰρ οὐδεὶς δουλίῳ χρῆται ζυγῷ.
αὕτη δέ, πολλῶν χρημάτων ἐξαίρετον
ἄνθος, στρατοῦ δώρημ᾽, ἐμοὶ ξυνέσπετο.
ἐπεὶ δ᾽ ἀκούειν σου κατέστραμμαι τάδε,
εἶμ᾽ ἐς δόμων μέλαθρα πορφύρας πατῶν.   885
ΚΛ. ἔστιν θάλασσα—τίς δέ νιν κατασβέσει;—
τρέφουσα πολλῆς πορφύρας *ἰσάργυρον
κηκῖδα παγκαίνιστον, εἱμάτων βαφάς.
*ἅλις δ᾽ ὑπάρχει τῶνδε σὺν θεοῖς, ἄναξ,
ἔχειν· πένεσθαι δ᾽ οὐκ ἐπίσταται δόμος.   890

πολλῶν πατησμὸν δ' εἱμάτων ἂν ηὐξάμην,
δόμοισι προὐνεχθέντος ἐν χρηστηρίοις,
ψυχῆς κόμιστρα *σῆς γε* μηχανωμένη.
ῥίζης γὰρ οὔσης φυλλὰς ἵκετ' ἐς δόμους
σκιὰν ὑπερτείνασα Σειρίου κυνός·   895
καὶ σοῦ μολόντος δωματῖτιν ἑστίαν,
θάλπος μὲν ἐν χειμῶνι σημαίνεις μολόν·
ὅταν δὲ τεύχῃ Ζεὺς ἀπ' ὄμφακος πικρᾶς
οἶνον, τότ' ἤδη ψῦχος ἐν δόμοις πέλει
ἀνδρὸς τελείου δῶμ' ἐπιστρωφωμένου.   900
Ζεῦ, Ζεῦ τέλειε, τὰς ἐμὰς εὐχὰς τέλει·
μέλοι δέ τοι σοὶ τῶνπερ ἂν μέλλῃς τελεῖν.

ΧΟ.   τίπτε μοι τόδ' ἐμπέδως   στρ. α'.
     δεῖμα προστατήριον
     καρδίας τερασκόπου ποτᾶται,   905
μαντιπολεῖ δ' *ἀκέλευστον ἄμισθον ἀοιδάν,*
     οὐδ' ἀποπτύσαι, δίκαν
     δυσκρίτων ὀνειράτων,
     θάρσος εὐπιθὲς ἵζει
φρενὸς φίλον θρόνον; χρόνος δ' ἐπὶ   910
     πρυμνησίων *ξυνεμβολαῖς
     ψαμμίας ἀκάτας παρή-
‖βησεν, εὖτε ναυβάτας
‖ὦρθ' ὑπ' Ἴλιον   στρατός.
     πεύθομαι δ' ἀπ' ὀμμάτων   ἀντ. α'.
     νόστον, αὐτόμαρτυς ὤν·   916
     τὸν δ' ἄνευ λύρας ὅμως*μονῳδεῖ
θρῆνον Ἐρινύος αὐτοδίδακτος ἔσωθεν
     θυμός, οὐ τὸ πᾶν ἔχων
     ἐλπίδος φίλον θράσος.   920
     σπλάγχνα δ'*οὔτι ματάζει,
‖πρὸς ἐνδίκοις φρεσὶν   κυκλούμενον
‖δίναις κέαρ τελεσφόροις.

εὔχομαι δ' ἀπ' ἐμᾶς *τοιαῦτ'
ἐλπίδος ψύθη πεσεῖν   925
ἐς τὸ μὴ τελεσφόρον.   (1000)
μάλα γέ τοι *τὸ μεγάλας ὑγείας ἀκόρετον*   στρ. β'.
τέρμα, νόσος γὰρ †ἀεὶ† γει-
των ὁμότοιχος ἐρείδει,
καὶ πότμος εὐθυπορῶν   930
ἀνδρὸς †ὑπὲρ βιότου
‖ κύματ'† ἔπαισεν ἕρμ' ἄφαντον.
καὶ τὸ μὲν πρὸ χρημάτων
‖ κτησίων ἀπ' εὐμέτρου
‖ σφενδόνας *ὄκνῳ βαλὼν
οὐκ ἔδυ πρόπας δόμος   935
πημονᾶς γέμων ἄγαν,
οὐδ' ἐπόντισε σκάφος.
πολλά τοι δόσις
ἐκ Διὸς ἀμφιλαφής τε καὶ ἐξ ἀλόκων ἐπετειᾶν
νῆστιν ὤλεσεν νόσον.   940
‖ἐπὶ δὲ γᾶν πεσὸν ἅπαξ θανάσιμον τὸ πρόπαρ ἀν-   ἀντ. β'.
δρὸς μέλαν αἷμα, τίς ἂν *τοῦτ'
ἀγκαλέσαιτ' ἐπαείδων;
οὐ δὲ τὸν ὀρθοδαῆ
τῶν φθιμένων ἀνάγειν   945
Ζεὺς *κατέπαυσ' ἐπ' εὐλαβείᾳ;
εἰ δὲ μὴ τεταγμένα
μοῖρα μοῖραν ἐκ θεῶν
εἶργε μὴ πλέον φέρειν,
προφθάσασα καρδία   950
γλῶσσαν ἂν τάδ' ἐξέχει.
νῦν δ' ὑπὸ σκότῳ βρέμει
θυμαλγής τε καὶ
οὐδὲν ἐπελπομένα ποτὲ καίριον ἐκτολυπεύσειν
ζωπυρουμένας φρενός.   955

ΑΓΑΜΕΜΝΩΝ.

ΚΛ. εἴσω κομίζου καὶ σύ· Κασάνδραν λέγω·
ἐπεί σ' ἔθηκε Ζεὺς ἀμηνίτως δόμοις
κοινωνὸν εἶναι χερνίβων, πολλῶν μετὰ
δούλων σταθεῖσαν κτησίου βωμοῦ πέλας.
ἔκβαιν' ἀπήνης τῆσδε, μηδ' ὑπερφρόνει.   960
καὶ παῖδα γάρ τοι φασὶν Ἀλκμήνης ποτὲ
πραθέντα τλῆναι, καὶ ζυγῶν θιγεῖν βίᾳ.
εἰ δ' οὖν ἀνάγκη τῆσδ' ἐπιρρέποι τύχης,
ἀρχαιοπλούτων δεσποτῶν πολλὴ χάρις·
οἳ δ' οὔποτ' ἐλπίσαντες ἤμησαν καλῶς,   965
ὠμοί τε δούλοις πάντα καὶ παρὰ στάθμην.
ἔχεις παρ' ἡμῶν οἷά περ νομίζεται.
ΧΟ. σοί τοι λέγουσα παύεται σαφῆ λόγον.
ἐντὸς δ' *ἁλοῦσα μορσίμων ἀγρευμάτων
πείθοι' ἄν, εἰ πείθοι'· ἀπειθοίης δ' ἴσως.   970
ΚΛ. ἀλλ' εἴπερ ἐστὶ μή, χελιδόνος δίκην,   (1050)
ἀγνῶτα φωνὴν βάρβαρον κεκτημένη,
ἔσω φρενῶν λέγουσα πείθω νιν λόγῳ.
ΧΟ. ἕπου· τὰ λῷστα τῶν παρεστώτων λέγει.
πείθου, λιποῦσα τόνδ' ἁμαξήρη θρόνον.   975
ΚΛ. οὔ τοι θυραίαν τήνδ' ἐμοὶ *σχολὴν πάρα
τρίβειν· τὰ μὲν γὰρ ἑστίας μεσομφάλου
†ἥγισμέν' ἡμῖν ἐστι, ποιμνίων δ' ἄπο†
ἕστηκεν ἤδη μῆλα πρὸς σφαγὰς πυρός,
ὡς οὔποτ' ἐλπίσασι τήνδ' ἕξειν χάριν.
σὺ δ' εἴ τι δράσεις τῶνδε, μὴ σχολὴν τίθει·   980
εἰ δ' ἀξυνήμων οὖσα μὴ δέχει λόγον,
*ἀλλ' ἀντὶ φωνῆς φράζε καρβάνῳ χερί.
ΧΟ. ἑρμηνέως ἔοικεν ἡ ξένη τοροῦ
δεῖσθαι· τρόπος δὲ θηρὸς ὡς νεαιρέτου.
ΚΛ. ἦ μαίνεταί γε καὶ κακῶν κλύει φρενῶν,   985
ἥτις λιποῦσα μὲν πόλιν νεαίρετον
ἥκει, χαλινὸν δ' οὐκ ἐπίσταται φέρειν

Κ. Α.   3

34   ΑΙΣΧΥΛΟΥ

πρὶν αἱματηρὸν ἐξαφρίζεσθαι μένος.
οὐ μὴν πλέω ῥίψασ' ἀτιμωθήσομαι.

ΧΟ.   ἐγὼ δ', ἐποικτείρω γάρ, οὐ θυμώσομαι.   990
      ἴθ', ὦ τάλαινα, τόνδ' ἐρημώσασ' ὄχον,
      *εἴκουσ' ἀνάγκῃ τῇδε καίνισον ζυγόν.

                    ΚΑΣΑΝΔΡΑ.

            ὀτοτοτοῖ, πόποι, δᾶ.   στρ. α'.
            ὦ 'πολλον, ὦ 'πολλον.
ΧΟ.   τί ταῦτ' ἀνωτότυξας ἀμφὶ Λοξίου;   995
      οὐ γὰρ τοιοῦτος ὥστε θρηνητοῦ τυχεῖν.
ΚΑ.   ὀτοτοτοῖ, πόποι, δᾶ.   ἀντ. α'.
            ὦ 'πολλον, ὦ 'πολλον.
ΧΟ.   ἥδ' αὖτε δυσφημοῦσα τὸν θεὸν καλεῖ,
      οὐδὲν προσήκοντ' ἐν γόοις παραστατεῖν.   1000
ΚΑ.   Ἀπόλλων, Ἀπόλλων   στρ. β'.
            ἀγυιᾶτ', ἀπόλλων ἐμός·
      ἀπώλεσας γὰρ οὐ μόλις τὸ δεύτερον.
ΧΟ.   χρήσειν ἔοικεν ἀμφὶ τῶν αὑτῆς κακῶν·
      μένει τὸ θεῖον δουλίᾳ *περ ἐν φρενί.   1005
ΚΑ.   Ἀπόλλων, Ἀπόλλων   ἀντ. β'.
            ἀγυιᾶτ', ἀπόλλων ἐμός.
      ἃ ποῖ ποτ' ἤγαγές με; πρὸς ποίαν στέγην;
ΧΟ.   πρὸς τὴν Ἀτρειδῶν· εἰ σὺ μὴ τόδ' ἐννοεῖς,
      ἐγὼ λέγω σοι· καὶ τάδ' οὐκ ἐρεῖς ψύθη.   1010
ΚΑ.   ἃ ἅ,   στρ. γ'.
      μισόθεον μὲν οὖν, πολλὰ συνίστορ' *αὐ-
            τοκτόνα κακὰ κάρτάνας
      ἀνδροσφαγεῖόν θ' αἱμάτων ῥαντήριον.
ΧΟ.   ἔοικεν εὔρις ἡ ξένη, κυνὸς δίκην,   1015
      εἶναι· ματεύει δ' ὧν *ἀνευρήσει φόνον.
ΚΑ.   *ἃ ἅ,*   ἀντ. γ'.
      μαρτυρίοισι γὰρ τοῖσδ' ἐπιπείθομαι,—

κλαιόμενα *βρέφη σφαγὰς
ὀπτάς τε σάρκας πρὸς πατρὸς βεβρωμένας. 1020
ΧΟ.   ἦ μὴν κλέος σοῦ μαντικὸν πεπυσμένοι
*ἦσμεν· προφήτας δ' οὔτινας *ματεύομεν·
ΚΑ.   ἰώ, πόποι, τί ποτε μήδεται;   στρ. δ'. (1100)
τί τόδε *νῦν ἄχος *νέον;
μέγ' ἐν δόμοισι τοῖσδε μήδεται κακόν,   1025
ἄφερτον φίλοισιν, δυσίατον· ἀλκὰ δ'
ἑκὰς ἀποστατεῖ.
ΧΟ.   τούτων ἄιδρίς εἰμι τῶν μαντευμάτων·
ἐκεῖνα δ' ἔγνων· πᾶσα γὰρ πόλις βοᾷ.
ΚΑ.   ἰώ, τάλαινα, τόδε γὰρ τελεῖς;   ἀντ. δ'.
τὸν ὁμοδέμνιον πόσιν   1031
λουτροῖσι φαιδρύνασα—πῶς φράσω τέλος;
τάχος γὰρ τόδ' ἔσται. προτείνει δὲ χεὶρ ἐκ
χερὸς *ὀρέγματα.
ΧΟ.   οὔπω ξυνῆκα· νῦν γὰρ ἐξ αἰνιγμάτων   1035
ἐπαργέμοισι θεσφάτοις ἀμηχανῶ.
ΚΑ.   ἔ, ἔ, παπαῖ, παπαῖ, τί τόδε φαίνεται;   στρ. ε'.
*μὴ δίκτυόν τί γ' "Αιδου;
ἀλλ' ἄρκυς ἡ ξύνευνος, ἡ ξυναιτία
*λοιγοῦ. στάσις δ' *ἀκόρετος γένει   1040
κατολολυξάτω θύματος λευσίμου.
ΧΟ.   ποίαν Ἐρινὺν τήνδε δώμασιν κέλει   στρ. στ'.
ἐπορθιάζειν; οὔ με φαιδρύνει λόγος.
ἐπὶ δὲ καρδίαν ἔδραμε κροκοβαφὴς
σταγών, ἅτε *καιρία πτώσιμος   1045
ξυνανύτει βίου δύντος αὐγαῖς.
ταχεῖα δ' ἄτα πέλει.
ΚΑ.   ἆ ἆ, ἰδού, ἰδού· ἄπεχε τῆς βοὸς   ἀντ. ε'.
τὸν ταῦρον· ἐν πέπλοισιν
*μελαγκέρῳ λαβοῦσα μηχανήματι   1050
τύπτει· πίτνει δ' *ἐν ἐνύδρῳ *κύτει.

δολοφόνου λέβητος τύχαν σοι λέγω.

ΧΟ. οὐ κομπάσαιμ' ἂν θεσφάτων γνώμων ἄκρος ἀντ. στ'.
εἶναι· κακῷ δέ τῳ προσεικάζω τάδε.

ἀπὸ δὲ θεσφάτων τίς ἀγαθὰ φάτις   1055
βροτοῖς στέλλεται; κακῶν γὰρ *διαὶ
πολυεπεῖς τέχναι θεσπιῳδὸν
φόβον φέρουσιν μαθεῖν.

ΚΛ. ἰὼ ἰὼ ταλαίνας κακόποτμοι τύχαι·   στρ. ζ'.
τὸ γὰρ ἐμὸν θροῶ πάθος ἐπεγχέασ'.   1060
*ἆ ποῖ με δεῦρο τὴν τάλαιναν ἤγαγες;
οὐδέν ποτ' εἰ μὴ ξυνθανουμένην· τί γάρ;

ΧΟ. φρενομανής τις εἶ θεοφόρητος, ἀμ-   στρ. η'.
φὶ δ' αὑτᾶς θροεῖς
νόμον ἄνομον, οἷά τις *ξουθᾶς   1065
‖ ἀκόρετος βοᾶς φεῦ ταλαίναις Ἴτυν
‖ φρεσὶν Ἴτυν στένουσ' ἀμφιθαλῆ κακοῖς
ἀηδὼν βίον.

ΚΛ. ἰὼ ἰὼ λιγείας μόρον ἀηδόνος·   ἀντ. ζ'.
*περίβαλον γάρ οἱ πτεροφόρον δέμας   1070
θεοί, γλυκύν τ' *αἰῶνα κλαυμάτων ἄτερ·
ἐμοὶ δὲ μίμνει σχισμὸς ἀμφήκει δορί.

ΧΟ. πόθεν ἐπισσύτους θεοφόρους ἔχεις   ἀντ. η'. (1150)
ματαίους δύας,
τὰ δ' ἐπίφοβα δυσφάτῳ κλαγγᾷ   1075
μελοτυπεῖς, ὁμοῦ τ' ὀρθίοις ἐν νόμοις;
πόθεν ὅρους ἔχεις θεσπεσίας ὁδοῦ
κακορρήμονας;

ΚΛ. ἰὼ γάμοι, γάμοι   στρ. θ'.
Πάριδος, ὀλέθριοι φίλων.   1080
ἰὼ Σκαμάνδρου πάτριον ποτόν·
τότε μὲν ἀμφὶ σὰς ἀϊόνας τάλαιν'
ἠνυτόμαν τροφαῖς·
νῦν δ' ἀμφὶ Κωκυτόν τε κἀχερουσίους

ὄχθους ἔοικα θεσπιῳδήσειν τάχα.   1085

XO.   τί τόδε τορὸν ἄγαν ἔπος ἐφημίσω;   στρ. ί.
καί τις νεόγονος ἂν μάθοι.
πέπληγμαι δ᾽ ὑπαὶ δήγματι φοινίῳ,
δυσαλγεῖ τύχᾳ μινυρὰ θρεομένας,
θαύματ᾽ ἐμοὶ κλύειν.   1090

ΚΑ.   ἰὼ πόνοι, πόνοι   ἀντ. θ.
πόλεος ὀλομένας τὸ πᾶν.
ἰὼ πρόπυργοι θυσίαι πατρός,
πολυκανεῖς βοτῶν ποιονόμων. ἄκος δ᾽
οὐδὲν ἐπήρκεσαν   1095
τὸ μὴ πόλιν μέν, ὥσπερ οὖν ἔχει, παθεῖν·
ἐγὼ δὲ *θερμὸν οὖς* τάχ᾽ ἐν πέδῳ βαλῶ.

XO.   ἑπόμενα *προτέροις τάδ᾽ *ἐπεφημίσω.   ἀντ. ί.
καί τις σὲ *κακοφρονῶν τίθη-
σι δαίμων, *ὕπερθεν βαρὺς* ἐμπίτνων,   1100
μελίζειν πάθη γοερὰ *θανάσιμ᾽, ὦν
τέρματ᾽* ἀμηχανῶ.

ΚΑ.   καὶ μὴν ὁ χρησμὸς οὐκέτ᾽ ἐκ καλυμμάτων
ἔσται δεδορκώς, νεογάμου νύμφης δίκην·
λαμπρὸς δ᾽ ἔοικεν ἡλίου πρὸς ἀντολὰς   1105
πνέων ἐσῄξειν, ὥστε κύματος δίκην
*κλύζειν πρὸς αὐγὰς τοῦδε πήματος πολὺ
μεῖζον· φρενώσω δ᾽ οὐκέτ᾽ ἐξ αἰνιγμάτων.
καὶ μαρτυρεῖτε συνδρόμως ἴχνος κακῶν
ῥινηλατούσῃ τῶν πάλαι πεπραγμένων.   1110
τὴν γὰρ στέγην τήνδ᾽ οὔποτ᾽ ἐκλείπει χορὸς
ξύμφθογγος, οὐκ εὔφωνος· οὐ γὰρ εὖ λέγει.
καὶ μὴν πεπωκώς γ᾽, ὡς θρασύνεσθαι πλέον,
βρότειον αἷμα, κῶμος ἐν δόμοις μένει
δύσπεμπτος ἔξω ξυγγόνων Ἐρινύων.   1115
ὑμνοῦσι δ᾽ ὕμνον δώμασιν προσήμεναι,
πρώταρχον ἄτην· ἐν μέρει δ᾽ ἀπέπτυσαν

εὐνὰς ἀδελφοῦ τῷ πατοῦντι δυσμενεῖς.
ἥμαρτον, ἢ *κυρῶ τι τοξότης τις ὥς;
ἢ ψευδόμαντίς εἰμι θυροκόπος φλέδων; 1120
ἐκμαρτύρησον προὐμόσας τό μ᾽ εἰδέναι
λόγῳ παλαιὰς τῶνδ᾽ ἁμαρτίας δόμων.

ΧΟ. καὶ πῶς ἂν ὅρκος, *πῆγμα γενναίως παγέν,
παιώνιον γένοιτο; θαυμάζω δέ σου,
πόντου πέραν τραφεῖσαν ἀλλόθρουν πόλιν 1125
κυρεῖν λέγουσαν ὥσπερ εἰ παρεστάτεις. (1201)

ΚΑ. μάντις μ᾽ Ἀπόλλων τῷδ᾽ ἐπέστησεν τέλει.

ΧΟ. μῶν καὶ θεός περ ἱμέρῳ πεπληγμένος;

ΚΑ. προτοῦ μὲν αἰδὼς ἦν ἐμοὶ λέγειν τάδε.

ΧΟ. ἁβρύνεται γὰρ πᾶς τις εὖ πράσσων πλέον. 1130

ΚΑ. ἀλλ᾽ ἦν παλαιστὴς κάρτ᾽ ἐμοὶ πνέων χάριν.

ΧΟ. ἦ καὶ τέκνων εἰς ἔργον ἦλθετον νόμῳ;

ΚΑ. ξυναινέσασα Λοξίαν ἐψευσάμην.

ΧΟ. ἤδη τέχναισιν ἐνθέοις ᾑρημένη;

ΚΑ. ἤδη πολίταις πάντ᾽ ἐθέσπιζον πάθη. 1135

ΧΟ. πῶς δῆτ᾽; *ἄνατος ἦσθα Λοξίου κότῳ;

ΚΑ. ἔπειθον *οὐδέν᾽ οὐδέν, ὡς τάδ᾽ ἤμπλακον.

ΧΟ. ἡμῖν γε μὲν δὴ πιστὰ θεσπίζειν δοκεῖς.

ΚΑ   ἰοῦ ἰοῦ, ὢ ὢ κακά.
ὑπ᾽ αὖ με δεινὸς ὀρθομαντείας πόνος 1140
στροβεῖ, ταράσσων φροιμίοις *ἐπισσύτοις.
ὁρᾶτε τούσδε τοὺς δόμοις ἐφημένους
νέους, ὀνείρων προσφερεῖς μορφώμασιν;
παῖδες θανόντες ὡσπερεὶ πρὸς τῶν φίλων,
χεῖρας κρεῶν πλήθοντες οἰκείας βορᾶς, 1145
ξὺν ἐντέροις τε σπλάγχν᾽, ἐποίκτιστον γέμος,
πρέπουσ᾽ ἔχοντες, ὧν πατὴρ ἐγεύσατο.
ἐκ τῶνδε ποινάς φημι βουλεύειν τινὰ
λέοντ᾽ ἄναλκιν ἐν λέχει στρωφώμενον
οἰκουρόν, οἴμοι, τῷ μολόντι δεσπότῃ 1150

ἐμῷ· φέρειν γὰρ χρὴ τὸ δούλιον ζυγόν.
νεῶν τ᾽ *ἔπαρχος Ἰλίου τ᾽ ἀναστάτης
οὐκ οἶδεν *οἵα γλῶσσα μισήτης κυνὸς
λείξασα κἀκτείνασα φαιδρὸν οὖς, δίκην
Ἄτης λαθραίου, *δήξεται κακῇ τύχῃ.   1155
*τοιαῦτα τολμᾷ· θῆλυς ἄρσενος φονεὺς
ἐστίν—τί νιν καλοῦσα δυσφιλὲς δάκος
τύχοιμ᾽ ἄν; ἀμφίσβαιναν, ἢ Σκύλλαν τινὰ
οἰκοῦσαν ἐν πέτραισι, ναυτίλων βλάβην,
θύουσαν Ἅιδου μητέρ᾽, ἄσπονδόν τ᾽ *Ἄρην 1160
φίλοις πνέουσαν; ὡς δ᾽ ἐπωλολύξατο
ἡ παντότολμος, ὥσπερ ἐν μάχης τροπῇ.
δοκεῖ δὲ χαίρειν νοστίμῳ σωτηρίᾳ.
καὶ τῶνδ᾽ ὅμοιον εἴ τι μὴ πείθω· τί γάρ;
τὸ μέλλον ἥξει. καὶ σύ *μ᾽ ἐν* τάχει παρὼν 1165
ἄγαν ἀληθόμαντιν οἰκτείρας ἐρεῖς.

ΧΟ.   τὴν μὲν Θυέστου δαῖτα παιδείων κρεῶν
ξυνῆκα καὶ πέφρικα· καὶ φόβος μ᾽ ἔχει
κλύοντ᾽ ἀληθῶς οὐδὲν ἐξηκασμένα·
τὰ δ᾽ ἄλλ᾽ ἀκούσας ἐκ δρόμου πεσὼν τρέχω. 1170

ΚΑ.   Ἀγαμέμνονός σέ φημ᾽ ἐπόψεσθαι μόρον.

ΧΟ.   εὔφημον, ὦ τάλαινα, κοίμησον στόμα.

ΚΑ.   ἀλλ᾽ οὔτι Παιὼν τῷδ᾽ ἐπιστατεῖ λόγῳ.

ΧΟ.   οὔκ, εἰ παρέσται γ᾽· ἀλλὰ μὴ γένοιτό πω.

ΚΑ.   σὺ μὲν κατεύχει, τοῖς δ᾽ ἀποκτείνειν μέλει. 1175

ΧΟ.   τίνος πρὸς ἀνδρὸς τοῦτ᾽ ἄχος πορσύνεται; (1251)

ΚΑ.   ἦ *κάρθ᾽ ὅρον παρεσκόπεις* χρησμῶν ἐμῶν.

ΧΟ.   τοῦ γὰρ τελοῦντος οὐ ξυνῆκα μηχανήν.

ΚΑ.   καὶ μὴν ἄγαν γ᾽ Ἕλλην᾽ ἐπίσταμαι φάτιν.

ΧΟ.   καὶ γὰρ τὰ πυθόκραντα, *δυσμαθῆ δ᾽ ὅμως. 1180

ΚΑ.   παπαῖ οἷον τὸ πῦρ· ἐπέρχεται δέ μοι.
ὀτοτοῖ Λύκει᾽ Ἄπολλον· οἳ ἐγώ, ἐγώ.
αὕτη *δίπους λέαινα, συγκοιμωμένη

λύκῳ, λέοντος εὐγενοῦς ἀπουσίᾳ,
κτενεῖ με τὴν τάλαιναν, ὡς δὲ φάρμακον   1185
τεύχουσα κἀμοῦ μισθὸν ἐνθήσει κότῳ.
ἐπεύχεται *δέ, φωτὶ θήγουσα ξίφος,*
ἐμῆς ἀγωγῆς ἀντιτίσασθαι φόνον.
τί δῆτ᾽ ἐμαυτῆς καταγέλωτ᾽ ἔχω τάδε
καὶ σκῆπτρα καὶ μαντεῖα περὶ δέρῃ στέφη;   1190
*σφὼ μὲν πρὸ μοίρας τῆς ἐμῆς διαφθερῶ.
ἴτ᾽ ἐς φθόρον πεσόντ᾽· *ἐγὼ δ᾽ ἅμ᾽ ἔψομαι.*
ἄλλην τιν᾽ *ἄταις ἀντ᾽ ἐμοῦ πλουτίζετε.
ἰδοὺ δ᾽, Ἀπόλλων αὐτὸς ἐκδύων ἐμὲ
χρηστηρίαν ἐσθῆτ᾽, ἐποπτεύσας δ᾽ *ὅμως   1195
κἀν τοῖσδε κόσμοις καταγελωμένην *μ᾽ ἔτλη*
φίλων ὕπ᾽ ἐχθρῶν *τ᾽ οὐ διχορρόπως μάτην.
καλουμένη δὲ φοιτάς, ὡς ἀγύρτρια,
πτωχός, τάλαινα, λιμοθνὴς ἠνεσχόμην.
καὶ νῦν ὁ μάντις, μάντιν ἐκπράξας ἐμέ,   1200
ἀπήγαγ᾽ ἐς τοιάσδε θανασίμους τύχας·
βωμοῦ πατρῴου δ᾽ ἀντ᾽ ἐπίξηνον μένει
θερμῷ *κοπείσῃ φοινίῳ προσφάγματι.
οὐ μὴν ἄτιμοί γ᾽ ἐκ θεῶν τεθνήξομεν.
ἥξει γὰρ ἡμῶν ἄλλος αὖ τιμάορος,   1205
μητροκτόνον φίτυμα, ποινάτωρ πατρός·
φυγὰς δ᾽ ἀλήτης τῆσδε γῆς ἀπόξενος
κάτεισιν, ἄτας τάσδε θριγκώσων φίλοις·
ὁμώμοται γὰρ ὅρκος ἐκ θεῶν μέγας,
ἄξειν νιν ὑπτίασμα κειμένου πατρός.   1210
τί δῆτ᾽ ἐγὼ *κάτοικτος ὧδ᾽ ἀναστένω,
ἐπεὶ τὸ πρῶτον εἶδον Ἰλίου πόλιν
πράξασαν ὡς ἔπραξεν, οἳ δ᾽ *εἷλον πόλιν,
οὕτως ἀπαλλάσσουσιν ἐν θεῶν κρίσει;
ἰοῦσα πράξω, τλήσομαι τὸ κατθανεῖν.   1215
Ἅιδου πύλας δὲ *τάσδ᾽ ἐγὼ* προσεννέπω.

ἐπεύχομαι δὲ καιρίας πληγῆς τυχεῖν,
ὡς ἀσφάδαστος, αἱμάτων εὐθνησίμων
ἀπορρυέντων, ὄμμα συμβάλω τόδε.

ΧΟ. ὦ πολλὰ μὲν τάλαινα, πολλὰ δ' αὖ σοφὴ   1220
γύναι, μακρὰν ἔτεινας· εἰ δ' ἐτητύμως
μόρον τὸν αὑτῆς οἶσθα, πῶς θεηλάτου
βοὸς δίκην πρὸς βωμὸν εὐτόλμως πατεῖς;

ΚΑ. οὐκ ἔστ' ἄλυξις, οὔ, ξένοι, *χρόνον πλέω.

ΧΟ. ὁ δ' ὕστατός γε τοῦ χρόνου πρεσβεύεται.   1225

ΚΑ. ἥκει τόδ' ἦμαρ· σμικρὰ κερδανῶ φυγῇ.   (1301)

ΧΟ. ἀλλ' ἴσθι τλήμων οὖσ' ἀπ' εὐτόλμου φρενός.

ΚΑ. οὐδεὶς ἀκούει ταῦτα τῶν εὐδαιμόνων.

ΧΟ. ἀλλ' εὐκλεῶς τοι κατθανεῖν χάρις βροτῷ.

ΚΑ. ἰώ, πάτερ, σοῦ τῶν τε γενναίων τέκνων.   1230

ΧΟ. τί δ' ἐστὶ χρῆμα; τίς σ' ἀποστρέφει φόβος;

ΚΑ. φεῦ, φεῦ.

ΧΟ. τί τοῦτ' ἔφευξας; εἴ τι μὴ φρενῶν στύγος.

ΚΑ. *φόνον δόμοι πνέουσιν αἱματοσταγῆ.

ΧΟ. καὶ πῶς τόδ' ὄζει θυμάτων ἐφεστίων;   1235

ΚΑ. ὅμοιος ἀτμὸς ὥσπερ ἐκ τάφου πρέπει.

ΧΟ. οὐ Σύριον ἀγλάϊσμα δώμασιν λέγεις.

ΚΑ. ἀλλ' εἶμι κἀν δόμοισι κωκύσουσ' ἐμὴν
Ἀγαμέμνονός τε μοῖραν. ἀρκείτω βίος.
ἰώ, ξένοι.   1240
οὔ τοι δυσοίζω, θάμνον ὡς ὄρνις, φόβῳ
*ἄλλως· θανούσῃ μαρτυρεῖτέ μοι τόδε,
ὅταν γυνὴ γυναικὸς ἀντ' ἐμοῦ θάνῃ,
ἀνήρ τε δυσδάμαρτος ἀντ' ἀνδρὸς πέσῃ.
ἐπιξενοῦμαι ταῦτα δ' ὡς θανουμένη.   1245

ΧΟ. ὦ τλῆμον, οἰκτείρω σε θεσφάτου μόρου.

ΚΑ. ἅπαξ ἔτ' εἰπεῖν ῥῆσιν, *οὐ θρῆνον θέλω
ἐμὸν τὸν αὑτῆς. ἡλίῳ δ' ἐπεύχομαι
πρὸς ὕστατον φῶς, τοῖς *φίλων τιμαόροις

42 ΑΙΣΧΥΛΟΥ

*ἐχθροὺς φονεῦσι *τὸν φόνον* τίνειν ὁμοῦ   1250
δούλης θανούσης, εὐμαροῦς χειρώματος.
ἰὼ βρότεια πράγματ'· εὐτυχοῦντα μὲν
σκιᾷ τις ἂν πρέψειεν· εἰ δὲ δυστυχῇ,
βολαῖς ὑγρώσσων σπόγγος ὤλεσεν γραφήν.
καὶ ταῦτ' ἐκείνων μᾶλλον οἰκτείρω πολύ.   1255

ΧΟ.   τὸ μὲν εὖ πράσσειν ἀκόρεστον ἔφυ
πᾶσι βροτοῖσιν· δακτυλοδείκτων δ'
οὔτις ἀπειπὼν εἴργει μελάθρων,
μηκέτ' *ἐσέλθῃς, τάδε φωνῶν.
καὶ τῷδε πόλιν μὲν ἑλεῖν ἔδοσαν   1260
μάκαρες Πριάμου,
θεοτίμητος δ' οἴκαδ' ἱκάνει·
νῦν δ' εἰ προτέρων αἷμ' ἀποτίσει,
καὶ τοῖσι θανοῦσι θανὼν ποινὰς
ἄλλων θανάτων *ἀπάνευθε κρανεῖ,*   1265
τίς *ποτ' ἂν εὔξαιτο βροτῶν ἀσινεῖ
δαίμονι φῦναι, τάδ' ἀκούων;
ΑΓ.   ὤμοι, πέπληγμαι καιρίαν πληγὴν ἔσω.
ΧΟ.   σῖγα· τίς πληγὴν ἀϋτεῖ καιρίως οὐτασμένος;
ΑΓ.   ὤμοι μάλ' αὖθις, δευτέραν πεπληγμένος.   1270
ΧΟ.   τοὔργον εἰργάσθαι δοκεῖ μοι βασιλέως οἰμώγματι·
ἀλλὰ κοινωσώμεθ' *ἄν πως ἀσφαλῆ βουλεύματα.
ΧΟ.   α'. ἐγὼ μὲν ὑμῖν τὴν ἐμὴν γνώμην λέγω,
πρὸς δῶμα δεῦρ' ἀστοῖσι κηρύσσειν βοήν.
ΧΟ.   β'. ἐμοὶ δ' ὅπως τάχιστά γ' ἐμπεσεῖν δοκεῖ,   1275
καὶ πρᾶγμ' ἐλέγχειν ξὺν νεορρύτῳ ξίφει.   (1351)
ΧΟ.   γ'. κἀγώ, τοιούτου γνώματος κοινωνὸς ὤν,
ψηφίζομαί *τι δρᾶν· τὸ μὴ μέλλειν δ' ἀκμή.
ΧΟ.   δ'. ὁρᾶν πάρεστι· φροιμιάζονται γὰρ ὡς
τυραννίδος σημεῖα πράσσοντες πόλει.   1280
ΧΟ.   ε'. χρονίζομεν γάρ· οἱ δὲ τῆς *μελλοῦς κλέος
*πέδοι πατοῦντες οὐ καθεύδουσιν χερί.

AΓAMEMNΩN. 43

ΧΟ. στ'. οὐκ οἶδα βουλῆς ἧστινος τυχὼν λέγω.
τοῦ δρῶντός ἐστι καὶ τὸ βουλεῦσαι περί.
ΧΟ. ζ'. κἀγὼ τοιοῦτός εἰμ᾽, ἐπεὶ δυσμηχανῶ   1285
λόγοισι τὸν θανόντ᾽ ἀνιστάναι πάλιν.
ΧΟ. η'. ἦ καὶ βίον *τείνοντες ὧδ᾽ ὑπείξομεν
δόμων καταισχυντῆρσι τοῖσδ᾽ ἡγουμένοις;
ΧΟ. θ'. ἀλλ᾽ οὐκ ἀνεκτόν, ἀλλὰ κατθανεῖν κρατεῖ·
πεπαιτέρα γὰρ μοῖρα τῆς τυραννίδος.   1290
ΧΟ. ι'. ἦ γὰρ τεκμηρίοισιν ἐξ οἰμωγμάτων
μαντευσόμεσθα τἀνδρὸς ὡς ὀλωλότος;
ΧΟ. ια'. σάφ᾽ εἰδότας χρὴ τῶνδε *μυθεῖσθαι πέρι·
τὸ γὰρ τοπάζειν τοῦ σάφ᾽ εἰδέναι δίχα.
ΧΟ. ιβ'. ταύτην ἐπαινεῖν πάντοθεν πληθύνομαι,   1295
τρανῶς Ἀτρείδην εἰδέναι κυροῦνθ᾽ ὅπως.
ΚΛ. πολλῶν πάροιθεν καιρίως εἰρημένων,
τἀναντί᾽ εἰπεῖν οὐκ ἐπαισχυνθήσομαι.
πῶς γάρ τις ἐχθροῖς ἐχθρὰ πορσύνων, φίλοις
δοκοῦσιν εἶναι, *πημονῆς ἀρκύστατ᾽ ἂν*   1300
φράξειεν ὕψος κρεῖσσον ἐκπηδήματος;
ἐμοὶ δ᾽ ἀγὼν ὅδ᾽ οὐκ ἀφρόντιστος πάλαι
*εὐχῆς παλαιᾶς ἦλθε, σὺν χρόνῳ γε μήν.
ἕστηκα δ᾽ ἔνθ᾽ ἔπαισ᾽ ἐπ᾽ ἐξειργασμένοις.
οὕτω δ᾽ ἔπραξα, καὶ τάδ᾽ οὐκ ἀρνήσομαι,   1305
ὡς μήτε φεύγειν μήτ᾽ *ἀμύνεσθαι μόρον.
ἄπειρον ἀμφίβληστρον, ὥσπερ ἰχθύων,
περιστιχίζω, πλοῦτον εἵματος κακόν.
παίω δέ νιν δίς· κἂν δυοῖν *οἰμωγμάτοιν
μεθῆκεν *αὐτοῦ κῶλα· καὶ πεπτωκότι   1310
τρίτην ἐπενδίδωμι, τοῦ κατὰ χθονὸς
Ἅιδου, νεκρῶν σωτῆρος, εὐκταίαν χάριν.
οὕτω τὸν αὑτοῦ θυμὸν ὁρμαίνει πεσών·
κἀκφυσιῶν ὀξεῖαν αἵματος σφαγὴν
βάλλει μ᾽ ἐρεμνῇ ψακάδι φοινίας δρόσου,   1315

χαίρουσαν οὐδὲν ἧσσον ἢ *διοσδότῳ
γάνει* σπορητὸς κάλυκος ἐν λοχεύμασιν.
ὡς ὧδ' ἐχόντων, πρέσβος Ἀργείων τόδε,
χαίροιτ' ἄν, εἰ χαίροιτ', ἐγὼ δ' ἐπεύχομαι.
εἰ δ' ἦν, *πρεπόντως ὥστ' ἐπισπένδειν νεκρῷ,   1320
τάδ' ἂν δικαίως ἦν, ὑπερδίκως μὲν οὖν·
*τοσόνδε κρατῆρ' ἐν δόμοις κακῶν ὅδε
πλήσας ἀραίων αὐτὸς ἐκπίνει μολών.

ΧΟ.   θαυμάζομέν σου γλῶσσαν, ὡς θρασύστομος,
ἥτις τοιόνδ' ἐπ' ἀνδρὶ κομπάζεις λόγον.   1325 (1400)

ΚΛ.   πειρᾶσθέ μου γυναικὸς ὡς ἀφράσμονος·
ἐγὼ δ' ἀτρέστῳ καρδίᾳ πρὸς εἰδότας
λέγω—σὺ δ' αἰνεῖν εἴτε με ψέγειν θέλεις,
ὅμοιον—οὗτός ἐστιν Ἀγαμέμνων, ἐμὸς
πόσις, νεκρὸς δὲ τῆσδε δεξιᾶς χερός,   1330
ἔργον δικαίας τέκτονος. τάδ' ὧδ' ἔχει.

ΧΟ.   τί κακόν, ὦ γύναι,   στρ.
χθονοτρεφὲς ἐδανὸν ἢ ποτὸν
πασαμένα ῥυτᾶς ἐξ ἁλὸς ὅρμενον
τόδ' ἐπέθου θύος δημοθρόους τ' ἀράς;   1335
ἀπέδικες ἀπέταμές *τ',
*ἀπόπολις δ' ἔσει,
μῖσος ὄβριμον ἀστοῖς.

ΚΛ.   νῦν μὲν δικάζεις ἐκ πόλεως φυγὴν ἐμοὶ
καὶ μῖσος ἀστῶν δημόθρους τ' ἔχειν ἀράς,   1340
οὐδὲν *τότ' ἀνδρὶ τῷδ' ἐναντίον φέρων·
ὃς οὐ προτιμῶν ὡσπερεὶ βοτοῦ μόρον,
μήλων φλεόντων εὐπόκοις νομεύμασιν,
ἔθυσεν αὐτοῦ παῖδα, φιλτάτην ἐμοὶ
ὠδῖν', ἐπῳδὸν Θρῃκίων *ἀημάτων.   1345
οὐ τοῦτον ἐκ γῆς τῆσδε *χρῆν σ' ἀνδρηλατεῖν,
μιασμάτων ἄποιν'; ἐπήκοος δ' ἐμῶν
ἔργων δικαστὴς τραχὺς εἶ. λέγω δέ σοι

τοιαῦτ᾽ ἀπειλεῖν, ὡς παρεσκευασμένης
ἐκ τῶν ὁμοίων χειρὶ νικήσαντ᾽ ἐμοῦ   1350
ἄρχειν· ἐὰν δὲ τοὔμπαλιν κραίνῃ θεός,
γνώσει διδαχθεὶς ὀψὲ γοῦν τὸ σωφρονεῖν.

ΧΟ.   μεγαλόμητις εἶ,   ἀντ.
    περίφρονα δ᾽ ἔλακες, ὥσπερ οὖν
φονολιβεῖ τύχᾳ φρὴν ἐπιμαίνεται,   1355
λῖπος ἐπ᾽ ὀμμάτων αἵματος *ἐμπρέπειν
    ἀτίετον· ἔτι σε χρὴ
    στερομέναν φίλων
    τύμμα *τύμματι τῖσαι.

ΚΛ. καὶ τήνδ᾽ ἀκούεις ὁρκίων ἐμῶν θέμιν·   1360
μὰ τὴν τέλειον τῆς ἐμῆς παιδὸς Δίκην,
Ἄτην τ᾽ Ἐρινύν θ᾽, αἷσι τόνδ᾽ ἔσφαξ᾽ ἐγώ,
οὔ μοι φόβου μέλαθρον ἐλπὶς *ἐμπατεῖν,
ἕως ἂν αἴθῃ πῦρ ἐφ᾽ ἑστίας ἐμῆς
Αἴγισθος, ὡς τὸ πρόσθεν εὖ φρονῶν ἐμοί.   1365
οὗτος γὰρ ἡμῖν ἀσπὶς οὐ σμικρὰ θράσους.
κεῖται γυναικὸς τῆσδε λυμαντήριος
†ἀνήρ, ὁ πασῶν ἐκφανὴς ἰδεῖν στρατῷ†
Χρυσηΐδων μείλιγμα τῶν ὑπ᾽ Ἰλίῳ·
ἥ τ᾽ αἰχμάλωτος ἥδε καὶ τερασκόπος,
καὶ κοινόλεκτρος τοῦδε, θεσφατηλόγος   1370
πιστὴ ξύνευνος, *ναυτίλοις δὲ σελμάτων
*ἰσοτριβής. ἄτιμα δ᾽ οὐκ ἐπραξάτην·
ὁ μὲν γὰρ οὕτως· ἡ δέ τοι, κύκνου δίκην,
τὸν ὕστατον μέλψασα θανάσιμον γόον
κεῖται φιλήτωρ *τῷδ᾽, ἐμοὶ δ᾽ ἐπήγαγεν   1375
*εὐναῖς παροψώνημα τῆς ἐμῆς χλιδῆς.

ΧΟ. φεῦ, τίς ἂν ἐν τάχει, μὴ περιώδυνος,   στρ. α´.
    μηδὲ δεμνιοτήρης,
μόλοι τὸν αἰεὶ φέρουσ᾽ ἐν ἡμῖν   (1450)
μοῖρ᾽ ἀτέλευτον ὕπνον, δαμέντος   1380

φύλακος εὐμενεστάτου,
καὶ *πολύ γε* τλάντος γυναικὸς διαί;
πρὸς γυναικὸς δ' ἀπέφθισεν βίον.
    ἰὼ ἰὼ *παράνους Ἑλένα   στρ. β'.
μία τὰς πολλάς, τὰς πάνυ πολλὰς   1385
ψυχὰς ὀλέσασ' ὑπὸ Τροίᾳ·
νῦν δὲ τελείαν . . .
[desunt versus aliquot]
†καὶ† πολύμναστον ἐπηνθίσω   [στρ. γ'.]
†Πλεισθενίδαισι μίασμα† δι' αἷμ' ἄνιπτον,
    *τάν τ' ἔριν ἃ δόμοισιν   1390
τότ' ἦν ἄδματος*, ἀνδρὸς οἰζύς.

ΚΛ. μηδὲν θανάτου μοῖραν ἐπεύχου   στρ. δ'.
τοῖσδε βαρυνθείς·
μηδ' εἰς Ἑλένην κότον ἐκτρέψῃς,
ὡς ἀνδρολέτειρ', ὡς μία πολλῶν   1395
ἀνδρῶν ψυχὰς Δαναῶν ὀλέσασ',
ἀξύστατον ἄλγος ἔπραξεν.

ΧΟ. δαῖμον, ὃς ἐμπίτνεις δώμασι καὶ *διφυί-   ἀντ. α'.
οισι Τανταλίδαισιν,
κράτος τ' ἰσόψυχον ἐκ γυναικῶν   1400
*καρδιόδηκτον ἐμοὶ κρατύνεις,
*ἴδ' ἐπὶ σώματος δίκαν
μοι κόρακος ἐχθροῦ *σταθεῖσ' ἐκνόμοις*
ὕμνον ὑμνεῖν ἐπεύχεται *νόμοις.

ΚΛ. νῦν δ' ὤρθωσας στόματος γνώμην,   ἀντ. δ'.
τὸν τριπάχυιον   1406
δαίμονα γέννης τῆσδε κικλήσκων·
ἐκ τοῦ γὰρ ἔρως αἱματολοιχὸς
*νείρᾳ τρέφεται, πρὶν καταλῆξαι
τὸ παλαιὸν ἄχος, νέος ἰχώρ.   1410

ΧΟ.   ἦ μέγαν *ἐν μελάθροις*   στρ. ε'.
δαίμονα καὶ βαρύμηνιν αἰνεῖς,

φεῦ, φεῦ, κακὸν αἶνον ἀτηρᾶς τύχας ἀκορέστου.
ἰώ, ἰή, διαὶ Διὸς
παναιτίου, πανεργέτα·   1415
τί γὰρ βροτοῖς ἄνευ Διὸς
τελεῖται; τί τῶνδ'
οὐ θεόκραντόν ἐστιν;
    ἰὼ ἰώ,   στρ. στ'.
βασιλεῦ, βασιλεῦ, πῶς σε δακρύσω;   1420
φρενὸς ἐκ φιλίας τί ποτ' εἴπω;
κεῖσαι δ' ἀράχνης ἐν ὑφάσματι τῷδ'
ἀσεβεῖ θανάτῳ βίον ἐκπνέων.
ὤ μοί μοι, κοίταν τάνδ' ἀνελεύθερον,   στρ. ζ'.
δολίῳ μόρῳ δαμεὶς   1425
ἐκ χερὸς ἀμφιτόμῳ βελέμνῳ.
ΚΛ. αὐχεῖς εἶναι τόδε τοὔργον ἐμόν.   στρ. η'.
μὴ δ' ἐπιλεχθῇς
'Αγαμεμνονίαν εἶναί μ' ἄλοχον·
φανταζόμενος δὲ γυναικὶ νεκροῦ   1430 (1500)
τοῦδ' ὁ παλαιὸς δριμὺς ἀλάστωρ
'Ατρέως, χαλεποῦ θοινατῆρος,
   τόνδ' ἀπέτισεν,
τέλεον νεαροῖς ἐπιθύσας.
ΧΟ. ὡς μὲν ἀναίτιος εἶ   ἀντ. ε'.
τοῦδε φόνου, τίς ὁ μαρτυρήσων;   1436
πῶ; πῶ; πατρόθεν δὲ συλλήπτωρ γένοιτ' ἂν ἀλάστωρ.
βιάζεται δ' ὁμοσπόροις
ἐπιρροαῖσιν αἱμάτων
μέλας "Αρης, ὅποι *δίκαν   1440
προβαίνων* πάχνᾳ
κουροβόρῳ παρέξει.
   ἰὼ ἰώ,   ἀντ. στ'.
βασιλεῦ, βασιλεῦ, πῶς σε δακρύσω;
φρενὸς ἐκ φιλίας τί ποτ' εἴπω;   1445

48 ΑΙΣΧΤΛΟΤ

κεῖσαι δ' ἀράχνης ἐν ὑφάσματι τῷδ'
ἀσεβεῖ θανάτῳ βίον ἐκπνέων.
ὦ μοί μοι, κοίταν τάνδ' ἀνελεύθερον,   ἀντ. ζ'.
δολίῳ μόρῳ δαμεὶς
ἐκ χερὸς ἀμφιτόμῳ βελέμνῳ.   1450
ΚΛ.   οὐδὲ γὰρ οὗτος δολίαν ἄτην   ἀντ. η'.
οἴκοισιν ἔθηκ';
ἀλλ' ἐμὸν ἐκ τοῦδ' ἔρνος ἀερθὲν
‖ τὴν πολύκλαυτον *ἀνάξια δρασας
‖ Ἰφιγένειαν, πάσχων ἄξια*   1455
μηδὲν ἐν "Αιδου μεγαλαυχείτω,
ξιφοδηλήτῳ
θανάτῳ τίσας ἅπερ ἦρξεν.
ΧΟ.   ἀμηχανῶ, φροντίδος στερηθεὶς   στρ. θ'.
εὐπαλάμων μεριμνᾶν,   1460
ὅπα τράπωμαι, πίτνοντος οἴκου.
δέδοικα δ' ὄμβρου κτύπον δομοσφαλῆ
τὸν αἱματηρόν· ψακὰς δὲ λήγει.
*δίκην δ' ἐπ' ἄλλο πρᾶγμα *θηγάνει βλάβης
πρὸς ἄλλαις θηγάναισι Μοῖρα.   1465
ἰὼ γᾶ, γᾶ, εἴθε μ' ἐδέξω,   ἀντ. β'.
πρὶν τόνδ' ἐπιδεῖν ἀργυροτοίχου
δροίτας κατέχοντα χαμεύναν.
τίς ὁ θάψων νιν, τίς ὁ θρηνήσων;
ἢ σὺ τόδ' ἔρξαι   1470
τλήσει, κτείνασ' ἄνδρα τὸν αὐτῆς
ἀποκωκῦσαι, ψυχῇ τ' ἄχαριν
χάριν ἀντ' ἔργων
μεγάλων ἀδίκως ἐπικρᾶναι;
.   .   .   .   [ἀντ. γ'.]
τίς δ' *ἐπιτύμβιον αἶνον* ἐπ' ἀνδρὶ θείῳ   1476
ξὺν δακρύοις ἰάπτων

Post 1451 codd. dant οὔτ' ἀνελεύθερον οἶμαι θάνατον | τῷδε γενέσθαι.

ἀλαθεία φρενῶν πονήσει;

ΚΛ. οὐ σὲ προσήκει τὸ μέλημα λέγειν   στρ. ι'. (1550)
     τοῦτο· πρὸς ἡμῶν   1480
     κάππεσεν, *ἡμεῖς καὶ καταθάψομεν,
     οὐχ ὑπὸ κλαυθμῶν τῶν ἐξ οἴκων,
     (duo versus desunt)
     ἀλλ' Ἰφιγένειά νιν ἀσπασίως
     θυγατήρ, ὡς χρή,
     πατέρ' ἀντιάσασα πρὸς ὠκύπορον   1485
     πόρθμευμ' ἀχέων
     περὶ *χεῖρε βαλοῦσα φιλήσει.

ΧΟ. ὄνειδος ἥκει τόδ' ἀντ' ὀνείδους,   ἀντ. θ'.
     δύσμαχα δ' ἐστὶ κρῖναι·
     φέρει φέροντ', ἐκτίνει δ' ὁ καίνων.   1490
     *μένει δέ, μίμνοντος ἐν χρόνῳ Διός,
     παθεῖν τὸν ἔρξαντα· θέσμιον γάρ·
     τίς ἂν γονὰν *ἀραῖον ἐκβάλοι δόμων;
     κεκόλληται γένος *πρὸς ἄτα.*

ΚΛ. εἰς τόνδ' *ἐνέβης ξὺν ἀληθείᾳ   ἀντ. ι'.
     χρησμόν· ἐγὼ δ' οὖν   1496
     ἐθέλω, δαίμονι τῷ Πλεισθενιδᾶν
     ὅρκους θεμένη, τάδε μὲν στέργειν,
     δύστλητά περ ὄνθ'· ὁ δὲ λοιπόν, ἰόντ'
     ἐκ τῶνδε δόμων ἄλλην γενεὰν   1500
     τρίβειν θανάτοις αὐθένταισιν.
     κτεάνων τε μέρος
     βαιὸν ἐχούσῃ πᾶν ἀπόχρη μοι
     ‖μανίας μελάθρων
     ‖ἀλληλοφόνους ἀφελούσῃ.   1505

ΑΙΓΙΣΘΟΣ.

ὦ φέγγος εὖφρον ἡμέρας δικηφόρου·
φαίην ἂν ἤδη νῦν βροτῶν τιμαόρους
θεοὺς ἄνωθεν γῆς ἐποπτεύειν ἄχη,

Κ. Α.   4

ἰδὼν ὑφαντοῖς ἐν πέπλοις Ἐρινύων
τὸν ἄνδρα τόνδε κείμενον φίλως ἐμοί,   1510
χερὸς πατρῴας ἐκτίνοντα μηχανάς.
Ἀτρεὺς γὰρ ἄρχων τῆσδε γῆς, τούτου πατήρ,
πατέρα Θυέστην τὸν ἐμόν, ὡς τορῶς φράσαι,
αὑτοῦ δ' ἀδελφόν, ἀμφίλεκτος ὢν κράτει,
ἠνδρηλάτησεν ἐκ πόλεώς τε καὶ δόμων.   1515
καὶ προστρόπαιος ἑστίας μολὼν πάλιν
τλήμων Θυέστης μοῖραν ηὕρετ' ἀσφαλῆ,
τὸ μὴ θανὼν πατρῷον αἱμάξαι πέδον
*αὐτός· ξένια δὲ τοῦδε δύσθεος πατὴρ
Ἀτρεὺς προθύμως μᾶλλον ἢ φίλως πατρὶ   1520
τῷ 'μῷ, κρεουργὸν ἦμαρ εὐθύμως ἄγειν
δοκῶν, παρέσχε δαῖτα παιδείων κρεῶν.
τὰ μὲν ποδήρη καὶ χερῶν ἄκρους κτένας
*ἔκρυπτ' ἄνωθεν ἀνδρακὰς καθήμενος·
ἄσημα δ' αὐτῶν †μόρια τῷ δυσδαίμονι   1525
φαγεῖν ἔπεμψ'· ὁ δ'† αὐτίκ' ἀγνοίᾳ λαβὼν
ἔσθει βορὰν ἄσωτον, ὡς ὁρᾷς, γένει.
κἄπειτ' ἐπιγνοὺς ἔργον οὐ καταίσιον,
ᾤμωξεν, ἀμπίπτει δ' ἀπὸ σφαγῆς *ἐμῶν·   (1600)
μόρον δ' ἄφερτον Πελοπίδαις ἐπεύχεται,
λάκτισμα δείπνου ξυνδίκως τιθεὶς *ἀράν,   1530
οὕτως ὀλέσθαι πᾶν τὸ Πλεισθένους γένος.
ἐκ τῶνδέ σοι πεσόντα τόνδ' ἰδεῖν πάρα,
κἀγὼ δίκαιος τοῦδε τοῦ φόνου ῥαφεύς·
τρίτον γὰρ *ἐπὶ τοῖνδ'* ὄντα μ' ἀθλίῳ πατρὶ
ξυνεξελαύνει τυτθὸν ὄντ' ἐν σπαργάνοις,   1535
τραφέντα δ' αὖθις ἡ δίκη κατήγαγε.
καὶ τοῦδε τἀνδρὸς ἡψάμην θυραῖος ὤν,
πᾶσαν ξυνάψας μηχανὴν δυσβουλίας.
οὕτω καλὸν δὴ καὶ τὸ κατθανεῖν ἐμοὶ
ἰδόντι τοῦτον τῆς δίκης ἐν ἔρκεσιν.   1540

ΧΟ. Αἴγισθ᾽, ὑβρίζειν ἐν κακοῖσιν οὐ σέβω.
σὺ δ᾽ ἄνδρα τόνδε φὴς ἑκὼν κατακτανεῖν,
μόνος δ᾽ ἔποικτον τόνδε βουλεῦσαι φόνον.
οὔ φημ᾽ ἀλύξειν ἐν δίκῃ τὸ σὸν κάρα
δημορριφεῖς, σάφ᾽ ἴσθι, λευσίμους ἀράς. 1545

ΑΙ. σὺ ταῦτα φωνεῖς νερτέρᾳ προσήμενος
κώπῃ, κρατούντων τῶν ἐπὶ ζυγῷ δορός;
γνώσει, γέρων ὤν, ὡς διδάσκεσθαι βαρὺ
τῷ τηλικούτῳ, σωφρονεῖν εἰρημένον.
δεσμὸς δὲ καὶ τὸ γῆρας αἵ τε νήστιδες 1550
δύαι διδάσκειν ἐξοχώταται φρενῶν
ἰατρομάντεις. οὐχ ὁρᾷς ὁρῶν τάδε;
πρὸς κέντρα μὴ λάκτιζε, μὴ *παίσας μογῇς.

ΧΟ. ‖*εὐνὴν σὺ τοῦδ᾽ οἰκουρὸς αἰσχύνας ἅμα
‖γυναικὶ τοὺς ἥκοντας ἐκ μάχης τρέων* 1555
ἀνδρὶ στρατηγῷ †*τ᾽ αἰσχρὸν ἔρραψας φόνον*†.

ΑΙ. καὶ ταῦτα τἄπη κλαυμάτων ἀρχηγενῆ.
᾽Ορφεῖ δὲ γλῶσσαν τὴν ἐναντίαν ἔχεις·
ὁ μὲν γὰρ ἦγε πάντ᾽ ἀπὸ φθογγῆς χαρᾷ,
σὺ δ᾽ ἐξορίνας *νηπίοις ὑλάγμασιν 1560
ἄξει· κρατηθεὶς δ᾽ ἡμερώτερος φανεῖ.

ΧΟ. ὡς δὴ σύ μοι τύραννος ᾽Αργείων ἔσει,
ὅς, *οὐδ᾽ ἐπειδὴ τῷδ᾽ ἐβούλευσας μόρον,
δρᾶσαι τόδ᾽ ἔργον οὐκ ἔτλης αὐτοκτόνως.

ΑΙ. τὸ γὰρ δολῶσαι πρὸς γυναικὸς ἦν σαφῶς· 1565
ἐγὼ δ᾽ ὕποπτος ἐχθρὸς ἦ παλαιγενής.
ἐκ τῶν δὲ τοῦδε χρημάτων πειράσομαι
ἄρχειν πολιτῶν· τὸν δὲ μὴ πειθάνορα
ζεύξω βαρείαις οὔτι μὴ σειραφόρον
κριθῶντα πῶλον, ἀλλ᾽ ὁ δυσφιλὴς *σκότῳ 1570
λιμὸς ξύνοικος μαλθακόν σφ᾽ ἐπόψεται.

ΧΟ. *σὺ δὴ τὸν ἄνδρα τόνδ᾽ ἀπὸ ψυχῆς κακῆς
οὐκ αὐτὸς ἠνάριζες, ἀλλὰ σὺν γυνή,

52 ΑΙΣΧΥΛΟΥ ΑΓΑΜΕΜΝΩΝ.

χώρας μίασμα καὶ θεῶν ἐγχωρίων,
ἔκτειν᾽· Ὀρέστης ἀρά που βλέπει φάος, 1575
ὅπως κατελθὼν δεῦρο πρευμενεῖ τύχῃ
ἀμφοῖν γένηται τοῖνδε παγκρατὴς φονεύς ;

ΑΙ. ἀλλ᾽ ἐπεὶ δοκεῖς τάδ᾽ ἔρδειν *κοὐ λέγειν, γνώσει τάχα.

ΧΟ. †οὐ γάρ, εἰ γέροντές ἐσμεν, τοῖς κακοῖς ὑπείξομεν.† 1579 (1650)

ΑΙ. εἶα δή, φίλοι λοχῖται, τοὔργον οὐχ ἑκὰς τόδε.

ΧΟ. εἶα δή, ξίφος πρόκωπον πᾶς τις εὐτρεπιζέτω.

ΑΙ. ‖ἀλλὰ μὴν κἀγὼ πρόκωπος οὐκ ἀναίνομαι θανεῖν.

ΧΟ. δεχομένοις λέγεις θανεῖν σε· τὴν τύχην δ᾽ *αἱρούμεθα.

ΚΛ. μηδαμῶς, ὦ φίλτατ᾽ ἀνδρῶν, ἄλλα δράσωμεν κακά·
ἀλλὰ καὶ τάδ᾽ ἐξαμῆσαι πολλὰ δύστηνον θέρος· 1585
πημονῆς ἅλις γ᾽ ὑπάρχει· μηδὲν αἱματώμεθα.
στεῖχε καὶ σὺ χοἱ γέροντες πρὸς δόμους πεπρω-
μένους,
πρὶν παθεῖν ἔρξαντες· *ἀρκεῖν χρῆν τάδ᾽ ὡς ἐπράξαμεν·
εἰ δέ τοι μόχθων γένοιτο τῶνδ᾽ ἅλις, *δεχοίμεθ᾽ ἄν,
δαίμονος *χηλῇ βαρείᾳ δυστυχῶς πεπληγμένοι.
ὧδ᾽ ἔχει λόγος γυναικός, εἴ τις ἀξιοῖ μαθεῖν. 1591

ΑΙ. ἀλλὰ τούσδ᾽ ἐμοὶ ματαίαν γλῶσσαν ὧδ᾽ ἀπανθίσαι,
κἀκβαλεῖν ἔπη τοιαῦτα *δαίμονος πειρωμένους,
σώφρονος γνώμης δ᾽ *ἁμαρτεῖν, τὸν κρατοῦντά †θ᾽
ὑβρίσαι.† 1594

ΧΟ. οὐκ ἂν Ἀργείων τόδ᾽ εἴη, φῶτα προσσαίνειν κακόν.

ΑΙ. ἀλλ᾽ ἐγώ σ᾽ ἐν ὑστέραισιν ἡμέραις μέτειμ᾽ ἔτι.

ΧΟ. οὐκ, ἐὰν δαίμων Ὀρέστην δεῦρ᾽ ἀπευθύνῃ μολεῖν.

ΑΙ. οἶδ᾽ ἐγὼ φεύγοντας ἄνδρας ἐλπίδας σιτουμένους.

ΧΟ. πρᾶσσε, πιαίνου, μιαίνων τὴν δίκην· ἐπεὶ πάρα.

ΑΙ. ἴσθι μοι δώσων ἄποινα τῆσδε μωρίας χάριν. 1600

ΧΟ. κόμπασον θαρσῶν, ἀλέκτωρ *ὥστε θηλείας πέλας.

ΚΛ. μὴ προτιμήσῃς ματαίων τῶνδ᾽ ὑλαγμάτων· †ἐγὼ†
καὶ σὺ θήσομεν κρατοῦντε τῶνδε δωμάτων †καλῶς†.

TRANSLATION

WITH NOTES EXPLANATORY AND ILLUSTRATIVE.

TRANSLATION.

[Inclosed numerals refer to the Greek text.]

AGAMEMNON.

[SCENE: *the royal palace at Argos: opposite to the central door is the altar of Apollo Aguieus: near it, on each side, altars of other deities. On the flat roof of the palace, or, perhaps, on a tower reared above it, is seen a* WATCHMAN, *in recumbent posture, with head resting on his hands, gazing towards the east. The time is night, but near to morning.*]

PROLOGOS.

WATCHMAN.

STILL do I ask the gods deliverance from these toils
throughout my long year's watch, whereto I lay me down

Prologos. In this prologue the poet has three chief objects in view : a. to announce the capture of Troy by the beacon-blaze and the watchman's outcry; β. to bring Clytaemnestra to the notice of his audience as a woman of masculine character and strong will (10); γ. to prepare them for future evil by hinting the misconduct of those who rule the palace in the absence of Agamemnon (18, 19, 36—39).

2. μῆκος, accus. of duration. Some would have it to depend on ἐτείας, taking φρουρᾶς in apposition to πόνων. Others read μῆχος, *remedy*, in appos. to ἀπαλλαγήν.

whereto &c. ἣν κοιμώμενος, a construction (κοιμᾶσθαι φρουράν) of the cognate or contained accus. The verb has the meaning of κεῖσθαι only.

upon the Atreidae's roof, arm-rested, like a dog,
and know by heart the congress of the nightly stars,
with those which bring to men winter and summer-tide,   5
bright potentates, *their sheen* conspicuous in the sky
beholding, whensoe'er they set and rise again.
and now I'm watching for the signal of a torch,
the blaze of fire, that bringeth a report from Troy,
a voice announcing capture : for e'en so commands   10
a woman's manly-planning heart in hopeful mood.
but whensoe'er I keep this nightly-restless couch
of mine, all drenched with dew, by dreams unvisited—

3. *arm-rested*, ἄγκαθεν. Hesychius and another grammarian, followed
by some editors, consider this to be a form of ἀνέκαθεν, *aloft.* Some place
ἀνέκαθεν in the text. We think Cod. F. and Pal. right in regarding it as =
Homeric ἐπ' ἀγκῶνος, on the elbow.

5, 6. The watchman, reclining on the palace-roof nightly through the
year, and looking eastward, would (as Professor Adams kindly tells us)
have the opportunity of studying all the constellations lying not far from
the Equator : the most conspicuous being,—among the zodiacal, Taurus,
Gemini, Leo, Virgo, Scorpio,—among the extra-zodiacal, Andromeda,
Orion, Canis Major and Minor, Aquila. As the constellations so seen
would vary according to the seasons, a poet might say that they bring
summer and winter. This would not apply to the planets, Jupiter, Venus
and Mars, which would also become conspicuous in the course of the year,
but not as connected with particular seasons. Some stars more distant
from the Equator would also engage the observer's attention, as Capella in
Auriga, Arcturus in Bootes, and Vega in Lyra.

6. *potentates*, δυνάστας. Most explain this of the sun and moon. But
the sun would not be seen in the night, and the moon has nothing to do
with the change of seasons. It is however possible that Aesch., thinking
most of the sun, may have meant to say that the watch, beginning at sunset,
and ending at sunrise, would teach the various hours at which these took
place. Others refer δυνάστας to larger fixed stars which would in the
course of the year come within the watchman's field of view as he lay down
with his face towards the east. See these in the last note.

7. On this verse and on verse 17 see *Conspectus Lectionum* and *Notes
on Lection.*

10. *so commands*, ὧδε κρατεῖ, Herm., to which version we see no valid
objection. One whose will rules or prevails may be said to command.

for terror in the stead of sleep beside me stands,
so that in sleep I may not soundly close mine eyes—   15
and when I think to sing a song or hum a tune,
providing this one music-antidote to sleep,
then do I wail with groans the evils of this house,
not, as of yore, in noblest wise administer'd.
but now may't come, my fortunate release from toils,   20
when through the dark with joyous message gleams the fire,

(The beacon-blaze is descried on Mt. Arachnaeus: the Watchman starts to his feet, and cries.)

Hail, O thou shiner of the night, exhibiting
a day-light splendour, and in Argos garniture
of many a dancing choir, to honour this event.
                    hurrah! hurrah!   25
to Agamemnon's wife clear token do I give
that from her couch she rise with earliest speed, and lift,
for *all* the house *to hear*, a happy-omened cry
this torchlight loudly greeting, since that Ilion's town
is taken, as the beacon-message plainly tells.   30
and I myself too will perform a prelude-dance;

14. *terror,* φόβος, i.e. fear of punishment for sleeping on his watch.

16. ἀείδειν, *to sing* words; μινύρεσθαι, *to hum a tune* without words.

24. συμφορὰ is used in its original sense, *occurrence, event,* which here is a happy one. But, by a well-known Greek euphemism, it most frequently means *a calamitous event, a misfortune,* as above, 18.

25. Some think that the watchman now descends by an unseen stair to the proscenium, and there ends his speech, afterwards entering the palace by one of the lesser doors. We do not take this view. If he had been watching on a turret, he descends from it, and perhaps shouts through a trap-door in the roof to the queen and family, then, concluding his speech on the roof, he quits it by an unseen stair.

28. λαμπάδι depends on the ἐπὶ in ἐπορθιάζειν, *to shout aloud on.*

30. *plainly tells,* ἀγγέλλων πρέπει, *distinctly announces.* πρέπειν expresses distinctness in what is seen or heard. See ἐμπρέποντας above, 6.

31. Here the watchman performs some steps of a dance.

for lucky shall I count the fortunes of our lords,
now that this beacon-watch has thrown me triple sice.
and so, when he, the king who rules the palace, comes,
my lot be with this hand to hold his well-loved hand.   35
of all the rest I'm silent: on my tongue hath stepp'd
a mighty ox; the house itself, if voice it found,
would give the clearest evidence; since I by choice
speak to the knowing, to the unknowing I forget.

PARODOS.

[*The Watchman leaves the palace roof. An interval of time is now supposed.
Daylight has arrived. Clytaemnestra, acquainted with the tidings of the
beacon, has sent messengers commanding incense to be burnt before all the
shrines of Argos, in token of thanksgiving. The Chorus, consisting of
the chief councillors of the state, attend at the palace to learn the news.
Each χορευτὴς carries a staff (βακτηρία). They enter the orchestra by
the passage between the stage and the spectators' seats (θέατρον) on the
right hand of the latter, and, moving on the circumference of a quadrant,
ascend the choral platform, which extends from the central thymele (altar
of Bacchus) to the proscenium. There, standing in their usual order,
they chant their opening song. The passage by which they enter is called
Parodos, and the song then sung receives the same technical name. In
this drama it has three parts, 1. Anapaests; 2. Pro-ode; 3. Ode.*]

32, 33. θήσομαι, *I shall reckon* or (as Pal.) *score. lucky*, εὖ πεσόντα, *to
have had a lucky cast*: the metaphor is continued in the next verse. *triple
sice*, τρὶς ἕξ. The dice (κύβος) of the Greeks were like our own; and,
when they played with three, the best throw was three sixes, which the
Romans called Venus. The lowest was τρεῖς κύβοι (three aces), in Latin,
Canis.

35. *to hold*, βαστάσαι, lit. *to lift or bear up.* The use of this verb
seems to shew that the inferior greeted his lord by laying his hand under
that of the latter, and respectfully pressing it upward.

36. *on my tongue* &c. The origin of this metaphor, an ox treading on
the tongue, which expresses enforced silence, is unknown.

37. *the house* &c. See Luke xix. 40: 'I tell you that, if these
should hold their peace, the stones would immediately cry out.'

39. *I forget*, λήθομαι. Ital. *non mi ricordo*; which, since a famous
occasion in 1820, has almost passed into a proverb for convenient silence.
It might be rendered *hold my peace* here.

CHORUS.

1. *Anapaests.*

Now is the tenth year *on its passage,*   40
since Priam's great opponent,
king Menelaus with king Agamemnon,
—a stalwart yoke-pair, sons of Atreus, *holding*
from Zeus the honour of two thrones, two sceptres,—
an Argive armament of thousand vessels   45
from out this country
despatch'd, a militant reprisal,
a mighty war-cry shouting in their fury,
in mood like vultures,
which in their lonely sorrows for their children   50
high o'er their eyrie whirl in circles

40. In the anapaestic system (or series of systems, if a versus paroe-miacus be regarded as the terminus of a system) with which the Parodos commences, the Chorus says : that ten years have passed since the expedition against Troy sailed out under Agamemnon and Menelaus, whose wrath for the loss of Helen was like that of a pair of vultures robbed of their young : that an avenging deity espoused their cause : that war and bloodshed ensued, of which the end was not reached, but punishment could not fail to visit the unholy performance of sacred rites. The old age of the Chorus, which had kept its members at home, is described as a second childhood. Finally they address Clytaemnestra (who, during their recitative, has probably come out of the palace and begun to light the altars before it), inquiring why the order for burning incense is gone forth, and begging her to relieve the anxiety with which their minds are disturbed.

41. *opponent,* ἀντίδικος, properly in a suit (δίκη). This is specially applicable to Menelaus, who had been robbed of his wife, and whose name is first mentioned. Agamemnon is then added, as his brother espousing his cause, and as commander-in-chief; but the two continue to be mentioned as forming one yoke-pair, ζεῦγος 'Ατρειδᾶν, in apposition with which gen. stands τιμῆς and its epithets. The construction is remarkable.

50. *lonely,* ἐκπατίοις. This is variously explained : the derivation (ἐκ πάτου, out of the usual path) suggests the sense we give.

51. *high o'er,* ὕπατοι, for ὕπερθε, an unusual expression. 'Επάνω is a conjecture worthy of consideration, as ὕπατοι follows, 55.

with oary pinions rowing,
since they have lost *their labour,*
the couch-observing labour of their nestlings.
but hearing from on high, perchance Apollo   55
or Pan or Zeus, the shrilly-crying bird-wail
of these sky-sojourners,
unto transgressors sendeth
an after-punishing Erinys.
e'en so the mightier Zeus, of guest-law guardian,   60
sends forth the sons of Atreus,
about a many-suitored woman
appointing limb-subduing struggles countless
of knee that in the dust is planted
and spear-shaft snapping in the onsets   65
alike for Trojans and for Danaans.
as things are now, so are they, and fulfilled
shall be as Destiny hath willed ;
†*nor e'er shall any man*† by secret soothing
of burnt-oblation or of wine-libation   70
avert of fireless rites the strong-set indignation.

55. It has been suggested, that Apollo favours the vultures as augural
birds; Pan, as birds that hunt; Zeus, as birds of royal nature. Τις 'Απόλ-
λων κ.τ.λ. = τις ἢ 'Απ. ἤ κ.τ.λ.

57. *sky-sojourners*, μετοίκων. The vultures are settlers in the sky,
where the gods dwell. Apollo, Pan, Zeus, are their patrons (προστάται).
But τῶνδε μετοίκων may possibly be a gloss.

60. *the mightier,* ὁ κρείσσων, i.e. Ζεὺς ξένιος (of guest-law guardian),
who is assumed, in that character, to be still mightier than the Zeus (τις)
who favoured the vultures.

62. *many-suitored*, πολυάνορος. Helen had many suitors : and, after
the death of Paris, she married Deiphobus.

65. *onsets*, προτελείοις. Hesychius has : προτέλεια, αἱ πρὸ τοῦ γάμου
τελούμεναι θυσίαι. Hence the word is used here metaphorically for a
skirmish beginning a battle : in 204, for a sacrifice before a voyage.

71. *fireless rites.* The meaning of ἀπύρων ἱερῶν has been disputed.
There seems to be no safer explanation than this—that the poet thus
designates all unholy rites, such as the marriage-rites of Paris and Helen,

but we, by aged frames exempted,
left of the force behind which then *was mustered*,
remain, our child-like strength on staves supporting.
for the young marrow leaping upward   75
within the bosom,
ere martial vigour holds its place, is eld-like ;
and far-gone eld, what time the foliage withers,
ways triple-footed walketh,
and, than a child no stronger,   80 (83)
a day-seen dream, each *old man* wanders.
but thou, Tyndareus' daughter,
queen Clytaemnestra, what is this occasion?
what new thing *has befallen* ?
what hast thou noted, trusted in what tidings,   85
that thus thou sendest round an incense-stirring *message?*
for now of all the gods both city-ruling,
supernal, infernal,
and o'er the mart presiding,
the altars are ablaze with offerings: 90 (93)
the torch on this side and on that uplifteth
its skyward-reaching stature,
drugged with the soft and guileless suasions

---

which, being hasty and illegal, took place without the usual burnt-offerings.
The wrath of these will mean the wrath of the deities to whom such offerings
were due.   The sacrifice of Iphigenia may also be glanced at.

72. *exempted*, ἀτίται.   This word ἀτίτης (ἀ τίω) is explained to mean,
not liable to pay a due ; here, ' not fit for military service.'

79. *triple-footed*, τρίποδας.   An allusion to the riddle of the Sphinx,
solved by Oedipus, ἔστι δίπους ἐπὶ γῆς καὶ τέτραπος...καὶ τρίπος.   The biped
man, when he crawls as an infant, is four-footed; when he takes a crutch
in old age, three-footed.

93. *guileless*, ἀδόλοισι.   The true contrast implied by this epithet has
been generally overlooked.   Some poorly render it *genuine ;* others suppose
the guile of orators to be glanced at.   In our opinion (looking at φαρμ. χρ.
ἁγνοῦ) Aeschylus refers to the φάρμακα δόλια of sorceresses (φαρμακευτρίαι).
See Theocr. *Id.* II. Verg. *Ecl.* VIII.   He means to say that the tidings

of holy ointment,
the clot from out the royal store-room.   95
of these things what thou canst, and what to utter
is lawful, speak, †*shew something certain*†,
and of this care become a healer,
which now is sometimes evil-boding,
but soon again from sacrifices   100 (103)
hope shining mild drives thought away, that sorrows
insatiate *still*, a soul-consuming mischief.

2. *Pro-ode.*

Empowered am I to sing aloud   *Strophe.*
the lucky might of stalwart heroes,
boded by a wayside omen,   10
(for still my life, with strength connurtured,

made known by Clytaemnestra's illumination are true. The queen is no
deceiving sorceress.

95. *clot,* πέλανος, a soft essential substance, such as butter or lard.

store-room, μυχόθεν, from the μυχός, interior of the palace, where the
store-rooms were, near the ἑστία : lit. 'the royal clot from the μυχός.'

101. *that sorrows,* lit. of sorrow, λύπης.

102 (106). On changes made in these Anapaests, glosses omitted (61,
71. 92), additions suggested (69, 101), corrections (67, 83, 97, 106), see
Consp. Lect. and *Notes on Lection.*

103. Why Clytaemnestra at this moment makes no reply to the Chorus,
is left to conjecture. Engaged with the altars, she may be supposed to have
moved during the recitation of the anapaests, and to be out of sight behind
the right-hand Periacte. The Pro-ode of the Parodos now sung describes
a wayside omen which occurred to Agamemnon and Menelaus on their
march to Chalcis, and its interpretation by the army-seer Calchas, who,
knowing by his skill that Artemis was displeased with the Atreidae, invoked
the aid of Apollo to pacify her, and prevent the evil consequences hinted
at in the concluding lines. The omen was that of two eagles (who represent
the Atreidae) devouring a pregnant hare. On wayside omens (ἐνόδια
σύμβολα) see Theophrast. *Char.* (ὁ δεισιδαίμων) and Hor. *C.* III. 27.

104. *stalwart heroes,* ἀνδρῶν ἐντελέων. See *Notes on Lection.*

105. *boded by a wayside omen,* ὅδιον.

106. *for still* &c. i.e. though old, I am strong enough to sing with
boldness.

by heavenly favour
upon me breathes the confidence of song),
how the twin-thronèd kingship of the Achaeans,
of Hellad youth a government harmonious,   110 (111)
with spear and hand exacting vengeance
a fiery bird to Teucrian land
conducts, the king of birds to kings of ships
—the black one and the white-tailed—manifest
nigh to the tents, upon the hand that wields the spear,   115
in a station seen of all,
feeding upon a hare with young ones big,
caught ere its closing race was over.
sing woe ! sing woe ! but be the good victorious !
Them when the skilful army-seer   *Antistrophe.*
beheld, the warlike sons of Atreus   121 (122)
two in number, twain in temper,
he understood the hare-devourers,
their earliest escort :
and thus, interpreting the portent, spake.   125
'this expedition captures Priam's city
in time : and all the herds before the fortress,
that fed the people with abundance,
shall fate with violence lay waste :

109.   *kingship*, κράτος (abstract for concrete) = βασιλέας.   So τάγαν, *leaders*.

111.   *exacting vengeance*, πράκτορι.

114.   Aristotle (*H. A.* IX.) distinguishes these eagles as μελανάετος and πύγαργος.   They symbolise the differing tempers of the two Atreidae, 121.

115.   *upon the hand that wields the spear*, χερὸς ἐκ δοριπάλτου, i.e. on the right hand.

116.   *station*, ἕδραι, an augural term.

118.   *caught*, βλαβέντα, neut. plur. referred to hare and young ones.

122.   *he understood*, ἐδάη, i.e. he learnt their meaning.

124.   *their earliest escort*, πομπᾶς ἀρχούς, i.e. the ominous birds which first met them, ἐνοδίους ὄρνιθας.   See *Notes on Lection*.

let only from the gods no envy cloud,   130 (129)
forestricken, Troy's great bit in arms encamp'd.
for spiteful to the house is Artemis the pure,
to her father's wingèd hounds,
a timid creature eating, young and all,
ere birth: and hates the meal of eagles.   135
sing woe! sing woe! but be the good victorious!
So kindly though she be, the Beauteous one,   *Epode.*
to dewdrops small of furious lions,
and to the udder-loving cubs
of all land-roaming beasts, she beggeth   140 (137)
the pleasing signs of these birds to fulfil,
visions of happy omen, but not blameless.
I call for aid from healing Paean,
that she may frame no stormful breezes
against the Danaans blowing,   145
long time the ships detaining,
the while a second sacrifice she speedeth,
a lawless one, unbanquetable,
kindred artificer of quarrels,

130. *cloud,* κνεφάσῃ. 'To cloud a bit' is a confused metaphor; but in tragedy the language of soothsayers is studiously dark. See it parodied by Aristophanes in the *Birds*. 'The bit' means the Greek army.

133. *winged hounds,* πτανοῖσιν κυσί. The eagle is called the hound of Zeus, as his constant attendant; and 'winged hound' (by a tragic idiom) to distinguish the metaphorical from the real dog. See *Prom.* 1042, Διὸς δέ τοι πτηνὸς κύων δαφοινὸς αἰετός. Soph. fr. 815, ὁ σκηπτοβάμων αἰετός, κύων Διός. Clytaemnestra is called δίπους λέαινα, 1187. Mr Paley says: "the eagles and the Atreidae are here viewed as identical, the one being portended by the other; and the anger of Artemis against the birds for killing the hare is indicative of her anger against Agamemnon for some offence which Aeschylus does not expressly mention, but Sophocles (*El.* 566) describes as the slaughter of a doe in hunting."

141. *these birds,* στρουθῶν τούτων. Here στρουθοί means 'large birds,' i. e. the eagles. See the word in Lexicon.

143. *healing Paean.* Apollo, as healing god, is named Παιάν. His epithet, ἰήιος, is variously explained. See it in Lex.

a husband not respecting: for there waiteth   150 (144)
a terrible recoiling anger,
house-guarding, treacherous, mindful, child-avenging.'
such things did Calchas shouting utter
with mighty blessings mingled,
as from the wayside birds predestined   155
unto the royal houses.
with these in concert
sing woe! sing woe! but be the good victorious!

Ode.

Zeus, whosoe'er he is, if by that title   *Str.* 1.
to be called himself delighteth,   160 (152)
even thus do I address him.
other name I cannot mention,
in the balance weighing all,

158. On the readings in this Ode (108, 121, 123, 136, 139—40) see *Consp. Lect.* and *Notes on Lection.*

159. The Chorus, in this Ode, begin with a profession of religious faith in Zeus as now the supreme ruler of heaven. Uranus and Kronos (they say) are past and powerless. It is wise to sing the praise of Zeus the conqueror, who taught mankind the truth that learning is gained by suffering. One instance of this is seen in that repentance which is forced on reluctant minds by the stings of conscious guilt, and which must be viewed as a blessing from the gods. Such is the case of Agamemnon. At the time when the Achaeans were detained in Chalcis by foul winds, with ruin to their health, and when Calchas laid before the chiefs the dread demands of Artemis,—Agamemnon exclaimed : 'terrible is the choice between disobedience and the murder of a child: for how can I leave my troops to their fate? how can I refuse to my allies the sacrifice they desire and demand?' Thus did he steel his heart to become the slayer of his daughter. The dire fact is then described with picturesque pathos: and the maxim repeated, that the fruit of suffering is learning. But how this will be shown in the Future, none can foretell. A time will come for knowing; till then, lamentation is premature. May the issue be prosperous, in accordance with the wishes of her who is now singly guarding this Apian land.

K. A.   5

save Zeus, if from my thought the idle burden
I may reject with true *decision.* 165
If one there was in former ages mighty, *Ant.* 1.
with all-battling prowess teeming,
proofless now his ancient being:
and who afterward existed
found a conqueror, and is gone. 170 (160)
but any shouting gladly 'Zeus the victor,'
shall gain the full award of wisdom:
Him who the way of wisdom showed to mortals, *Str.* 2.
who stablished *as* a valid *maxim,*
by suffering they must purchase learning. 175
yea, e'en in slumber o'er the heart
sad memory of evil trickles,

168. Aeschylus could not mean that Uranus, one of the μάκαρες θεοὶ αἰὲν ἐόντες, had ceased to exist. In the *Prometheus* he says of Uranus and Kronos,

οὐκ ἐκ τῶνδ' ἐγὼ
δισσοὺς τυράννους ἐκπεσόντας ᾐσθόμην;

What he says in this place is, that Uranus has become a mere tradition, while Kronos has been conquered and expelled.

169 (58). *who afterward existed:* i.e. Κρόνος (Saturn), the father of Zeus, deposed and expelled from Olympus by his son, according to the Hellenic mythology. In the *Eumenides* 584 κ.τ.λ., when Apollo, defending Orestes against the Furies, declares that he himself obeyed the command of Zeus in directing Orestes to take vengeance on Clytaemnestra for the murder of Agamemnon, the Furies in reply twit him with this act of Zeus,

πατρὸς προτιμᾷ Ζεὺς μόρον, τῷ σῷ λόγῳ·
αὐτὸς δ' ἔδησε πατέρα πρεσβύτην Κρόνον.

Apollo answers by saying that Zeus did not incur the irretrievable guilt of bloodshed.

170. *a conqueror,* τριακτῆρος. Τριακτήρ, from τριάζειν, *to throw thrice* in a wrestling-match, which decided the victory.

171. *shouting...Zeus the victor,* Ζῆνα—ἐπινίκια κλάζων, lit. 'shouting victory-songs on Zeus,' κλάζων having the two accusatives of thing and person. Mr Paley cites Aristoph. *Ach. uit.* τήνελλα καλλίνικον ᾄδοντές σε καὶ τὸν ἀσκόν.

and to the unwilling brings discretion;
such is the favour of the gods,
I ween, who on the sacred bench are seated.   180 (168)
And then the elder chief of ships Achaean,   *Ant.* 2.
no blame on any prophet casting,
conspiring with imperious fortunes,
what time the Achaean soldiery
with barrel-emptying stress of weather   185
were sorely troubled, occupying
the site to Chalcis opposite
on tide-reciprocating shores of Aulis—
When blasts that from the Strymon came,   *Str.* 3.
producing leisure mischievous, with famine,   190 (176)
bad anchorages, wanderings of mortals,
nor ships nor cables sparing,
time after lengthened time protracting,
were wasting with delay the flower of Argos—
when yet another remedy,   195
more grievous than the bitter wintry-wind,
unto the chiefs the prophet shouted,
before them casting Artemis,
that with their sceptres
the sons of Atreus smote upon the earth,   200 (185)
and stifled not the tear—
'Twas thus the elder chief exclaim'd: *Ant.* 3.
'a heavy fate indeed is disobedience,
and heavy too, if I my child shall slaughter,
my mansion's lovely darling,   205
a father's hands before the altar

178. *brings:* lit. comes.
181. *And then* &c. So far, this Ode has contained a religious and
moral digression affecting the crisis which the Chorus had reached at the
close of the Pro-ode. In its second antistrophe the story of Agamemnon
is now continued.
189. *from the Strymon,* i.e. from the N.E., most unfavourable for the
voyage to Troy.

with streaming gore of murdered maid polluting.
of these things, which is void of ill?
a fleet-deserter how can I become,
and fall away from my alliance?   210 (194)
for lawfully may they desire
with rage outrageous
a sacrifice wind-calming, virgin blood.
may all be for the best!'
So, when the harness of necessity   *Str.* 4.   215
he donned, an impious wind-change blowing,
impure, unholy, from that moment
he chose a new all-daring purpose.
for mortals, by its base monitions,
the wretched madness of first sin emboldens.   220 (202)
and so he had the hardihood
to be a daughter's sacrificer,
auxiliar to a woman-venging warfare,
and to the sailing ships
a rite inaugurating their departure.   225
Her prayers and invocations of her sire,   *Ant.* 4.
her maiden age, as nought they counted,
those war-enamoured arbitrators.
and, when the litany was ended,
the father told the priestly servants,   230 (209)
as lay she prostrate with her robes about her,
with all their heart to lift her high,
prone, as a kid, above the altar,

215. *harness,* λέπαδνον, lit. *breast-rein.*

216 (197). *wind-change,* τροπαίαν (αὔραν).

218 (199). μετέγνω. Μετὰ in composition often implies *change.*
Μεταγιγνώσκειν is to *adopt a new opinion* or *purpose* (γνώμη) which is described as τὸ παντότολμον φρονεῖν, *the having an all-daring mind.*

223 (203). *auxiliar,* ἀρωγάν, in apposition to the clause θυτὴρ γενέσθαι θυγατρός.

225 (204). *a rite* &c., προτέλεια. See 64.

and, watching o'er her lovely mouth, to stifle
with voiceless strength of gags   235
her shriek of execration on the houses.
But, to the earth down-dropping   *Str.* 5.
her saffron-tinctured veil, each sacrificer
she smote with piteous arrow from her eye,
as though 'twere in a picture, seeming   240 (219)
desirous to address them : since full often
in the large-tabled guest-hall of her sire
she sang, and virgin with pure voice did honour
fondly to her fond father's paean,
that ushered in   245
with happy fate the third libation.
What next—I saw not, speak not :   *Ant.* 5.
it was not unfulfill'd, the lore of Calchas.
to them that suffer Justice doth incline
the scale of learning : but the Future   250 (228)

234. If φυλακᾷ were read here, the construction would be simple.
But Mr Paley, keeping φυλακάν, makes it the subj. of κατασχεῖν, *that a
watch* &c. *should restrain* &c. This is possible : but, upon the whole, we
consider φυλακὰν a contained accus. depending on κατασχεῖν, which also
governs φθόγγον as object. This is rendered in effect by the English version, *watching* &c.

238. *saffron-tinctured veil.* The scholiasts say πέπλον, *robe* or mantle.
Some believe κρόκου βαφὰς to mean *blood*, and use χέουσα as an argument.
See *Consp. L.*

240. *as...in a picture.* In a later age, the sacrifice of Iphigenia was
the subject of a famous picture by Timanthes, who crowned his skill by
hiding the face of Agamemnon. See the description by Lucretius.

242. ἀνδρῶνας, properly the men's apartments, used here (with εὐτραπέζους) to imply the *guest-hall* which belonged to them,

243. *did honour,* ἐτίμα, i.e. *took part in.* See τίονται, 657.

244—246. Mr Paley says : "the σπονδὴ and the παιὰν were inseparable
adjuncts of a banquet, and the αὐλητρὶς was seldom left out." Probably
the paean was sung at the third libation ; hence it is called here τριτό-
σπονδος, and as that libation was sacred to Ζεὺς Σωτήρ, it is also called
εὔποτμος, *happy-fated.*

thou'lt hear when it is past; till then, farewell to't:
'tis quite as good as sorrowing ere the time;
for clear 'twill come with day-break: but of these things
the issue be success! so wisheth
of Apia's land   255
this nearest and sole-guarding bulwark.

EPEISODION I.

[*There is some difficulty in accounting for the silence of Clytaemnestra when
     addressed in the anapaests of the Parodos 82—102. Some think that
     she had not left the palace at that time; others that she was on the
     proscenium at l. 82, but quitted it before 102 without staying to reply,
     which is perhaps the truer view. At all events she now comes forward
     to the logeion, and is addressed by the Coryphaeus in the words with
     which the First Epeisodion begins.*]

CHORUS.

Thy power revering, Clytaemnestra, I am come:
for 'tis *but* justice to respect a ruler's wife
when the male throne is left without an occupant.
but, whether thou hast learnt some good, or, learning nought,
in hope of happy tidings incense offerest,   261 (239)
fain would I hear: yet shall thy silence not offend.

   256. *bulwark,* ἕρκος. It is very doubtful whether this expression is
applied by the Chorus to themselves as the Council of State or to Clytaemnestra, who now appears on the proscenium. We lean to the latter
view. On the various readings in this Ode (153, 157, 159, 167, 180, 190,
191, 216, 228—9, 231—2 and others) see *Consp. L.* and *Notes on Lection.*

   257. In this Epeisodion, Clytaemnestra, replying to the questions of
the Chorus, first describes the succession of beacons by which the news
of the capture of Troy has been transmitted to Argos; and then draws an
imaginary picture of the condition of things in the captured city. Her concluding words, like those of the watchman, are designed by the poet to
prepare the minds of the hearers for evil impending, which here is ascribed
to the possibly aroused displeasure of the deities.

   260. *thou hast learnt,* lit. *having learnt,* πεπυσμένη. The Chorus ask
whether the incense is offered in thanksgiving or in supplication.

CLYTAEMNESTRA.

With happy tidings, as the proverb *is*, indeed
may Morning from its mother Night arrive to birth!
but thou wilt hear a joy too great for hearer's hope;   265
the Argive *troops* have taken Priam's capital.

CHORUS.

What sayest thou? the word is lost for lack of faith.

CLYTAEMNESTRA.

That Troy belongs to the Achaeans:—speak I plain?

CHORUS.

Joy steals upon my *senses*, calling forth a tear.

CLYTAEMNESTRA.

'Tis true: thine eye declares thy loyal sentiment. 270 (248)

CHORUS.

What is't thou trustest? hast thou proof of this event?

CLYTAEMNESTRA.

I have: why should I not, unless a god deceived?

CHORUS.

Do phantoms *seen* in dreams convince thy reverent soul?

CLYTAEMNESTRA.

I would not earn the credit of a sleepy mind.

---

264. The name Εὐφρόνη (which stands to Νύξ in some such relation
as Εὐμενίδες to ʼΕρινύες) suggests εὐαγγέλια.

271. This verse is usually printed as one question: *what trustworthy
proof* &c.? Others place a first interrogation after γάρ; *how then? hast
thou* &c.? Clytaemnestra's reply suggests the punctuation in our text.
ʻ I have a τέκμαρ,ʼ she says, and ends her speech by saying τέκμαρ τοιοῦτον
ξύμβολόν τε σοὶ λέγω 315 (291).

274. Most editors render this: *I would not accept the fancy of a dozing
mind.* This is unobjectionable in itself, but the tone of the next lines leads
us to prefer what appears in our version: *I have no wish to be thought a
dreamer of dreams.*

CHORUS.

Has then some wingless voice enriched thee *with the news?* 275

CLYTAEMNESTRA.

My intellect, as some young girl's, thou scornest sore.

CHORUS.

Declare within what time the city has been sack'd.

CLYTAEMNESTRA.

Within this night, I say, that bore the present dawn.

CHORUS.

What messenger is he that could achieve such speed?

CLYTAEMNESTRA.

Hephaestos, forth from Ida sending a bright light. 280 (258)
and beacon ever hitherward from courier fire
sent beacon: Ida first to the Hermaean cliff
of Lemnos: from that isle the mighty faggot-blaze
in order third the Athoan height of Zeus received,
and thence the travelling torch's strength, high-elevate 285
so as to skim the surface of the sea, lay full
before the gladdened view, transmitting, like some sun,
a golden-beaming blaze unto Makistus' towers.
nor did he, dallying, or by heedless sleep o'ercome,
forego the duty that beseems a messenger: 290 (268)

275. *wingless voice,* ἄπτερος φάτις, a voice conveyed to the mental ear
by no bird, i.e. a kind of presentiment. On omens conveyed by the cry
of birds see Soph. *Oed. T.* 966, *Antig.* 1001, 1021.

277. *within what time,* ποίου χρόνου ; The gen. has this force.

279. *could achieve such speed?* Some render, *could arrive so soon ?*

280. *Hephaestos,* Ἥφαιστος, the fire-god Vulcan. The succession of
beacons is (1) M. Ida in the Troad: (2) M. Hermaeus in Lemnos, westward : (3) M. Athos on the peninsula Acte, westward: (4) M. Makistus
in Euboea, southward: (5) M. Messapius in Boeotia, south of west: (6) M.
Cithaeron in Boeotia, south of west: (7) M. Aegiplanctus in Megaris, west
of south : (8) M. Arachnaeus in Argolis, west of south: (9) the palace-roof
at Argos, westward.

but to Euripus' streams far flies the beacon flame,
and makes its signal to Messapius' sentinels.
they, answering blaze with blaze, the tidings forwarded
by lighting up with fire a pile of aged heath.
so in its vigour still the torch, not yet bedimmed,   295
across the plain of the Asopus took its leap,
like the bright moon, unto Cithaeron's cliff, and there
awoke another *new* relay of missive flame.
nor did that watch-post disallow the far-sent light,
kindling a larger blaze than any named before.   300 (278)
forthwith beyond the lake Gorgopis shot the light,
and coming to its point on Aegiplanctus' mount
it urged an increase of the stablished fire-supply,
so, lighting up with stintless energy, they send
a mighty beard of flame, †*and one possessing strength*   305
so masterful as† with its onward-rushing blaze
the very headland to surmount that overlooks
the gulf Saronic: then it shot, until it reach'd
mount Arachnaeus, city-neighbouring beacon-site:
and last unto this roof of the Atreidae shoots   310 (287)
this light, not undescended from Idaean fire.
such are the well-adapted laws of torch-bearers,
from one to other in succession *due* fulfilled.
and the first winneth, though 'tis hindmost in the race.

312. *laws of torch-bearers.* The arrangements of the famous torch-race at Athens present some difficulties. We know two things, (1) that the winner must reach the goal with his torch alight: (2) that racers handed over their lighted torches to other racers under some law of succession, as here διαδοχαῖς, and in Lucretius, et quasi cursores, vitai lampada tradunt. The contending tribes, therefore, must have provided at least two runners each; the second of whom should receive the lighted torch from the first, perhaps to carry it back to the starting place, if the course was like that of the δίαυλος δρόμος. Or there might be several successive runners on parallel straight courses divided at equal intervals.

314 (290). *and the first winneth, though 'tis hindmost in the race.* This, we doubt not, means that the beacon of Ida, which looks down on the captured city, is on that account the winner. The victory is there.

such is to you the proof and token that I tell,   315
a message by my husband sent from Troy to me.

CHORUS.

The gods hereafter, lady, shall receive my prayers.
but for this tale—I fain would hear again, and crown
my wonder, how thou'lt tell it to the very close.

CLYTAEMNESTRA.

The Achaeans are the occupants of Troy this day.
a noise unmixed, I ween, is in the city heard.   321 (298)
should you pour vinegar and oil within one rim,
a variant you would call them, not a friendly pair.
so of the captives and the capturers distinct
the voices may be heard, a two-fold circumstance.   325
for on the one side they around the corpses flung
prostrate of husband or of brethren, children some
of aged parents, from a throat no longer free
the destiny bewail of these their dearest ones.
the others night-fatigue ensuing upon fight   330 (307)
sets famished down to breakfasts of whate'er the town
contains, no token placing them in order due,
but just as every man hath drawn the lot of chance.
within the captured habitations now of Troy
they're dwelling, from the chilly frosts of open sky   335
and from the dews delivered : thus divinely blest
they'll slumber all the night without a sentinel.
and, if they worship well the city-keeping gods,
those of the taken land, and shrines of deities,
they, captors, will not be made captive in their turn.   340 (317)
but let no prior lust prevail upon the host
to plunder what they ought not, overcome by greed :
for to their homes they must obtain a safe return,
to round the second member of the double-race.
and, if the army come obnoxious to the gods,   345
the sufferings of the slain may *then* be wakened up,

e'en if there happen *to them* no immediate ills.
from me, a woman *as I am*, such *thoughts* you hear.
but may the good prevail in no divided shape ;
for the delight of many blessings is my choice.   350 (327)

CHORUS.

Sagely thou speakest, lady, like a prudent man ;
but, after hearing from thy *mouth* the trusty signs,
I *now* prepare me duly to address the gods.
for joy is wrought of worth equivalent to toils.

STASIMON I.

1. *Anapaests.*

O Zeus the king, O night the friendly,   355

354. On the readings in Epeisodion I. (265, 281, 283—5, 313, and others) see *Consp. Lect.* and *Notes on Lection.*

355. Stas. 1. In the Anapaests introducing this Stasimon, the Chorus praises Zeus, who, by the event of the past night, has executed the retribution long prepared against Troy and its people for the guilt of Paris. The Ode begins with reasserting the same truth. Impious is the man who says the gods are indifferent to the conduct of mankind. A sinner's family feel the consequences, when the license of wealth tempts him to guilt. Sinless contentment is true wisdom : for wealth cannot protect the criminal who spurns the altar of justice. He is driven on by mad lust to irretrievable crime and final ruin, which a god inflicts. Such an óne was Paris, when he stole Helen from her home. She went, leaving war to her people, and carrying destruction to Troy, while the Achaean prophets deplored the affliction of the deserted and inconsolable husband. This is beautifully depicted in the second strophe and antistrophe. Next are described the miseries arising from war to the Grecian multitudes. Their friends are slain in battle; if they return home at all it is only in the shape of dust within their funereal urns. Hence the leaders of the war, the sons of Atreus, incur popular odium, and the Erinyes exact vengeance for the blood of the slain. Happy they who are exempt from the evils of war, either as conquerors or as conquered. In the Epode the Chorus expresses some doubt as to the certainty of the news. A woman, they say, is liable to believe too readily all tidings of a gratifying kind.

of mighty glories winner,
who flungest on the Trojan fortress
a net so closely meshed
that neither one full-grown
nor any child might overreach   360 (336)
slavery's vast snare of all-subduing ruin!
great Zeus I venerate, of guest-law guardian,
who wrought these *issues*, long since bending
his bow on Alexander in such wise
that nor before the seasonable moment,   365
nor yet above the stars
might shoot, without effect, his arrow.

2. *Ode.*

The stroke of Zeus they have: this *truth* to tell   *Str.* 1.
is easy, and to trace it out.
they fared as he decreed. there was who said   370 (347)
that gods disdain to take regard of mortals
by whom the grace of things inviolable
is trodden down: but impious he.
'tis shown to the descendants
of such as, daring what may not be dared,   375
breathe Ares with more might than justice,
their houses overflowing
beyond the measure that is good.
best 'tis not, no, nor free from wrong,
that it can be sufficing   380 (356)
to one of prudent temper.
for what defence are riches to a man,

366. *above the stars,* ὑπὲρ ἄστρων, i.e. *beside the mark,* seemingly a
proverbial phrase.

376. *breathe Ares,* Ἄρη πνεόντων, i.e. are inspired with the daring and
violent temper ascribed to the influence of the Wargod Ares.

382. *for what defence* &c. Whether the emendation of the text here
adopted be exact or not, the sense of the passage is correctly represented in

who insolently spurneth out of sight
the mighty altar-throne of Justice?
The wretched suasive impulse drives him on,   *Ant.* 1. 385
fore-counselling, resistless child
of fatuous sin : all remedy is vain.
the mischief is not hidden ; plain it showeth,
a light of baleful gleam : like ill-mixed copper
if rubbing is applied, the man   390 (365)
black-grainèd is, when tested ;
since, boy-like, he pursues a flying bird,
insufferable tribulation
upon his city bringing :
and to his prayers no god gives ear,   395
but overthrows the unrighteous man
with things like these familiar.
and such an one was Paris,
what time unto the home of Atreus' sons
he came, and by the stealing of a wife   4cc (374)
the hospitable board polluted.
Then, leaving to the citizens   *Str.* 2.
shields clashing, spearmen, sailors arming,
to Ilion taking ruin for a dower,
†*of cities twain one migrant curse,*†

the Greek and in the translation. *To spurn the altar of justice out of sight*
means (as Mr Paley says) 'to get rid of all distinction between right and
wrong.'

386. *fore-counselling, resistless child of fatuous sin,* προβουλόπαις ἄφερτος
ἄτας. Some render προβ. 'devising beforehand woe for children :' in which
latter sense (says Pal.) "the doctrine will be that the consequences of crime
descend to generations unborn: while in the former sense, which is to be
preferred, ἄτη is said τίκτειν and to have a child πειθώ," see 700. Karst.,
Weil., Dav., read πρόβουλος, παῖς, which Mr Paley does not disapprove.

391. *black-grained,* μελαμπαγής. "Bronze, when composed of a due
proportion of copper and tin, has a green rust (*aerugo*), and becomes bright
by friction; whereas, if mixed with zinc, it turns quite black externally,
and is liable to become dim and speckled, after being polished." Paley.

404, 2. Verg. Aen. II. 573. Troiae et patriae communis Erinys.

swiftly through the gates she's gone,   405
daring a thing undareable ;
and thus with many a groan they spake,
the prophets of the dwelling :
" alas ! alas !
o palace, palace, and ye chiefs !   410 (381)
alas, o bed and all ye traces
of husband-loving *kindness !*
silent in his dishonour, unupbraiding
he standeth, all that *once* was sweetest gone :
and in his longing for *the wife* o'er sea   415
a phantom shall appear to rule the palace.
the gracefulness of fine-formed statues
is held in detestation,
and for the husband, in the want of eyes,
all loveliness hath perished.   420 (389)
And pensive fancies dream-displayed   *Ant.* 2.
arrive, presenting vain enjoyment.
for vainly—when one seems to look on bliss
†*by sweet dreams visited in sleep*†—
swiftly-sliding through the hands
'tis gone, the vision—afterward   425
attendant with its wings no more
upon the paths of slumber."
and such indeed
are they, the sorrows *that are felt*
beside the palace-hearth and others   430 (396)
yet more than these afflictive.
but for the masses—them that sailed together

---

413. *silent* &c. In attempting to correct a passage so corrupt as this,
no scholar would venture to suppose he was restoring the exact words of the
poet. We have been guided, in great measure, by our opinion of the sense
which the place requires.

419. *in the want of eyes,* ὀφθαλμῶν ἐν ἀχηνίαις. We have changed
our opinion as to the interpretation of this phrase.

from forth the land of Hellas—in the home
of every one heart-aching grief is seen.
yea, many are the things that touch the heart-core :　　435
some doth a *friend* full well remember
he sent erewhile *to battle*,
but to the home of each, instead of men,
come urns and ashes *only*.
The War-god, who for gold exchangeth bodies,　440 (405) *Str.* 3.
and holds the scales in combat of the spear,
burnt dust for friends to mourn with heavy tears
from Ilion sendeth, freighting
the jars, in place of men, with well-stowed ashes.
so they bemoan their heroes, praising *each :*　　445
this one, for being skilled in warfare,
and that, for having nobly fall'n
in bloodshed through another's wife.
such is their secret fretting ;
and grudging grief steals silent on　　　　450 (415)
against the wrong-redressing sons of Atreus.
but others on the spot, around the fortress,
in their own forms hold tombs of Ilian land,
yet, holding, by the foeman's soil are hidden.
The talk of spiteful citizens is noisome,　　455 *Ant.* 3.
and worketh as a people-sanctioned curse.
my care expects some night-wrapt thing to hear :
for of the many-slaying

451. *wrong-redressing*, προδίκοις, plaintiffs or champions in a suit (δίκη); i.e. principals and leaders in the Trojan war, a war of vengeance for wrong.

453. *in their own forms*, εὔμορφοι in codd. The word certainly stands in contradistinction to the burnt ashes of other slain; hence we suspect that Aesch. wrote ἔμμορφοι, *in their own forms*, i.e. unburnt.

456. *people-sanctioned curse*, δημοκράντου ἀρᾶς. Mr Paley says: "the custom of execrating the public enemies of the Athenians in their assemblies is well known. Demost. 270 οὐχ ὧν ἔτυχεν ἦν, ἀλλ' οἶς ὁ δῆμος καταρᾶται."

the deities are never unobservant,
and in due time the black Erinyes   460 (424)
one who was lucky without justice
by luck-reversing brunt of life
make dark, and when among the unknown
he lies, no succour waits him.
renown o'er-great is perilous: 465
for by the eyes of Zeus a bolt is darted.
my choice is happiness devoid of envy:
neither a city-sacker may I be,
nor see the light of life, to others captive.
By the good tidings of the fire   *Epode.* 470 (435)
a quick report has travelled through the city.
who knows if truly *told*,
or if it be some fallacy divine?
yet who so childish or so shorn of sense,
as, by the new-sent beacon-message   475
inflamed in heart, through variant news
to be dejected afterward?
it suits a woman's *eager* mind
before the evident assurance
to welcome a delight.   .   480 (444)
the feminine decision on its march
too credulously trustful

466. *by the eyes of Zeus*, ὅσσοις διόθεν. So we render with Mr Paley. Others make ὅσσοις = *against the eyes* (of the many-slaying).

478. *eager mind*, αἰχμᾶ. Of this word Mr Paley says on *Prom.* 412, 'In Aesch. it appears to signify *indoles*, from ἀΐσσω, like θυμὸς from θύω, in both the notion of impulse prevailing, according to the natural temperament of the Greeks.'

481—3. Our old version followed Donaldson, who shews (*New Crat.* § 174) that ἐπινέμομαι can be used passively. But this use seems excluded here by ταχύπορος, which suits the deponent sense *encroaching* (by an invading army or epidemic) but not the passive, *encroached on.* 'The female limit' is a metaphor, implying 'the sentiment determining the mind of woman.'

goes swiftly ; but swift-fated too
a woman-bruited glory perisheth.

EPEISODION II.

CHORUS.

Soon shall we know the things by torches carrying light   485
transmitted, and by beacon-watches and by fire,
whether indeed they're true, or whether dream-like came
this blaze, and with its pleasantness beguiled our minds.
yon herald I behold approaching from the shore
with olive-boughs o'ershaded, while the thirsty dust,   490 (454)
brother of mud, and closely bordering, attests

484. For the emendations in this ch.ode (which corruption in some
parts renders necessary, as in 346, 355– 363, 383—4, 388—9, 397—8, 402,
427, and others) and on the additions suggested after 376, 392, see *Consp.
Lect.* and *Notes on Lection.*

485. In this Epeisodion the Chorus notices the arrival of the herald
Talthybius, who, on entering, salutes his native city, its deities, edifices
and statues. He notifies the approaching return of Agamemnon, and extols
the greatness of his victory. A conversation (στιχομυθία, line for line)
ensues between him and the Chorus, in which they hint the disquietude of
feeling in Argos. The herald then recounts the sufferings of the army at
Troy during the war, which are now compensated by brilliant results, for
which thanksgivings are due to the gods. Clytaemnestra then approaches
and claims credit for the confidence she placed in the beacon-message.
She sends a hypocritical greeting to Agamemnon, declaring her own
fidelity during his absence : and then probably retires. The Chorus enquire
about Menelaus. In his replies, Talthybius is obliged to confess that the
Grecian fleet has been shattered and dispersed by a storm, and that the
ship of Menelaus has disappeared. He speaks, however, with confident
hope of his safe return ere long; and now goes into the palace.

489. *from the shore.* The herald comes in therefore by the entrance
of the stage to the left of the spectators.

490. *the thirsty dust, brother of mud, and closely bordering* &c.
A strange mode of intimating that the herald's boots &c. are covered with
mud, and his other garments with dust.

K. A.   6

that neither mute, nor lighting flame of mountain wood,
will he give signal unto thee by smoke of fire;
but rather, he will either speak and utter joy,
or—but the word opposed to this my soul abhors: 495
for to the good displayed be each addition good!
who for this city offers prayer of other kind,
be his, himself to reap the error of his heart.

HERALD.

O thou paternal threshold of the Argive land,
to thee in this tenth yearly sunlight I am come,   500 (463)
now, after many hopes were wreck'd, of one possess'd.
for ne'er was I expecting in this Argive land
to be in death the sharer of a blessèd tomb.
now do I give thee greeting, land, now, sunlight, thee,
and Zeus the country's highest, and the Pythian king,   505
no longer aiming arrows at us with his bow.
enough upon Scamander's banks wast thou unkind:
in other mood a saviour now and healer be,
o king Apollo; and the gods address I all
o'er games presiding: Hermes too, my champion,   510 (473)
dear herald, and by heralds all a name revered,
and heroes who despatch'd us, that in kindliness
they will receive the host surviving from the war.
o thou the dwelling of our kings, belovèd roof,
and holy seats, and ye, sun-facing deities,   515
if e'er of old, with these your eyes of happy cheer
in order due receive ye the long absent king.
for, bringing light in darkness equally to you
and to all present here, king Agamemnon's come.
salute him duly then, for so it well beseems,   520 (483)
since with the spade of justice-righting Zeus—whereby
the champaign hath been tilled—he has uprooted Troy.
the altars are extinct, and shrines of deities,

and perisheth at once the seed of all the land.
on Troy's *neck* has he thrown such yoke, and now he's come—
the royal elder-son of Atreus, happy man ;   526
and worthiest to be honoured of all mortals he
that live : for neither Paris nor his citizens
can boast their doing greater than their suffering.
for, worsted in a suit of rapine and of theft,   530 (493)
he lost his ravished pledge, and mowed unto the ground
his father's house in utter ruin, land and all.
doubly did Priam's children pay the price of sin.

CHORUS.

Joy to thee, herald of the Achaeans from the host.

HERALD.

I do rejoice : now may the gods decree my death.   535

CHORUS.

Desire of this thy fatherland hath harassed thee?

HERALD.

Ay, so that tears are in mine eyes from this delight.

CHORUS.

Then ye too were infected with that sweet disease.

HERALD.

How so? by teaching I shall master this thy speech.

---

528. συντελὴς πόλις seems to mean no more than *the city to which he belonged*, i.e. *his fellow-citizens*.

531. *ravished pledge*, ῥύσιον, what is violently taken, properly as a pledge, to be restored on conditions. Here it can only mean a *booty* wrongfully taken, i.e. Helen and her wealth.

mowed, ἔθρισεν for ἐθέρισεν from θερίζω.

534. *from the host*, τῶν ἀπὸ στρατοῦ, an extremely daring 'praegnans locutio,' for τῶν ἐν στρατῷ, αὐτὸς ἀπὸ στρατοῦ μολών.

535. *now may the gods* &c. τεθνᾶναι δ' οὐκέτ' ἀντερῶ θεοῖς, a bold expression, incapable of literal rendering in a few words : '(as to) dying, I will no longer debate against it with the gods.'

CHORUS.

Smitten with love of those who answered you with love.

HERALD.

This land, you mean, was longing for the longing host.   541 (504)

CHORUS.

Yea! so that oft I groaned aloud in gloom of heart.

HERALD.

Whence came that sullen gloom upon the citizens?

CHORUS.

Silence I long have held an antidote to harm.

HERALD.

How? were there any that you feared, the kings away?   545

CHORUS.

As you were saying, e'en to die were great delight.

HERALD.

Yes, we have been successful: but in lengthened time
of these things one may say some fell out happily,
while others were not free from fault; but who, save gods,
is unafflicted through a whole eternity?   550 (513)
our labours were we to recite, and lodgings vile,
our scanty spaces, poorly strown—when were we not
groaning and shouting any fraction of a day?
then to our land-life even more disgust attached:

543. *upon the citizens*, πόλει, as we read here for στρατῷ (codd.),
which we regard as a senseless gloss.

547. What moved Aesch. to assign to the herald a style so disjointed
as we find in some places? Perhaps the heraldic office, sacrosanct as it was,
had, like that of modern beadles and town-criers, a comic side in popular
regard: and, while it was the function of heralds to recite grand words
put into their mouths by authority, they were not supposed to be fluent
expounders of their own thoughts.

552. *spaces*, παρήξεις, which, Mr Paley says, "seem to mean the narrow
passages along the deck between the rowers."

553. *shouting*, λάσκοντες, our conjecture for the unmeaning λαχόντες.

for near the foemen's fortress-walls our couches lay,   555
and *rains* from heaven, and meadow-dews *that rose* from earth,
were drenching us, a constant mischief of our clothes,
our hair like that of wild-beasts making : and if one
should tell the tale of bird-destroying winter-time,
like that which Ida's snow made unendurable,   560 (523)
or heat, what time upon the windless couch of noon
the sea without a billow sank and went to sleep—
these things what boots it to lament? 'tis past and gone,
the labour ; first for those who've died 'tis past and gone,
so that they will not care to come to life anew.   565
why need one make a calculation of the slain?
why should the living grieve for adverse fortune's chance?
†*of these things I suggest to take no further thought*†,
and to misfortunes I commend a long farewell.
but to ourselves, survivors of the Argive host,
gain hath the vantage, loss presents no counterpoise, 570 (533)
and fitly to this present sunlight may we boast,
while over sea and over land our flight we take :
"Troy having captured now at last, the Argive host
these spoils unto the gods that are *adored* in Greece
nailed in their temples, *to remain* an antique joy."   575
our city and its captains ought you to extol,
such actions hearing, and the grace of Zeus that wrought
these things shall have its honour.   All my words are said.

556.   *rains*, understood from δρόσοι by zeugma.

566.   *make a calculation*, ἐν ψήφῳ λέγειν, lit. *to tell on the pebble* (calculus), i.e. by counters.

567.   After this line, before καὶ, it is evident that a verse is lost.

574.   adored *in Greece*.   On their way home, and after their return, the several chiefs would dedicate spoils to the gods with inscriptions of this nature.   Probably Virgil, a student of the Greek drama, had this passage in view when he makes Aeneas dedicate Grecian spoils at Actium with the inscription, 'Aeneas haec de Danais victoribus arma,' *Aen.* III. 288.

CHORUS.

Defeat by force of argument I do not grudge:
for useful learning to the old is ever young.　　　580 (543)
but justly for this house and Clytaemnestra chief
these things have interest, and impart to me their joy.

CLYTAEMNESTRA.

Long since indeed I shouted loud a joyous cry,
when the first nightly messenger of fire arrived,
telling of Ilion's capture and its ruined fate,　　　585
and some one spake and censured me:—'relying then
on beacon-watchers, now thou deemest Troy is sacked?
how like a woman, to be thus elate of heart!'
such language clearly meant that I was led astray:
yet sacrifice I rendered, and in female strain　　　590 (553)
one here, one there, a shout of joy the city through
with pious words uplifted, while they lulled to rest
in shrines of gods the incense-preying odorous flame.
and now why needest thou prolong to me thy tale?
from the king's self I shall obtain a full account.　　　595
but I will haste with every honour possible
to greet my venerated lord on his return:

579. *defeat I do not grudge*, νικώμενος οὐκ ἀναίνομαι. The latter verb, like αἰσχύνομαι, has various constructions, the participle, as here, being one.

582. *and impart to me their joy;* lit. "and (it is fit) that along with them (ξὺν) they (ταῦτα) should enrich (=gladden) me." Such is Klausen's view of the construction, which seems correct.

583. Here Clytaemnestra advances to the λογεῖον and takes part in the dialogue.

590. *in female strain*, γυναικείῳ νόμῳ. The ὀλολυγμὸς was mostly the cry of women, but men might take part in it.

592. *lulled to rest*, i.e. extinguished by pouring wine on them, as Mr Paley says, though nothing is known of the custom.

595. *from the king's self* &c. Thus again the poet escapes tedious repetition, giving the first touch of that hypocrisy which the queen carries on to the full in the next lines. On these see *Notes on Lection.*

for what light can a woman see more sweet than this,
when heaven has brought her husband safe from his campaign,
the gates to open? take this message to my lord: 600 (563)
say to the city he is come supremely dear,
† *seeing that first of all in Argos he will* find
a people† faithful when he comes, at home a wife
such as he left her, watch-dog of his royal house,
gentle to him, a foe to such as wish him ill,
and in all other points alike, no sacred seal   605
having in this long interval of time disturbed.
pleasure from other man, nay, scandalous report
I know no more of than the art of dyeing brass.
such is my boast, and, laden to the full with truth,
no shameful one for any noble lady's mouth.   610 (573)

CHORUS.

To you, a learner, thus indeed she makes her speech,
to those who thoroughly interpret, speciously.
but, herald, say—of Menelaus 'tis I ask—
if on his homeward voyage safe returning back
he will arrive with you, this country's much-loved lord.   615

HERALD.

I could not possibly by speech make false news good,
that friends should reap the joy for long-continued time.

608. *the art of dyeing brass,* χαλκοῦ βαφάς. This seems to be a proverbial expression for unattainable knowledge.

611—12. These words are studiously obscure, for the Chorus could not
tell the herald plainly that Clyt. was not speaking truly.

616—17. *I could not possibly,* οὐκ ἔσθ᾽ ὅπως λέξαιμι. Mr Paley cites
appositely: οὐκ ἔστιν ὅτῳ μείζονα μοῖραν νείμαιμ᾽ ἤ σοι *Prom.* 299. οὐκ ἔστιν
ὅστις πλὴν ἐμοῦ κείραιτό νιν, *Cho.* 164. Peile justly ascribes this idiom of
the opt. to 'indefinite generality,' and Mr Paley with equal justice observes
that this character especially belongs to negative propositions.

The constructions τὰ ψευδῆ καλὰ in 616 and κεδνὰ ταληθῆ in 618 claim
particular attention. Here we think Mr Paley mistaken when he says

CHORUS.

How much I wish your speech could make true tidings good.
but these things severed are not easily concealed.

HERALD.

The chief hath disappear'd from the Achaean fleet,   620 (583)
his vessel and himself; I tell you no untruth.

CHORUS.

Had he set sail from Ilion in your sight, or did
a storm, a common trouble, snatch him from the host?

HERALD.

E'en as a first-rate archer, you have hit the mark,
and of a long woe given a concise report.   625

CHORUS.

Was it as living or as dead there went about
a rumour of him by the other mariners?

HERALD.

None knoweth so as clearly to declare the fact
save him—the Sun—that nourisheth the growths of earth.

" there is no grammatical objection to taking κεδνὰ τὰ ἀληθῆ = καλὰ τὰ μὴ ψευδῆ (ὄντα), opposed to τὰ ψευδῆ καλὰ preceding (which he has rendered 'good news which is false'): 'would then you could tell us good news which is true.' " We admit that τὰ ψευδῆ καλὰ is capable of being rendered 'false good-news,' treating καλὰ as a subst. and ψευδῆ as its attribute : and if l. 618 did not follow (with κεδνὰ τἀληθῆ), we might well be satisfied with that rendering. But the parallel of κεδνὰ τἀληθῆ is a trait of light, proving at once that καλὰ is not to be treated as the subst. The subst. is τὰ ψευδῆ, opposed to τἀληθῆ, and καλὰ = κεδνά, each being predicative in position and adverbial (or proleptic) in sense. We disapprove also the view taken of 618 by Herm. Pei. Well. πῶς δῆτ' ἄν, εἰπὼν κεδνά, τἀληθῆ τύχοις (εἰπών). Our view is, 616 οὐκ ἔσθ' ὅπως λέξαιμι τὰ ψευδῆ (ὡς ὄντα) καλά, ' I could not speak false news (as) good ' (which is equivalent to 'false good news'): 618 πῶς δῆτ' ἂν τύχοις εἰπὼν τἀληθῆ (ὡς ὄντα) κεδνά; how I wish you could succeed in speaking true news (as) good' (equivalent to ' true good news ').

CHORUS.

Will you then tell me, to the naval host how came   630 (593)
a storm by rancour of the gods, and ended how?

HERALD.

A day for words well-omened it beseemeth not
to desecrate by tongue that telleth evil news :
divided is the honour of the deities.
but when a sad-faced messenger to any town   635
brings of a smitten host abhorr'd calamities—
saying that one, the public wound, hath struck the state,
while many men from many a home are *victims* gone
devoted by the two-thong'd scourge, that Ares loves,—
a double-spearèd curse, a bloody pair of ills;—   640 (602)
when one is laden with a heap of woes like these,
'tis fit to sing this paean of the Erinyes.
but when a joyful bearer of victorious news
has reach'd a city gladdened with felicity—
how shall I mingle good with ill, the while I tell   645
the Achaeans' storm not unarous'd by wrath of gods?
for Fire and Sea, the greatest enemies before,
conspired together, and showed pledges of their faith
by the destruction of the hapless Argive host.
ills of a billowy sea had risen in the night,   650 (612)
for Thracian storm-blasts still against each other crushed
the vessels, and ·they, butted with this violence
by furious hurricane and rush of beating rain,
had gone, by evil shepherd driven, out of view.
but, when the sun's bright light returned, the Aegean deep   655
we see with corpses blooming of Achaean men,
and naval wrecks: ourselves however and our ship,

    637. *the public*, τὸ δήμιον. Aesch. here dwells on the distinction of
public and private calamities. In a former passage (396 τὰ μὲν κατ' οἴκους
...τὸ πᾶν δὲ &c.) he had compared those of the great families and the
popular masses.

an unscathed hull, did some one stealthily withdraw,
or beg us off, some god, not man, that grasp'd the helm.
and saviour Fortune on the ship perch'd willingly :   660 (623)
that neither did we feel the beating of the surge
at anchor, nor were stranded on a rock-bound coast.
but after we had thus escaped a watery grave,
in the white daylight, little confident of fate,
we in our thoughts were brooding o'er the late mishap   665
of our afflicted and unkindly shattered fleet.
and now if any one of them is breathing still,
they speak of us as having perish'd : for why not?
and we imagine them to suffer the same fate.
but may things issue for the best ! yea, first of all   670 (633)
and chief, expect that Menelaus will arrive.
at least if any sunbeam knoweth aught of him
living and seeing light by the design of Zeus,
whose will it is not yet to extirpate the race,
some hope there is that he will reach his home again.   675
so much you've heard, and be assured you hear the truth.

STASIMON II.

CHORUS.

1. *Ode.*

Who was it that with truth so perfect—   *Str.* 1.

676.   On the corrections in Epeisodion II. (506, 516, 564—5) and on the
proposed additions after 530, 564 see *Consp. Lect.* and *Notes on Lection.*

677.   As Stasimon I. depicted the character and crime of Paris with its
causes, its circumstances and fatal consequences, so Stasimon II. deals
with the same general subject, the elopement, but with special reference to
the character and the sin of Helen.   The Chorus begin by saying that she
is justly called ʹΕλένη (the capturer, from ἑλεῖν), seeing that through her were
captured ships and men and a city.   Her marriage with Paris *marred* the
city of Priam and the lives of its citizens.   As a young lion reared in a
house, tame and gentle at first, becomes afterwards ravenous and blood-

was it not one, we do not see,
with thoughts forecasting destiny
the tongue directing happily?—   680 (642)
gave name to her, the war-bride, the debated,
the captivating Helen?
since verily ship-captivating,
men-captivating, city-captivating,
from forth her richly-sumptuous curtains   685
she with the breeze of land-born Zephyr sailed,
and many shield-accoutred huntsmen
were on the track of those
who brought to land the disappearing oar
upon the coast of Simois leaf-bestrown,   690 (651)
for *her, the cause of* bloody strife.
But wrath accomplishing its purpose   *Ant.* 1.
on Ilion a marriage forced
of name too true, in after time
exacting vengeance for the scorn   695

thirsty, such was Helen at Troy, lovely and charming when she came, at
the last a curse and a destroying fury. The ode concludes with moral re-
flections probably suggested by the chequered character and fortunes of the
race of Pelops. Excessive wealth, it is said, results in woe: but the
Chorus deems it more important to observe that one crime is wont to
produce another: insolence grows out of insolence, and engenders arrogance
and audacity. Justice abhors the mansions of vicious wealth, and loves to
dwell with the pious poor.

682. the captivating *Helen*. The epithet 'captivating' (not in the
Greek) is introduced to favour the rendering of the adjectives drawn from
the name Ἑλένη. Our learned and ingenious friend Miss Swanwick, in
her able translation, has employed the same artifice: 'Helen, the captor.'
A play upon names and words is adopted often by the tragic poets : Αἴας in
Soph. *Aj.*, Πενθεὺς in Eurip. *Bacch.* (also in Theocritus) are among the
instances. In this drama we find κῆδος ὀρθώνυμον 653; Ἀπόλλων ἐμός,
ἀπώλεσας γάρ 1011.

688. before κατ' ἴχνος und. ἔπλευσαν.

693. κῆδος has two meanings, (1) affinity by marriage, (2) woe.

done to the table and to Zeus hearth-sharing,
from them that honoured loudly
the spousal-celebrating music,
that novel hymen, which for bridesmen
the moment then was drawing on to sing.   700 (659)
but, learning a new dirgeful hymn,
Priam's old town, I ween,
with groanings loud its Paris ill-wived calls,
yea, having first a dirgeful life endured
for the sad blood of citizens.   705
E'en so some man hath nourished in his house   *Str.* 2.
reft of its mother's milk
yet udder-loving *still*, a lion's cub,
in life's primeval season
tame, unto the children kindly,   710 (669)
and to the aged an amusement.
so in the arms it oft was carried,
like to a new-rear'd infant child,
smiling upon the hand, and fawning
in stress of appetite.   715
But in the course of time the character   *Ant.* 2.
from parent stock derived
it showed; for paying fees to nurturers
by truculent sheep-slaughter,
it procured a feast unbidden;   720 (676)
and *all* the house with blood was spattered,
indomitable grief to servants,
a many-slaying mischief huge.
and thus 'twas bred within the mansion

699. We have, with some boldness, ventured to read νέον ὑμέν' for ὑμέναιον, in order to lengthen the final syllable in τίοντας, to which corresponds πρεπόντως in the strophe. The words ὑμὴν and ὑμέναιος are equally good for the song and for the deity; and the quantity of υ (in the former at least) is 'doubtful,' Ὑμὴν ὧ 'Ὑμέναιε. The epithet νέον is suitable to a second wedding. Some may prefer ὕμνον to ὑμέν'.

a priest of bale divine.   725
These things resembling I should say   *Str.* 3.
there came to Ilion's city
a temper of unruffled calm,
a gentle ornament of wealth,
a softly-darted eye-glance,   730 (683)
a flower of love heart-stinging.
but swerving from such state she wrought
a bitter end of marriage,
sent forth to be for Priam's race
ill-seated, ill-associated,   735
by mission of the guestlaw-guarding Zeus
a bride-deplored Erinys.
From ancient lore among mankind   *Ant.* 3.
is framed an aged maxim :
that, grown to fulness, a man's wealth   740 (689)
begets, and does not childless die ;
but from good fortune sprouteth
woe to the race, unsated.
but I from others differing
am lone in my opinion.   745
an impious deed engenders more
succeeding, and their stock resembling :
but righteous families at all times have
a happy fate in children.
And Insolence when old is wont to bear   *Str.* 4.   750 (698)
a youthful Insolence
in evil men displayed at this or that time
whene'er the destined season comes.
the young one genders Arrogance,
and that uncombated, unwarr'd,   755
unholy fiend Audacity,
black curses both for dwellings, like their parents.
But Justice shines in houses dark with smoke,   *Ant.* 4.
and honours virtuous life ;

while gold-bespangled seats, where hands are filthy,   760 (706)
she leaveth with averted eyes,
and unto pious homes repairs,
revering not the power of wealth
with spurious commendation stamp'd :
and each thing to its proper end she guideth.   765

[*At the close of this ode, Agamemnon and his suite enter the orchestra through
the Parodos on the left of the spectators. He is seated on a mule-car, in
which is also his prisoner Cassandra. The car approaches the steps
which on that side connect the orchestra with the proscenium ; and the
coryphaeus then addresses the king in the anapaests which follow.*]

2. *Anapaests.*

Now tell me, king, Troy's sacker, son of Atreus,
how I am to address thee, how revere thee,
not overstepping nor yet resting short of
the proper line of salutation ?
for many, after violating justice,   770 (716)
prize more the seeming than the being :
and every one is prompt to give the ill-fated
a groan of pity : but the sting of sorrow
in no case penetrateth to the heart-core :

766. These Anapaests introduce the Third Epeisodion, and might
almost be said to form a part of it. The Chorus march on their platform
towards the left-hand Parodos to greet the king and his train. In welcom-
ing him they express a fear lest they should say too much in the way of
flattery, or too little in the direction of joyful commendation. The prosperous have many insincere flatterers : but a good judge of character will
distinguish the true from the false. They own that their feeling was once
unfavourable to Agam., when he led so many forth to die, and sought to
embolden them by a cruel sacrifice. Now, as all's well that ends well, they
congratulate sincerely. In time (they add by way of warning) the king will
learn to discriminate wisely between loyal citizens and dangerous persons.

766. *Now tell me*, λέγε δή, a reading which we adopt in preference to the
vulgate ἄγε δή. The corruptions in these Anapaests seem to be numerous.

769. *proper line*, καιρόν, lit. season; i.e. just medium.

and to the semblance of congratulators   775
suiting themselves by straining smileless faces,
† *they cheat the undiscerning.* †
but whoso is a clever judge of cattle,
from such a person's eyes can ne'er be hidden
the natures that with water-mingled friendship
appear to fawn in loyalty of spirit.   780 (726)
and in those former days, when thou wast launching
an expedition for the sake of Helen,
by me thou wast depicted, I'll not hide it,
in colours most ill-favoured, as not wielding
the mental rudder well, from sacrifices   785
for men to death devoted
obtaining courage.
now therefore, with no feignèd feeling
nor any lack of love † *I praise thee, saying,* †
' all's well with toilers, when their toil's well ended.' 790 (734)
in time thou wilt distinguish by inquiry
the citizen who justly guarded
the city † *in thine absence* †,
and one of inconvenient *conduct.*

EPEISODION III.

AGAMEMNON.

Argos in first place and the country's deities   795

775. *to the semblance* &c. ξυγχαίρουσιν ὁμοιοπρεπεῖς, the former word
being dat. plur. of partic. συγχαίρων.

788. *with no feigned feeling*, οὐκ ἀπ' ἄκρας φρενός, not from the mere
surface of the mind.

790. *all's well* &c., lit. ' labour is cheerful to them that have ended it
well ': the play being on the double εὖ. Perhaps it is proverbial.

794. For corrections in Stasimon II. and the Anapaests following (658,
664, 666, 679, 699—704, 707—9, 712, 714, 716, 731) and for additions suggested at 722, 733, 735, see *Consp. Lect.* and *Notes on Lection.*

Epeisodion III. In reply to the anapaestic address of the Chorus,

'tis right that I salute, who help'd to win for me
return, and such reprisals as I justly took

Agamemnon begins by saluting his royal city and the gods who had given
him victory: next, referring to what the coryphaeus had said, he dwells on
the doubtful affection of friends, naming Ulixes as the only comrade on
whose support he could always rely: thirdly, he declares his intention to
settle affairs of state in a public council; and then prepares to leave the car,
enter the palace, and worship his domestic deities: concluding with a prayer
for continued success. Clytaemnestra, now advancing to the logeion, and
addressing the Chorus, states at some length 'the painful tenour of her life'
during Agamemnon's absence. She had been disturbed by evil rumours.
She had sent the young Orestes away to Phokis from fear of popular com-
motion: she had suffered in health from watching for the beacons, and
from restless and anxious nights. She welcomes her husband's return in
a series of far-fetched similes: inviting him to descend from the chariot and
enter the palace on a pathway laid down with purple embroideries. Replying to her, Agamemnon deprecates any such slavish homage and osten-
tatious splendour as Eastern despots were accustomed to: this, he says,
will displease the gods. Fame speaks for itself: prudence is man's best
endowment: and no man can be declared happy before the hour of death.
For himself, he would be of good cheer if he could always prosper as now.
A dialogue (in στιχομυθία) follows, in which Clytaemnestra, by dexterous
cross-examination, prevails on the king to accept the honour of a tapestried
pathway: 'Give me a sincere answer' (she says) 'to one question.'—'My
answer shall certainly be sincere.' 'In any fearful crisis, would you have
made a vow to do what I now ask?'—'Yes, no man knew better than
myself the time to announce that purpose.'—'And what do you think
Priam would have done if he had achieved such success?'—'I am very sure
he would have walked on embroideries.'—'Then do not dread public cen-
sure.' Agamemnon yields to his wife's insidious persuasion, and, after
recommending Cassandra to her care, stripping off his sandals he prepares
to descend from the chariot, and walk over the purple carpets to the palace.
The queen meanwhile says to him, that the sea is large enough to supply
any quantity of purple dye, and the royal house is rich enough to buy it.
She would have vowed tapestry without stint, at the suggestion of an
oracle, to obtain the assurance of his safety. A husband's return was like
warmth in the frosts of winter, or cool in the heats of the vintage-time.
She ends with an ambiguous prayer to Zeus the all-fulfiller, that he will
fulfil her present vow.

from Priam's city: for the gods our claim adjudged
by no tongue-sentence—ruin with the death of men
for Ilion—but into a bloody urn they cast   800 (743)
their votes without dissent, while to the opposing rim
hope of a hand drew ever near, but filled it not.
by smoke e'en yet the captured town is signalized:
alive are Ate's altar-steams; the dying ash
commingled with them sendeth forth fat reek of wealth.   805
unto the gods for these things it behoves to pay
thanks long remembered; since in fact we fortified
snares of relentless hate, and for a woman's sake
an Argive monster laid their city in the dust,
foal of a horse, a troop shield-brandishing, that took
its leap about the setting of the Pleiades: 811 (754)
yea, 'twas a bloody lion, that o'ersprang the wall,
and lapp'd to full content a draught of royal blood.
unto the gods my lengthened prelude is address'd:
but, for your feelings—all you said I bear in mind,   815
and *now* repeat it, and your views I advocate.
few men indeed have this implanted quality,
unenviously to regard a prosperous friend.
for surly venom, taking at the heart its seat,
doubleth his load who suffers from some fell disease:
sore laden is he with his own calamities,   821 (764)
and groaneth when he sees a neighbour's happiness.

---

798. *adjudged*, κρίνοντες, our reading for κλύοντες, the corruptness of
which we do not doubt. See *Notes on Lection.*

802. *hope of a hand*, ἐλπὶς χειρός, from which Mr Paley says 'no
intelligible sense can be extracted.' This is not just. Surely, if a voter
holding a ballot, goes up to two urns and seems for a moment to pause
before he drops it, we can quite understand what is meant by saying
that hope of a hand approached the urn which did not receive the
ballot.

811. *about the setting of the Pleiades*: i.e. the end of autumn, a stormy
time which, as Klausen says, accounts for the tempest.

K. A.   7

from knowledge I can speak, for well indeed I know
† *that of the men who sailed with me some showed themselves* †
a glass of friendship *merely*, shadow of a shade,
the while they seem'd to be my very loyal *friends.*
Ulixes only, who was voyaging against his will, 826
when yoked was wont to be my ready seconder,
whether I speak of one that's dead or living yet.
for all things else belonging to the state and gods,
in common council we shall institute debates, 830 (773)
and so determine, and the policy that's good,
how it may long last happily, we must advise:
but whatsoe'er has need of healing remedies,
by caustic 'or by kind appliance of the knife
we shall endeavour to avert diseaseful harm. 835
now to my palace and domestic hearth I'll go,
and first pay greeting homage to the deities,
who sent me forth and now have brought me home again.
may victory, since it followed me, for aye remain!

CLYTAEMNESTRA.

Men of the city, Argive elders present here, 840 (783)
my husband-loving habits it will shame me not
to speak before you; for in time fear fades away
from human natures: taught of none besides myself,
I shall avow the painful tenour of my life
as long as under Ilion's walls this *prince* abode. 845
first, for a woman, from her husband separate,
lone in the house to sit, is an enormous ill,
untoward rumours manifold compelled to hear;
now 'tis—that one man has arrived *with evil news*—

823—5. On the necessity of supplying τινὰς here to complete the
Greek construction see *Notes on Lection.*

827. σειραφόρος properly means a horse attached by a rope to help
the yoked horses. But as Ulixes is spoken of ζευχθείς, yoked, it is used
merely to express a staunch assistant, as our paraphrase expresses.

and next another, bearer of a worse account,   850 (792)
o'er all the palace publishing : and if indeed
this man had been receiver of as many wounds
as by report were ever dribbling to his house,
more numerous are his wounds than meshes of a net.
or had he died as many times as stories told,   855
a Geryon the Second he, three-bodied man,
a triple cloak of earth had boasted to obtain,
if in each form he had endured a single death.
by reason of untoward rumours such as these,   860 (802)
have others taken hold of me by violence,
and loosened many a halter fastened o'er my neck.
hence comes it that our son is not beside us here,
pledge of the mutual troth betwixt myself and thee,
Orestes, as was fit : and wonder not at this :   865
a war-friend well-affected to us nurtures him,
Strophius of Phokis, doubtful mischiefs unto me
foretelling, first thy peril under Ilion's walls,
and then *the chance*, if people-shouted anarchy
should hurl the council down, so natural it is   870 (812)
in men to give the fallen one a further spurn.
these reasons, trust me, carry with them no deceit.
to me however all the gushing founts of tears
are dried up at the source, and not a drop remains.
mine eyes, retiring late to bed, have taken harm,   875
the while I wept the beacon-watches set for thee
continually neglected : ever in my dreams
by the light buzzings of the swiftly-darting gnat
was I awakened, seeing still concerning thee
more woes than all *the minutes of* my sleeping time.   880 (822)

867. ἀμφίλεκτα, i.e. questionable; they might be this or that.

870. As at Paris in September, 1870, after the disaster of Sedan.

877. *neglected*, i.e. never lighted.

878. *by the light* &c., lit. *by the mosquito darting with its light buzzings*.

all this I bore: and now with sorrow-lightened mind
I can pronounce this man a watchdog of the stall,
a vessel's saving forestay, of a lofty roof
a strong-based pillar, of a father only child,
and land beyond their hope to mariners disclosed,   835
after a storm a day most beautiful to view,
to wayfarer athirst a fountain's gushing flow.
delightful is it to escape from any stress.
such greetings is he worthy of in my esteem:
and far be envy: many are the former woes   890 (832)
we were enduring. now at my desire, dear lord,
step from this mule-car forth, not setting on the earth
this foot, o king, that devastated Ilion.
why lag ye, maids, to whom the office is assigned
of strewing all the pathway's floor with tapestries?   895
a road forthwith be made with purple carpeting,
that Justice to his home unhoped may guide his steps.
what next ensues shall thought, not overcome by sleep,
as destined with the blessing of the gods, arrange.

AGAMEMNON.

Daughter of Leda, guardian of my *royal* house,   900 (842)
in keeping with my absence hast thou made thy speech:
for long was it extended: but in manner just
to praise, this meed from others it befits to come.
and, for the rest, with luxury do not pamper me
in woman's fashion, nor fall down and open-mouth'd   905
salute me with a shout, as some barbarian chief:

---

904. *with luxury* &c. In this episode we cannot doubt that Aesch.
bore in mind the startling events which had happened a few years before
he wrote it—the ambitious folly and tragic fate of Pausanias, the conqueror
at Plataea, whose open adoption of oriental pomp and luxury was the prelude to the treason meditated by him against Sparta and Hellas. The trap
laid by Clytaemnestra for her husband, with a view to draw down on him
the envy of gods and men, and so to make her crime easier, could not be
better chosen.

nor make my path, by strewing it with tapestries,
invidious: so 'tis right to venerate the gods;
but that a mortal upon splendid broideries
should walk, is in my judgment not exempt from fear. 910 (852)
as man I bid you do me reverence, not as god.
without foot-scraping carpets and embroidered shows
Fame cries aloud, and not to be unwise of heart
is God's chief gift: but happy must we call a man
who hath attain'd the close of life in blissful state. 915
if thus in all things I shall fare, my cheer is strong.

CLYTAEMNESTRA.

Well now: thy true thought not evading, answer me.

AGAMEMNON.

My true thought be assured I shall not falsify.

---

914. *happy* &c. This maxim is often repeated in Greek tragedy. Thus Sophocles concludes his *Oedipus Rex* with the warning—

μηδέν' ὀλβίζειν πρὶν ἂν
τέρμα τοῦ βίου περάσῃ μηδὲν ἀλγεινὸν παθών.

916 (858). Whether πράσσοιμ' ἂν or πράσσοιμεν (Dind. Franz) is the true reading may be questionable. Mr Paley takes πράσσοιμι in the sense of *acting—if in all things I shall act as discreetly as in this*. Perhaps he is right; and we leave this to the reader's judgment. Yet there is no impropriety in supposing that, having said 'no man can be deemed happy till after death,' Agamemnon might add, 'if in all respects I were to fare (i.e. succeed) as I have done in this instance, I should have good reason to confide in the continuance of prosperity to the hour of death.' And this sentiment of confidence would be more telling in its dramatic effect at a moment when his death was immediately to ensue.

917—920 (859—862). Our view of these lines is widely different from that in Mr Paley's notes. We have given reasons at large in the *Journal of Philology*, and we must in candour say that they are fully convincing to us. Our view is supported by the entire context, especially by comparison of 861 (Greek text) with 891. We believe ἐξειπεῖν to be the true reading in 862, but the change does not affect our general interpretation. See *Notes on Lection.*

CLYTAEMNESTRA.

Would'st thou in fear have vowed unto the gods such act?

AGAMEMNON.

Yes: skilled as well as any man to speak this vow.   920 (862)

CLYTAEMNESTRA.

What think'st thou Priam would have done, had he prevailed?

AGAMEMNON.

I think he surely would have walk'd on broideries.

CLYTAEMNESTRA.

Then do not stand in *any* dread of human blame.

AGAMEMNON.

And yet a people's loud report has mighty strength.

CLYTAEMNESTRA.

Ay, but the unenvied is unemulated too.   925

AGAMEMNON.

To covet war is not a woman's *attribute.*

CLYTAEMNESTRA.

But such as prosper may with grace accept defeat.

AGAMEMNON.

And dost thou really care for conquest in this strife?

CLYTAEMNESTRA.

Give way; consent at least to leave the power with me.

AGAMEMNON.

If such thy pleasure, then let some one instantly   930 (872)
pull off the sandals trodden slave-like by the foot:
lest, while with these I walk upon the seagrown dyes,
some envious eye of gods should strike me from afar.
for to waste substance is a grievous shame, with feet

921.   *had he prevailed;* lit. had he achieved these things.

destroying wealth and woven work of sumptuous price. 935
of this enough:—yon stranger woman kindly bring
within our house: the merciful in victory
with favouring eye the god beholdeth from afar:
for none with willing mind accepts a slavish yoke.
but she, the very flower select of mighty wealth, 940 (882)
the army's present, came a follower in my train.
now, since in this I'm subjugate to thy behest,
unto the palace I shall walk on purple floor.

CLYTAEMNESTRA.

There is a sea—and who shall e'er extinguish it?—
producing plenteous purple ooze for dyeing cloth, 945
precious as silver, constantly renewable.
of such things by the favour of the gods, o king,
our house hath ample store: it knows not penury.
the trampling of full many a cloth would I have vowed,
had this been to our house proposed in oracles, 950 (892)
contriving of thy life the ransom requisite.
for foliage, while the root exists, comes to a house,
spreading a shade against the dogstar Seirius.
and so, when thou returnest to thy palace hearth,
thou signifiest warmth is come in winter-time: 955
and from the bitter grape when Zeus createth wine,
then cool existeth in a house, and not till then,
when to his home returns an all-fulfilling man.
Zeus, Zeus the all-fulfiller, o fulfil my vows,
and be thy care the things thou meanest to fulfil. 960 (902)

[*Agamemnon enters the palace, followed by the queen.*]

960 (902). On the readings at 742, 747, 751, 759, 766, 767, 778, 791,
797, 799, 800, 831, 858, 862, 871, 876, 887, 889, 893, 897, 898, see *Conspectus Lect.* and *Notes on Lection.*

STASIMON III.

CHORUS.

Why doth this horror evermore　　　　　　　　*Str.* 1.
flit o'er my boding heart, a present power,
and prophesy with song
unbidden, unrewarded:
while these, like undecyphered dreams, to spurn　　965
persuasive boldness hath no seat
upon the dear throne of my heart?
time long hath left behind its youthfulness,
since cables from each ship together

Stasimon III. In the first strophe and antistrophe the Chorus avow that an unconquerable presentiment of coming evil disturbs their minds. In spite of the return of the army from Troy they cannot overcome their terror. In the next passages they say that, although the danger attending excessive prosperity may be averted by wise sacrifice of wealth, lifeblood once shed cannot be recalled: Zeus smote Asclepios, to hinder him from raising the dead. In the concluding lines they declare that their tongues are tied: they are not free to utter the alarm which afflicts their hearts.

961. *horror,* δεῖμα, so in F.: but in Fl. δεῖγμα, *phantom;* which Mr Paley and some others prefer.

964. *unrewarded,* ἄμισθον, lit. *unhired,* in allusion to the fees which poets like Pindar, the contemporary of Aeschylus, received for epinician odes, and those which dramatic poets, like himself, or dithyrambic like Simonides, obtained from the tribes competing in the Dionysiac contests. The meaning of the passage is that, when the return of Agamemnon and the army seems to call for a strain of jubilee, which would deserve reward, they find themselves enforced to sing a song of evil foreboding, which no one calls for (ἀκέλευστος) and no one will reward (ἄμισθος).

965—967. These words, simply rendered, mean: 'I have not the courage to dismiss this feeling, as if it were a vague dream.'

968. *time* &c. In this strangely expressed passage (χρ. παρήβησεν *time has outgone its youth,* ἐπὶ ξυνεμβολαῖς *after the castings-together,* πρυμνησίων *of the cables,* ψαμμίας ἀκάτας *of the vessel on the sands*) we may suspect some corruption: but there is nothing to suggest emendation unless it be ψαμμιᾶν ἀκατᾶν for ψαμμίας ἀκάτας, which is not essential.

ἐπὶ, *after;* see 1308 ἐπ' ἐξειργασμένοις.

were flung upon the sand,	970 (912)
as 'neath *the walls of* Ilion	
advanced the naval army.	
And now, from *teaching of* the eyes,	*Ant.* 1.
I know, myself a witness, their return.	
but still my soul within me	975
self-taught is chanting lyreless	
the dirge of an Erinys, having not	
hope's happy courage to the full.	
my inmost feelings are not vain,	
my heart, that on its truthful circlet beats	980 (922)
in eddies that suggest fulfilment.	
yet do I pray such *cares*	
may turn out false beyond my hope,	
and come not to completion.	
The limit of excessive health	*Str.* 2. 985
is truly most unsatisfied :	
and still against it leans disease,	
a neighbour with a party-wall :	
and a man's fate, a straight course steering	
†*across the waves of life*†,	
oft on a hidden rock has struck.	990 (932)
yet if in fear a house *o'erboard*	
from sling well-measured	

980. We have transposed the Greek words, being convinced that the concurrence of four dative cases is neither elegant nor perspicuous, but just what a misjudging transcriber would be likely to favour. See 1253—4.

φρεσίν. φρήν or φρένες physically means the midriff (διάφραγμα), the muscle which separates the heart and lungs from the abdominal viscera. The three lines imply: 'the beating of my heart is not unmeaning: it bodes something, against which I must pray.'

985. *health* (meaning here *prosperity*), ὑγεία for ὑγίεια or ὑγεία.

987. *and still*, lit. for still. Mr Paley says: "the γάρ depends (as is so often the case) on some suppressed sentiment. Men never think they have prosperity enough (regardless of the danger they incur): for &c."

has flung a portion of its hoarded wealth,
it hath not wholly sunk,
though laden deep with woe,   995
nor whelm'd its hull beneath the sea.
and truly gifts abundant
from Zeus and year-supplying furrows
have brought diseaseful famine to an end.
But the black blood before a man   *Ant.* **2.**   1000 (941)
that once upon the earth is spilt,
death-working—who may call back this
by incantation? did not Zeus
strike down and silence for precaution
him who had rightly learned   1005
the art of raising from the dead?
if now a pre-establish'd fate
had not forbidden
a fate arising from the gods to gain
the larger power, my heart
would have outstript my tongue,   1010 (950)

993. Tὸ μὲν means *some part.* Πρὸ......βαλὼν is a tmesis for προβαλών. This casting overboard of a portion of the freight to lighten a vessel in time of peril was called in Latin *iactura.* 'The house,' δόμος, is spoken of in the character of a vessel, as πότμος in 930. The metaphor is pushed very far, when in 937 the house is said not to sink *its hull* (σκάφος) within the deep. But the epithet κτησίων shows that no other word (as στόλος) must here take the place of δόμος.

1005. Respecting Asclepios struck by the bolt of Zeus, Mr Paley cites Ov. *Fast.* VI. 780,

> Iuppiter exemplum veritus direxit in illum
> fulmina, qui nimiae moverat artis opem.

1006. Mr Paley's version "if the appointed law of fate did not hinder fate from getting further assistance from the gods &c." is to us unintelligible. By τεταγμένα μοῖρα we understand, as he does, that 'superior destiny which even gods obey,' but we take ἐκ θεῶν as dependent on μοῖραν, and understand the 'fate from the gods' to imply the δεῖμα spoken of in the beginning of this song (see note there) and regarded as a τέρας sent by divine power. πλέον φέρειν means *to prevail, to get the better.*

and these things 'twould be pouring forth.
but darkly now it mutters,
soul-vex'd, and not expecting ever
aught to unravel from a breast on fire.

EPEISODION IV.

[*Cassandra remains in the mule-car while the Chorus are singing the
last Stasimon. Now the queen comes forth again, and summons Cassandra to the palace. The prophetess keeps her seat in obstinate silence:
and Clytaemnestra, full of indignation, after l. 1048 leaves the stage.
Cassandra, now complying with the advice of the coryphaeus, passes from
the car to the proscenium; and her interview with the Chorus fills up
the remainder of this Epeisodion.*]

CLYTAEMNESTRA.

Thou too (Cassandra 'tis I mean) convey thyself   1015
within: since Zeus hath made thee by a gentle doom
to be a sharer in our home of lustral bowls,
standing with many slaves the household altar nigh.
come from this mule-car forth, and be not overproud.
they say, d'ye mind, in old days even Alcmena's son   1020 (961)
bore to be sold, and underwent the yoke perforce.
if to such lot the stress of fortune's scale incline,
great blessing will be found in lords of antique wealth.
but they that reap rich harvest unexpectedly

1014.   On the readings at 904, 906, 907, 909, 910, 911, 913—14, 917,
921, 930—1, 924, 927—34, 941—46 see *Consp. Lect.* and *Notes on Lection.*
   1016.   *by a gentle doom*, ἀμηνίτως, lit. without wrath.
   1017.   *lustral bowls*, χερνίβων. "The χέρνιψ (*Eum.* 628) was the con-
secrated water dispensed to all" (Pal.) before the sacrifice to Ζεὺς κτήσιος,
the guardian of the family κτήματα, among which slaves are included.
Virtually, therefore, as Mr Paley observes, a taunt is conveyed in mention-
ing this privilege of Cassandra.
   1020.   *even Alcmena's son*, Heracles, sold as a slave to Omphale, queen
of Lydia.

are ever cruel to their slaves and out of rule: 1025
from us thou gettest all the customary dues.

CHORUS.

To thee it is she thus hath spoken a clear speech:
and since thou'rt caught within the toils of destiny,
obey thou wilt, if such thy will: perchance 'tis not.

CLYTAEMNESTRA.

Nay, if she doth not, swallow-like, possess a tongue   1030 (971)
barbarian, knowing none *beside*, I speak within
her comprehension, trying to prevail on her.

CHORUS.

Attend: she tells thee what is best in present case;
do as she bids, and leave this seat within the car.

CLYTAEMNESTRA.

I have no time, you see, to waste in converse here   1035
outside the door: for of the central palace-hearth
†*completed are our sanctities, and from the flocks*†
sheep stand even now for sacrifice of fire, as we

1027. *To thee* &c., lit. ' to thee indeed she ceases to speak a clear
word,' i.e. the speech *she has made* is clear.

1029. *perchance 'tis not:* lit. 'perchance thou wilt disobey.' ἂν is
carried on to ἀπειθοίης from πείθοι' ἄν.

1030. *swallow-like*, χελιδόνος δίκην. The Greeks found a resemblance
between the oriental (barbarian) speech and the twittering of swallows.
The allusion occurs repeatedly. See Herod. II. 57, Aristoph. *Ran.* 93,
678, Soph. *Antig.* 1002 βεβαρβαρωμένῳ.

1032. *trying to prevail on her*, πείθω νιν λόγῳ, lit. ' (try to) persuade
her by speech.' The verb does not express effectual persuasion, but the
endeavour to gain over by argument.

1033. *Attend*, ἕπου, lit. follow (with the mind what she says), a sense of
ἕπεσθαι frequent in Plato.

1035. On the whole of this speech of Clyt., which is corrupt, and on
959, 992, see *Consp. Lect.* and *Notes on Lection.*

1037. *as we could order best.* Such is the force of ὡς (ἡμῖν). The mean-

could order best, who ne'er had hoped to taste this joy.
if aught I tell thee thou wilt do, make no delay.
but if, for lack of knowledge, thou repliest not,   1040 (981)
give sign at least with foreign hand, instead of voice.

CHORUS.

This stranger seems to need a clear interpreter :
as of a newly-taken wild-beast, such her mood.

CLYTAEMNESTRA.

Sure she is mad, and hearkens to an evil mind,
who from a lately captured town is *hither* come,   1045
and knows not how to bear *the necessary* curb,
until her bloody violence be foam'd away.
howbeit I will not waste more words, and *thus* be scorn'd.

[*Exit* CLYTAEMNESTRA.

CHORUS.

But I will not be angry, for I pity her.
come, o unhappy *woman*, leave this chariot ;   105ɔ (991)
yield to the present stress and bear the novel yoke.

CASSANDRA.

Alas, alas, ye gods and earth !   *Str.* 1.
o Apollo, o Apollo !

ing is that, being taken by surprise, they got the sheep as well and as soon
as they could.

1040. *thou repliest not.* Such is the full force of οὐ δέχει λόγον, a
phrase used in dialectic discussion. Its correlative is δοῦναι λόγον.

1052. After (as we surmise) reaching the logeion, Cassandra bursts
forth into a series of wild outcries, partly prophetic, partly lamentative. She
first invokes Apollo with shrieks of horror, then sketches her dreadful visions
of the crimes heretofore perpetrated, and of those which now impend in the
palace of the Atreidae. Especially she foresees and in a series of dark outlines
describes the murder of Agamemnon by his cruel wife. She next foretells
her own coming death, bewails her sad fate, and with it that of her family
and fatherland. Alternately with the cries of the prophetess, the Chorus
utter their own feelings of terrified astonishment and sympathy. The
metres are for the most part lyric, but sometimes iambic.

CHORUS.

Why dost thou cry Alas concerning Loxias?
he is not one to need the chanter of a dirge.   1055

CASSANDRA.

Alas, alas, ye gods and earth!   *Ant.* 1.
o Apollo, o Apollo!

CHORUS.

Again with evil cries she calleth on the god,
who is not suited to attend at wailing times.

CASSANDRA.

Apollo, Apollo!   *Str.* 2.   1060 (1001)
o street-god, my Apollo!
not scantly hast thou ruined me, the second time.

CHORUS.

Of her own woes she seems about to prophesy.
the power divine abides, though in a mind enslaved.

CASSANDRA.

Apollo, Apollo!   *Ant.* 2.   1065
o street-god, my Apollo!
o whither is it thou hast brought me? to what roof?

CHORUS.

To that of the Atreidae: if thou know'st it not,
I tell thee this, nor wilt thou say 'tis falsity.

CASSANDRA.

     Woe, woe!   *Str.* 3.   1070 (1011)
to a god-hating one: conscious of many foul

1054. *cry Alas*, ἀνωτότυξας. ἀνοτοτύζω is one of the many verbs derived
from interjections: like ὤζω, οἰμώζω, αἰάζω, φεύζω (1237), ὀλολύζω and others.
Loxias is the title of Apollo as the god of prophecy.

1061—2. ἀπόλλων ἐμός· | ἀπώλεσας γὰρ κ.τ.λ. This play on the name
Apollo cannot be maintained in translation. See above 644. The final
syllable in ἐμός is lengthened in the interjectional construction.

family murders and halters and
a slaughter-house that sprinkles blood of men.

CHORUS.

Keen-scented as a hound the stranger woman seems
to be: she searches those, whose blood she will detect.   1075

CASSANDRA.

   Woe, woe!   *Ant.* 3.
ay! for the evidence which I believe is this:
babes for their slaughter who weep and wail,
and roasted flesh on which a father feeds.

CHORUS.

Ay, we had heard and known thy fame oracular: 1080 (1021)
but we are not in quest of any soothsayers.

CASSANDRA.

Alas, ye gods! what doth she meditate?   *Str.* 4.
what is this novel sorrow now?

1078. *babes*, βρέφη, the murdered children of Thyestes. See 1580 &c.
The disjointed construction is due to the speaker's phrensy. With Karsten
we reject both τάδε and τά. The scenes depicted (from 1065) are (1) Cassandra scents the blood shed in the palace: (2) she beholds in vision the
murderous banquet of Atreus: (3) she views Clytaemnestra meditating and
preparing her crime: (4) she sees her busied with the bath for Agamemnon:
(5) she sees her enveloping him with a treacherous ensnaring robe: horror-
stricken she calls the wife herself the snare, the accomplice of destruction
(λοιγοῦ), and invokes the Furies to raise their howl of exultation over a
sacrifice fit to be expiated by stoning (language anticipating a murder but
not yet expressly declaring it): (6) she beholds the perpetration of the
bloody deed, describing it under the image of a bull gored by an enraged
cow. The μελάγκερων μηχάνημα means the 'bipennis,' the double axe, of
which the two edges answer to the horns: with this she now smites
him, and he falls within the rim of a bath filled with water. This she
declares to be a δολοφόνος λέβης. That the Chorus do not yet fully understand a picture thus vividly exhibited must be ascribed to Cassandra's
destiny—not to be believed. Their doubts they politely veil in genera-
lities: and she goes on to foretell her own fate.

she meditates a mighty evil in this house,
to friends unbearable, and hard to cure: 1085
and help stands far aloof.

CHORUS.

Nought know I of these oracles: the former *facts*
I recognised: for with them all the city rings.

CASSANDRA.

Ah, wretched one! so wilt thou finish it?   *Ant.* 4.
the lord, the partner of thy bed,   1090 (1031)
with bath-streams cheering—how relate the end?
for speedily 'twill come: hand after hand
extends its stretchings forth.

CHORUS.

As yet I comprehend not: after riddling hints
I'm now perplexed by prophecies of import dark.   1095

CASSANDRA.

Ah, ah! alas, alas! what is this thing that appears?   *Str.* 5.
is 't not some net of Hades?
nay, but the bed-mate is the snare, the accomplice of
destruction: let a gang insatiate to the clan
loud o'er a victim shout *to be avenged* by stoning.   1100 (1041)

CHORUS.

What dire Erinys this thou biddest o'er the house   *Str.* 6.
to cry aloud? not cheering is the speech to me.
it rushes to my heart, the drop of ruddy dye,
which, welling from a mortal wound,

1103—5. This sentence, which appears to mean generally 'the life-blood rushes to my heart,' is in literal expression, 'and to my heart rushed the saffron-dyed drop, which falling with mortal effect (καιρία πτώσιμος) comes to its close together with the rays of setting life.' From the terrible presentiment thus inspired by Cassandra's pictures (see 904 τίπτε κ.τ.λ., and 921 σπλάγχνα κ.τ.λ.) the Chorus is led to say that 'woe cometh swift.'

ends with the rays of sinking life.   1105
speedily cometh woe.

CASSANDRA.

Ah, ah! behold, behold! keep from the heifer apart   *Ant.* 5.
the bull! in robèd raiment
she taketh, and with black-horn'd cunning instrument
she smiteth: he in water-holding vessel falls.   1110 (1051)
a treacherously-slaying laver's hap I tell thee.

CHORUS.

A first-rate judge of oracles I cannot boast   *Ant.* 6.
to be: but, this I liken to some evil thing.
for when is any good report from oracles
to mortals sent? through ills it is   1115
such wordy lore to learner brings
terrors of boding song.

CASSANDRA.

Alas, alas! a wretched woman's ill-starred lot!   *Str.* 7.
for my own woe, commingling, tell I loud:
o wherefore didst thou bring me wretched hither? 1120 (1061)
for nought, except to die with thee: what else?

CHORUS.

Soul-maddened one god-rapt thou art,   *Str.* 8.
and on thyself thou singest
music unmusical, most like
some nightingale, of delicate voice unsated,   1125
that with sad heart, alas, moans Itys, Itys,
through a life in woes abounding.

1108—1110 (1049, 1050). It is questionable whether λαβοῦσα should
have for its object τὸν ταῦρον, which gives a rendering *having caught him
in his robe-dress, she* &c., or μηχάνημα, which will be *she takes a dark-horned
instrument and slays him with it in his robe-dress.* The latter is favoured
by the position of λαβοῦσα, the former by the superior sense acquired, and
the idleness of ἐν πέπλοισιν unsustained by λαβοῦσα. This therefore we
adopt as logically better, though grammatically less probable.

K. A.   8

CASSANDRA.

Alas, alas! the fate of tuneful nightingale!   *Ant.* 7.
for with a wingèd body did the gods
enwrap her, and a sweet life void of weeping: 1130 (1071)
me waiteth rending with a two-edged spear.

CHORUS.

Whence on thee rushing hast thou these   *Ant.* 8.
vain griefs of inspiration,
and thy terrific melodies
framest in dismal shriek with loud notes blending?   1135
whence gainest thou the evil-worded limits
of a strain divinely guided?

CASSANDRA.

Alas, o spousals, spousals of Paris,   *Str.* 9.
the destruction of friends!
alas, o thou paternal water of Scamander!   1140 (1081)
then on thy brink indeed, unhappy maiden,
in nurture I was reared:
now near Cocytus and the shores of Acheron
eftsoons, it seemeth, I shall sing my fateful lays.

CHORUS.

What is this too clear word which thou hast uttered
            now?   *Str.* 10.   1145
even one new-born might learn *the meaning.*
stricken am I beneath with bloody sting,
while in distressful case thou mutterest low
amazing *words* for me to hear.

CASSANDRA.

Alas, o troubles, troubles that wholly   *Ant.* 9. 1150 (1091)
whelm in ruin a town!
alas, before the towers a father's sacrifices,

1131. *two-edged spear*, ἀμφήκει δορί. This means 'an axe.'

slayers of numerous herbage-grazing cattle!
yet they supplied no cure
to save the city from enduring all it doth: 1155
and I my glowing ear on earth shall quickly lay.

CHORUS.

Suited to those before are thy new-spoken words: *Ant.* 10.
an evil-minded demon makes thee,
heavily falling on thee from above,
to set to music doleful deadly woes,   1160 (1101)
the bounds of which I cannot guess.

CASSANDRA.

Now shall the oracle no more from out a veil
be looking, in the manner of a new-wed bride.

1156 (1097). Canter's emendation, followed by Hermann, θερμὸν οὖς
for vulg. θερμόνους, we defended at some length in our first edition. We
regard it now as so certain (all other suggestions being untenable and
Madvig's reading φαιδρὸν οὖς 1154 bringing support) that we spare the
repetition of our note.

1161. On the readings from 1052 (in 1005, 1012—24, 1034, 1038,
1040, 1045, 1051, 1060—1, 1065—6, 1087, 1097—1102) see *Consp. Lect.*
and *Notes on Lection.*

1162. Cassandra, now becoming calmer, tells the Chorus that her
oracle shall be declared to them in plainer terms. She does not, however,
speak with distinctness before l. 1229 (1171). She says now that a choir of
Furies, drunk with human blood, inhabit the Argive palace, and point with
abhorrence to the crime committed against a brother's marriage-bed.
Judging that this allusion to the feud of Atreus and Thyestes would be
understood by the Chorus, she challenges them to say whether she is familiar
or not with the legendary lore of Argos. When they admit her knowledge
with surprise, she tells them in a brief dialogue (στιχομυθία) how she came
to be endowed with the power of prophecy by Apollo, and to utter predictions which obtain no credit from the hearers. The Chorus express their
own belief in her veracity. Her first words 1162—66 (1103—07) say that
the oracle shall no longer peep from behind a veil, but shall be like a strong
morning wind, blowing in upon their minds brightly, and rolling onward
billows of woe ever greater and greater: meaning that the murder of
Agamemnon would surpass all their previous experience of melancholy
crime.

but, as it seems, to greet the rising of the sun
'twill come a brisk gale blowing, so that like a wave   1165
a woe still greater than this woe shall roll at dawn.
but I will teach your mind no more in riddling words.
and bear ye witness running by my side that I
scent out the trail of ills enacted long ago.
this roof there never quitteth an harmonious choir   1170 (1111)
but not melodious; for its words are far from sweet.
and after quaffing human blood, so as to be
the more audacious, in the halls a revelling troop
of sister Furies, hard to be expelled, abides:
who crouching in the mansion chant a song that speaks   1175
a curse original, and each in turn abhors
a brother's couches hostile to the trampler's *guilt.*
erred I, or, like some archer, do I hit the mark?
or am I some door-rapping cheat predicting lies?
bear witness with a previous oath that *well* I know   1180 (1121)
this dwelling's deeds of sin by ancient story told.

CHORUS.

What virtue could an oath, a pledge that honour gives,
possess? but thee I marvel at, that, bred o'er sea,
yet of a town that speaks another tongue thou dost
as truly talk, as if thou hadst been present there.   1185

CASSANDRA.

The seer Apollo made me mistress of this skill.

1178. *erred I?* The reason why Cassandra is made to put these questions, and to desire an oath from the Chorus testifying the truth of her
allusions to past history, is this. Apollo had, as a punishment, condemned
her to public discredit. She seeks therefore to bind the Chorus down by a
solemn declaration to receive what she says as the very truth. They avoid
such a pledge, asking what service it could do, while they recognize the
accuracy of her information.

1180. ἐκμαρτύρησον προυμόσας. This expression in some degree resem-
bles that in English law, 'testify on affidavit.'

1186. In codd. the lines marked in our Greek text 1127 and 1129 are

CHORUS.

Was it that he with love was smitten, though a god?

CASSANDRA.

Of these things 'twas a shame to me before to speak.

CHORUS.

Yes, every one while prospering is more delicate.

CASSANDRA.

He was a suitor, and he made strong love to me.   1190 (1131)

CHORUS.

And to his wishes didst thou yield in lawful wise?

CASSANDRA.

Consent I promised, but defrauded Loxias.

CHORUS.

Already with the arts of inspiration seized?

CASSANDRA.

All woes I was foretelling to the citizens.

CHORUS.

How then? wast thou unscathed by wrath of Loxias?   1195

CASSANDRA.

I gained belief from no one, after sinning thus.

CHORUS.

To us however seem thy bodings credible.

CASSANDRA.

Alas, alas: oh, oh, ye miseries!

continuously placed in the mouth of Cassandra, and 1128 and 1130 are similarly assigned to the Chorus.   Hermann rightly distributed them.

1195.   We have preferred the reception of Canter's ἄνατος for ἄνακτος to Wieseler's conjectural ἦσθα.

1196.   ὡς = ex quo, *from the time when.*

1198 &c.   Cassandra is again rapt with prophetic inspiration.   She sees in vision the monstrous crime of Atreus, the stealthy vengeance of

again the dreadful labour of true prophecy
whirls and disturbs my soul with preludes [rushing on].

1200 (1141)

do ye behold these infants seated at the house
like dream-discovered figures, children as it were
who by their friends were murdered? and their hands seem full
of their own flesh for viands, while a piteous load
they carry, vitals mixed with entrails, upon which   1205
a father feasted.   consequent on these events,
I say some dastard lion tossing in a bed,
house-guarding, plots revenge, alas, on him that's come,
my master, for one must abide the slavish yoke.
he, the fleet's captain, Ilion's wasting conqueror,   1210 (1152)
knows not the nature of a wanton hell-hound's tongue,
that licking first and stretching forth a jocund ear
shall, as some secret Ate, bite with foul success.
such deeds she dareth: murderess of a male is she,
a female—what abominable monster shall   1215
I fitly call her? ugly snake or one that dwells

Aegisthus, the approaching perpetration of Agamemnon's murder. The first
of these facts is recognized by the Chorus, the two latter are not understood.
Then Cassandra plainly says they will behold the death of Agamemnon.
Horrorstruck, they withhold belief, yet ask about the supposed perpetrator.
Cassandra taunts them with their slow comprehension of her language; and
then, once more subject to Apollo's influence, she breaks forth into a wild
disjointed speech of many lines, anticipating her own death at the hands of
Clytaemnestra.   Apollo, she says, is preparing her for it: she sees him in
vision stripping off her official decorations.   The Chorus behold this done
by her own hands alone.   She looks forward to a day when her murder
will be avenged.   And now (she says) she will enter the palace and die
there: for why should she survive her ruined country? only she prays for a
rapid and easy death.

   1205. *vitals mixed with entrails.* σπλάγχνα are the heart, liver and
lungs, ἔντερα the bowels &c.

   1211—1213.   See *Notes on Lection.*

   1216.   *ugly snake,* ἀμφίσβαινα, *the double-walker,* a harmless creature,
but uncanny to the eye.

in rocks, a Scylla, mischievous to mariners,
Death's raging mother, one that breathes a truceless war
to friends? how loud a shout she raised, the all-daring one,
as if 'twere in the crisis of the battle's rout.   1220 (1162)
she seems to be rejoicing at the safe return.
'tis all the same, if none of this convince; for why?
the future will arrive: and, witnessing ere long,
you'll say in pity that I am too true a seer.

CHORUS.

The banquet of Thyestes on his children's flesh   1225
I understood and shudder at, with terror thrill'd
to hear the tale told in its dread reality.
but, like a racer off the course, I heard the rest.

CASSANDRA.

I say that you will look on Agamemnon's death.

CHORUS.

To words well-omened, wretched woman, lull thy tongue.

                                              1230 (1172)

1217.   *Scylla.* See Hom. *Od.* XII. 85, Verg. *Ecl.* VI. Mr Paley refers
this superstitious legend to the existence of huge cuttle-fish in the Straits
of Messina.

1219—21. What a grandly terrible figure is Clytaemnestra here, raising
over her slaughtered husband a shout of triumph, like the battle-cry of an
excited warrior, and actually rejoicing in his safe return from Troy, because
it has given her the luxury of killing him.   To refer this ὀλολυγὴ to l. 548
and the μάχης τροπή to the fall of Troy, rendering δοκεῖ χαίρειν, 'she pre-
tends to rejoice,' seems to us absolutely to destroy the beauty of one of the
most splendid passages in this drama, one of the noblest samples of the poet's
genius.

1227.   *in its dread reality,* οὐδὲν ἐξηκασμένα, lit. not in mere resem-
blances.

1228.   *like a racer off the course,* ἐκ δρόμου πεσὼν τρέχω, lit. *having
heard the rest I run as a strayer from the course:* that is, I *heard* the
words but missed the sense, like a racer who has run off the course—has
lost the right track.

1230.   εὔφημον. Proleptic use of adj.

CASSANDRA.

Ah, but no healing god presideth o'er this speech.

CHORUS.

Not if it is to come: but may it ne'er befall!

CASSANDRA.

You turn to praying: but their business is to kill.

CHORUS.

What is the man by whom this grief is brought to pass?

CASSANDRA.

You quite o'erlooked the purport of my oracles.   1235

CHORUS.

The worker's plan it is I do not understand.

CASSANDRA.

Yet I am well acquainted with the Hellenic tongue.

CHORUS.

So are the Pythian oracles, yet hard to guess.

CASSANDRA.

Alas, what fire there is! and 'tis approaching me.
woe, woe! Apollo, God Lyceian! ah me, me!   1240 (1182)
this lioness, two-footed one, cohabiting,
in absence of the noble lion, with a wolf,
will slay me wretched: as a woman who prepares
a poison, she will mingle too my recompense

1243—46. We agree with Mr Paley that this place contains corruption: but we are disposed to find it in 1187 rather than in 1186 with Cod. F (i. e. Demetrius Triclinius) and Mr Paley. We suggest ἐπεύχεται δέ, φωτὶ θήγουσα ξίφος. The reading of Auratus, πότῳ for κότῳ, specious as it is, we do not adopt, deeming it less suitable to the place. Φόνον is the contained accus. with ἀντιτίσασθαι, the object αὐτὸν (φῶτα) being understood. See Eurip. *Med.* 259 πόσιν δίκην ἀντιτίσασθαι, *Heracl.* 852 ἀποτίσασθαι δίκην ἐχθρούς.

in her resentment: whetting for a man the sword,   1245
she vows with murder to revenge his bringing me.
why wear I these things still, a mockery of myself?
this staff, this chaplet round my throat oracular?
before my fate will I destroy you both. lie there
to ruin fallen: I shall follow close behind;   1250 (1192)
some other in my stead enrich with cursed woes.
lo, here! Apollo's self is stripping off from me
the dress prophetic: yet even in these ornaments
he bore to look upon me ridiculed by friends
and foes with undivided *minds, yet* erringly.   1255
like to some female conjuror, such terms I bore
as tramper, beggar, miserable half-starved wretch.
and now the seer-god, after making me a seer,
has led me forth to meet the doom of such a death.
yea, for the altar of my father's fate, a block   1260 (1202)
awaits me, smitten down with hot blood-spilling stroke.
yet shall I die not unregarded of the gods.
another in his turn shall come, redressing me,
a matricidal shoot, avenger of a sire.
an exiled wanderer, from this land a distant guest,   1265
he shall return to crown these cursed woes for friends:
for of the deities is sworn a mighty oath,
that his slain father's prostrate form shall bring him back.

1249. *you*, σφώ (for vulg. σε), *you twain*, i.e. the staff and the chaplet.

1250. Mr Paley's suggested ἀγ' ὦδ' as addressed to an imaginary executioner, seems to us impossible here. He asks how the corrupt reading of codd. ἀγαθώ δ' is to be accounted for. The state of these codd. hardly justifies such a challenge: yet here it seems evident that the antecedent in corruption of ἀγάθ' must have been ἄγεθ' in imaginary sequence to ἴτε. We follow Hermann's emendation.

1260. *altar of my father's fate*, βωμοῦ πατρῴου. We now deem it most probable that Cassandra refers here to the slaughter of Priam at his domestic altar by Neoptolemus. See Verg. *Aen.* II. 663, patrem qui obtruncat ad aras.

why am I groaning thus aloud in piteous wise,
since Ilion's city in the first place I beheld   1270 (1212)
faring as it did fare, and they who took the town
are in the judgment of the gods thus coming off?
I go to meet my fate, I will abide my death.
these as the gates of Hades greet I now by name.
and my petition is to meet a mortal stroke,   1275
that without palpitating struggle, while the blood
streams forth to easy dying, I may close this eye.

CHORUS.

O woman greatly wretched, also greatly wise,
thy speech hath been a long one : but if thine own end
thou truly knowest, to the altar how canst thou,   1280 (1222)
like an ox driven by a god, thus boldly walk?

CASSANDRA.

Escape is none, o strangers, for a longer time.

CHORUS.

But the last moments left of time are valued most.

CASSANDRA.

The day is come : 'tis little I shall gain by flight.

CHORUS.

Full sure thy patience testifies a valiant soul.   1285

CASSANDRA.

This commendation none of them that prosper hear.

1278. The Chorus express their astonishment that Cassandra, looking
for immediate death, could walk to meet it with so much determination.
She says that delay is useless. After a brief dialogue, she starts with horror
from the palace door, through which comes the scent of blood. Then re-
suming courage, and about to enter, she bids them remember her words when
later events occur. She prays before her last sunlight, that the avengers,
whose advent she looks for, may require atonement for her blood with that
of Agamemnon. Finally, before departure, she speaks of the instability of
human life. Prosperity is easily changed to adversity: and that is wiped
out by death.

CHORUS.

Yet glorious dying gratifies a mortal mind.

CASSANDRA.

Woe for thee, father, and thy noble progeny!

CHORUS.

What is the matter? what the alarm that makes thee shrink?

CASSANDRA.

Alas, alas!   1290 (1232)

CHORUS.

Whence came that sob? 'twas sure some horror of the heart.

CASSANDRA.

Blood-dripping murder from the house is steaming out.

CHORUS.

How cometh such a smell from incense on the hearth?

CASSANDRA.

It showeth even as a vapour from a tomb.

CHORUS.

Thou claimest for the house no Syrian luxury.   1295

CASSANDRA.

Well, I will go and mourn within the palace too
my own and Agamemnon's fate: enough of life!
alas, o strangers!
not with vain terror do I shudder, as a bird
doth at a bush: such witness bear this death of mine   1300 (1242)
whene'er a woman shall for me a woman die,
and for a man ill-wived another man shall fall.
this friendly part in dying hour I claim from you.

CHORUS.

Sad sufferer, for thy doom foretold I pity thee.

1293. *how cometh* &c. Another punctuation gives the rendering—
'how so? the smell is that of incense on the hearth.' What we have given
seems the better view.

Cassandra.

One saying more, no dirge of mine, I wish to speak.　　1305
unto the sun, in presence of his final light,
I pray, that to the friend-avenging murderers
foes at the same time may *with blood* the blood atone
of a slave-woman, easy conquest, done to death.
alas the lot of mortals! to a sketch one might,　　1310 (1252)
well-fortuned, liken it: but if ill fortune come,
a wetted sponge applied obliterates the draft:
and the first state far more I pity than the last.

ANAPAESTS.

Chorus.

Good fortune is insatiate in all mortals:
from finger-pointed mansions none excludes it,　　1315
crying, 'come here no more,' in words forbidding.
unto this *prince* to capture Priam's city
the blest ones granted;
and home he comes god-honoured:
but if he now shall expiate former bloodshed,　　1320 (1263)
and render to the dead by dying,
aloof from other deaths, full retribution,
what man of mortal nature
can ever boast, such *downfall* hearing,
that he was born with scathless fortune?　　1325

1311. *liken*, πρέψειεν. Photius has, 'πρέψαι, τὸ ὁμοιῶσαι Aesch.' Conington explained this passage of a sketch (σκιά): the sense, says Mr Paley, is 'that prosperity is as easily changed as the outline or cartoon of a picture, while adversity may be wiped out by one stroke, i.e. by death.'

1313. Cassandra pities 'the change from prosperity to adversity more than the sudden extinction of misery by death.' Pal. Here (as Ast, cited by Mr Paley, says) οὗτος refers to the more distant object, ἐκεῖνος to the nearer. This, though contrary to the general rule, is not infrequent.

1325. On the readings at 1121, 1136, 1141, 1153—5, 1177, 1186—8, 1191—7, 1203, 1211, 1216, 1224, 1248—50, 1253, 1264—6 see *Consp. Lect.* and *Notes on Lection.*

EPEISODION 5.

The cry of Agamemnon, murderously wounded by Clytaemnestra, is heard in the orchestra once and again. The coryphaeus calls on the choreutae for their opinions on the course to be taken: these are delivered, and by him briefly summed up. At this moment, by means of the stage-machine called eccyclema, the palace is opened and Clytaemnestra is disclosed stand-ing beside the veiled bodies of Agamemnon and Cassandra. She addresses the Chorus, declares her deed, describes, and exults in it. The remainder of this Epeisodion consists of the reproaches, complaints and lamentations of the Chorus on the one side, and the self-justifying replies of the queen on the other, partly in iambic measure, but chiefly in lyric metres. At the close Clytaemnestra expresses a desire to make peace with the Council.]

AGAMEMNON *(from within)*.
Alas me! smitten am I by a mortal blow.

CHORUS (Coryphæus).
Silence! who is this that crieth, wounded by a mortal stroke?

1326.   *blow.* We have not rendered the word ἔσω which codd. place at the close of this line, being displeased with each of the interpretations given to it. That Aesch. should make Agamemnon say, ' I am mortally wounded inside the house,' or ' I am mortally wounded inside my body,' seems hardly credible, though Schneidewin defends the latter, taking ἔσω = 'ictu valido, *deeply*.' Conjectures are: (1) ἔχω for ἔσω, with comma after πέπληγμαι, but we have not placed this in the text, as we would rather have the single verb πέπληγμαι for evident reasons: (2) ἐγώ for ἔσω. We think this might be defended as an emphatic pronoun, loudly uttered to draw attention. See Aristoph. *Ach.* 406, Δικαιόπολις καλεῖ σε Χολλίδης, ἐγώ.

1327.   Hermann and K. O. Müller were at issue respecting the number of choreutae in this play : and the controversy turned chiefly on the distribu-tion of speeches to the several members in this scene.   Hermann considered the whole number to be 15, assigning one trochaic line to each of the first three speakers, and two iambic lines to each of the others, the last being the coryphaeus.   The other view (which we follow) assigns to the cory-phaeus all the trochaic lines and the two last iambic: he is therefore the Χο. ιβ′ of our text, as well as the Χο. of (1269, 1271—2).

AGAMEMNON.

Alas once more! *I'm* smitten by a second blow.

CHORUS (Coryphaeus).

I suppose the deed is ended from the outcry of the king.
but let us by common counsel settle whatsoe'er is safe.

1330 (1272)

CHOREUTES 1.

I tell you my advice : that hither to the house
we notify the citizens to come with aid.

CHOREUTES 2.

I think that with our utmost speed we should rush in,
and sift the matter while the sword is reeking fresh.

CHOREUTES 3.

And I, too, sharing an opinion of this kind,   1335
vote we do something : 'tis no crisis for delay.

CHOREUTES 4.

'Tis clear to see : the prelude of their action shows
they are preparing for the town a tyranny.

CHOREUTES 5.

Ay, we are lingering : while they, trampling in the dust
restraining honour's scruples, ply the sleepless hand.

1340 (1282)

1330. *whatsoe'er* &c. The reading we take, ἄν πως for ἅ ἄν πως (ᾗ), *whatever may be*—and the other, ἄν πως (κοινωσώμεθα), *if we possibly can*—express much the same sense.

1332. *notify...to come with aid*, κηρύσσειν βοήν, lit. *to proclaim a cry*, the word βοήν, *cry*, having here the force of βοήθειαν, i.e. *a cry for aid*—as in English, help! murder! &c.; in French, au voleur! à l'assassin!

1334. *while the sword is reeking fresh*, ξὺν νεορρύτῳ ξίφει, lit. *with* (the help of) *the fresh-streaming sword*, taking the criminal *red-hand*, as it was once said.

1337. *'tis clear to see*: ὁρᾶν πάρεστι, lit. *it is possible to see*. See πάρα, 980.

CHOREUTES 6.

What happy counsel I can give I do not know.
the doer should have also plann'd the thing to do.

CHOREUTES 7.

Such is my mind too, since I lack ability
to bring a dead man back again to life by words.

CHOREUTES 8.

And shall we thus then, eking out our lives, submit   1345
to these for leaders, who pollute the family?

CHOREUTES 9.

No, that is not to be endured: 'twere best to die:
the stroke of fate is milder than a tyranny.

CHOREUTES 10.

And shall we upon evidence derived from groans
pronounce with seer-like certainty the man is dead?

1350 (1292)

CHOREUTES 11.

From thorough knowledge of the facts we ought to speak:
for guessing and assurance are two different things.

CHOREUTES 12 (Coryphaeus).

Most votes from all sides bid me recommend this *course,*
clearly to learn the present case of Atreus' son.

[CLYTAEMNESTRA *and the two veiled corpses are now disclosed
by the eccyclema.*]

1342. *the doer* &c. lit. *the doer's part is also the advising about* (the thing to be done).

1345. *eking out our lives,* βίον τείνοντες, i. e. in the endeavour to extend our lives—for the sake of lengthened life.

1348. *milder,* πεπαιτέρα, lit. 'softer,' πέπων expressing the softness of ripe fruit.

1353. *most votes* &c., lit. 'I am supplied with numbers (πληθύνομαι) from all sides to commend this (γνώμην)': i. e. 'the majority of opinions from every side bid me' &c.

1354. *to learn the present case of Atreus' son,* 'Ατρείδην εἰδέναι κυροῦνθ'

CLYTAEMNESTRA.

Much though I said erewhile adapted to the time,   1355
the contrary I shall not be ashamed to say.
for how, preparing hostile things for hostile men,
who seem as friends, shall any one erect a snare
of harm unto a height that cannot be o'erleapt?   1359 (1301)
not without thought long brooding o'er an ancient vow
this contest found me, though 'twas after lengthened time.
now where I struck I stand, upon a finished work.
so did I manage, and the fact I'll not deny,
that he should neither flee, nor guard himself from fate.
a casting-net, as that of fishes, issueless,   1365
I fasten round him, evil wealthiness of dress.
twice do I strike him; he with groaning outcries twain
his limbs relaxed; and on him, prostrate as he lay,
yet a third stroke I add, the votive gift of thanks
to Hades under earth, the saviour of the dead.   1370 (1312)

ὅπως (= ὅπως κυρεῖ). This pregnant brachylogy results from the idiomatic construction of οἶδα with participles.

At this point the palace opens by the action of the eccyclema, bringing out Clytaemnestra and the two corpses. It is thought by some scholars that the Chorus have at this time, while chanting the anapaests, left the orchestral platform for the proscenium, and that on Clytaemnestra's appearance they group themselves in two semicircles, as though about to surround her. These scholars hold that choral anapaests are always accompanied by a marching evolution of the chorus. If this be true in tragedy, which seems doubtful, it could not be so in comedy. For, although the Parabasis was preceded by a choral movement, it was chanted by a coryphaeus in station, addressing the spectators.

1359. *unto a height*, ὕψος, 'a height,' really in apposition to ἀρκύστατα. See *Consp. L.*

1368. Mr Paley reads αὐτοῦ, *on the spot* (implying, he says, 'at once').

1370. *to Hades...saviour of the dead*, Ἅιδου νεκρῶν σωτῆρος. Some editors for Ἅιδου read Διὸς with much plausibility. As the third libation at a banquet was sacred to Ζεὺς σωτήρ, Clytaemnestra, with horrible irony, says that the third blow of the axe dealt by her to Agamemnon was the votive honour of him (Hades or Ζεύς?) who beneath the earth is 'the saviour of the dead.'

thus having fallen, pants he forth his fretting soul,
and, breathing out of blood a rapid slaughter-tide,
he strikes me with a darksome drop of gory dew,
nor gladdens less than when, parturient of the bud,
the seed *rejoiceth in* the sky-descending rain.   1375
so stands the case; and ye, old men of Argos here,
be joyful, if ye will be joyful: I exult.
had it been fit to pour libation o'er the dead,
this had been justly, yea, 'twere more than justly, done:
so large a cup of cursèd evils for his house   1380 (1322)
had this man filled, and drains it, coming home, himself.

CHORUS.

We marvel at thy tongue, so daring-mouth'd it is,
that o'er a husband utterest this vaunting speech.

CLYTAEMNESTRA.

My powers ye're trying, as a woman's void of sense:
but I with heart undaunted say to knowing *men:*   1385
whether your pleasure be to praise me or to blame,
it is no matter: this is Agamemnon, *who*
lies here, my husband, and the corpse of this right-hand,
work of a just artificer.   The facts are so.

CHORUS.

Woman, what baleful edible earth-nourish'd,   *Str.* 1390 (1332)
or drink that issued from the liquid sea

1371. *pants he forth his fretting soul,* τὸν αὐτοῦ θυμὸν ὁρμαίνει.   Mr
Paley's rendering, 'he chafes in his mind,' is not commendable.   Θυμός,
meaning *life,* is frequent in the Homeric poems.

1388.   The punctuation which connects χερὸς with νεκρός, not with
ἔργον, is by far the more vigorous and Aeschylean.   Mr Paley adopts it.

1390. (1236).   The horrified Chorus ask Clytaemnestra, what baleful
drug she has eaten or drunk, that she has committed a crime which is only
to be expiated by her death as a murderess, with incense laid on her as
on an atoning sacrifice, accompanied by a form of public execration.

K. A.   9

hast tasted, that upon thyself thou placedst
this incense, with loud curses of the people?
pitiless didst thou fling and cleave:
and citiless thou shalt be,   1395
to citizens a hateful monster.

CLYTAEMNESTRA.

Now from the city thou adjudgest banishment
and hatred of the citizens for me to bear,
and execrations of the public voice; although
thou didst not then make opposition to this man,   1400 (1341)
who—caring for her fate as little as a beast's,
where sheep are most abundant in their fleecy flocks—
his own child, dearest offspring of my mother-throes,
did sacrifice, to disenchant the winds of Thrace.
ought you not this man to have banish'd from the land   1405
in payment of his foul misdeeds? but hearing of
my acts, thou art a stern judge: well—I bid thee speak
such threats, as deeming me prepared on equal terms

1392. ἐπέθου. Middle voice in double sense, (1) of indirect agency;
(2) reflexive; *didst cause to be laid on thyself.*

1394. ἀπέδικες. Some (as Pal.) place the question here, making ἀρὰs
object of ἀπέδικες (didst set at nought). We cannot concur: the three
compounds with ἀπὸ are, we think, connected, the first two suggesting the
third, as a *jeu de mots.* This we have tried to represent by introducing the
word *pitiless,* to precede *citiless.* The verbs express Clytaemnestra's murderous deed: having enveloped Agamemnon in the *cul-de-sac* bath-dress,
she suddenly flings him from her, seizes the axe, and cleaves him down
(ἀποτέμνει) with two blows.

1397. Clyt. in reply reproaches the Chorus with their indifference to
the guilt of Agememnon in sacrificing his daughter, and answers their
menace with a counter-threat.

1408. *as deeming* &c. ὡς κ.τ.λ. The construction is somewhat
involved: ἐμοῦ, coming last, seems to have a triple power; (1) as
absolute with παρεσκευασμένης; (2) as suggesting the object of νικήσαντα
(ἔμε); (3) as indicating the object of ἄρχειν (ἐμοῦ): i.e. ὡς (ἐμοῦ) παρεσκευασμένης ἐκ τῶν ὁμοίων (σέ) νικήσαντα (ἐμὲ) ἄρχειν ἐμοῦ. The words

for thee to govern when by force thou hast vanquish'd me.
but if the god should bring the contrary to pass,   1410 (1351)
thou'lt learn discretion, though *the lesson* be too late.

CHORUS.

Mighty art thou of counsel: haughty language   *Ant.*
is this which thou hast uttered (since indeed
thy heart as with blood-dripping fortune raves
distraught), that o'er thine eyes conspicuous showeth   1415
a smear of blood still unavenged.
yet must thou stroke with stroke
atone, of all thy friends forsaken.

CLYTAEMNESTRA.

This righteous sanction of my oaths thou too must hear:
I swear by the fulfilling Justice of my child,   1420 (1361)
by Ate and Erinys, unto whom I slew
this man, I ne'er expect to tread the hall of Fear,
so long as on my hearth Aegisthus burneth fire,
loyal in feeling to myself, as heretofore.
for he is no slight shield of confidence to me.   1425
low lies this woman's wife-insulting †*husband, whom*

ἐκ τῶν ὁμοίων suggest καὶ ἐμὲ νικήσασάν σε ἄρχειν σοῦ, to express τοὔμπαλιν
(the converse in l. 1351).

1413—16. The Chorus notice the blood-stain acknowledged by the
queen, and renew their threat. She 1419 defies them, expressing her
reliance on Aegisthus. Again she exults in the death of Agamemnon,
also in that of Cassandra, whom she loads with revolting imputations.

1422. This is a difficult line to interpret. Codd. have ἐμπατεῖ, which
Dind. and Franz keep: 'my hope treads not in the hall of fear,' i.e.
is not mingled with fear. Mr Paley makes φόβου depend on ἐλπίς,
meaning, 'I have no expectation of fear, that it tread my hall:' too harshly,
we think. Hermann reads οὔ μοι φόβου μέλαθρ' ἂν ἐλπὶς ἐμπατεῖν, 'I
have no expectation that fear will tread in my halls.' With some hesitation, reading ἐμπατεῖν, we render 'I have no expectation of setting my
foot in the hall of Fear,' a bold metaphor: but we see nothing better.

1426. *whom his staring army saw,* ὁ ἐκφανὴς ἰδεῖν στρατῷ, lit. 'who
(was) distinctly visible to the army.'

his staring army saw† the fondled favourite
of † *all* † Chryseis-girls in Ilion's neighbourhood:
and she, this captive woman, sign-interpreter
and paramour of this man, telling oracles
in faithful converse, wearing out in company   1430 (1371)
with sailor mates the benches. worthy their reward:
for he is—what ye see: she—mark me—like a swan,
after that she had sung her last funereal dirge,
his sweetheart, lieth here, and by this union brings
an added relish to my *feast* of luxury.   1435

CHORUS.

Alas! I would some fate not over-painful   *Str.* 1.

1432. *like a swan.* On the 'cycnus musicus' as distinct from the common swan, see Mr Paley's note.

1434. Hermann takes φιλήτωρ as an adj. and reads τῷδ' for τοῦδ' of codd. We follow him, as Mr Paley has done.

1435. Here by reading εὐναῖς, we are glad to rescue Clytaemnestra from the opprobrium of applying τῆς ἐμῆς χλιδῆς to her own union with Aegisthus. Wicked as she is, we have no right to ascribe to a proud queen language from which the lowest and worst of her sex would refrain. The 'luxury' she vaunts is that of gratified revenge and ambition, though it includes the legal recognition of her second marriage.

1436 The Chorus declare their wish to die: and apostrophise Helen as the fatal cause of many woes. Clytaemnestra finds fault with these sentiments. They address the demon of the house of Tantalus: and she agrees with them in ascribing the blood shed in the family to his influence. The Chorus suggest however that this influence is directed by Zeus 1473, without whom nothing is fulfilled. Then they break into a new lamentation of Agamemnon 1477 &c., which they repeat at 1501 &c. Clytaemnestra says 1485 &c. that the evil genius of Atreus has taken her form to execute vengeance for the murdered children. The Chorus will only admit to her that this evil spirit might be her aider and abettor. Kindred bloodshed would excite Ares to inflict vengeance. Clyt. declares 1511 &c. that Agamemnon has expiated the crime committed by him against his daughter Iphigeneia. The Chorus 1517 &c. express fresh doubts and anticipate greater calamities. Wishing they had died before seeing this deed, they ask who shall bury and lament Agamemnon. Will she, the murderous wife, dare to do this? Who will

nor couch-confining would arrive
and bring with speed amongst us
the everlasting endless sleep,
our kindest guardian being slain,   1440 (1381)
who through a woman much endured,
and by a woman lost his life.
ah, woe to thee, distracted Helen!   *Str.* 2.
who singly didst those many,
those very many lives 'neath Trojan walls destroy.   1445
    *   *   *   *   *

[a memorable †*stain for the Pleisthenidae*†   [*Str.* 3.]
to blossom thou didst bring through blood uncleansed,
and strife that in the palace
was then unquelled, a husband's sorrow.]

CLYTAEMNESTRA.

The fate of death be not invoking,   *Str.* 4.   1450 (1392)
distressed by these things;
nor yet on Helen turn thine anger;
that she, a manslayer, that she singly
destroying lives of many Danaans,
wrought unexampled anguish.   1455

pronounce the eulogy over his tomb? The queen tells them not to trouble
themselves with these matters 1537 &c.: they who slew will bury him
without domestic lamentation: his daughter Iphigeneia will meet and
embrace him on the shores of Acheron. The Chorus draw moral infer-
ences from these sad events 1546, and declare that the family is linked to
woe by an irretrievable destiny. Clytaemnestra concludes the dialogue by
an expression of desire for peace 1554 &c. She begs the evil genius to
quit their house in search of other victims, and would gladly resign much of
her wealth to escape future miseries of kindred murder. Her speeches are
all in anapaests; those of the Chorus chiefly lyric, sometimes anapaestic.

1446—9. Mr Paley justly says: "the text here is so corrupt that it
seems quite a vain attempt to explain or restore it." We have, like him,
offered a suggestion, which does not assume to be a restoration.

1455. *unexampled*, ἀξύστατος, an ἅπαξ λεγόμενον of which the sense is
rather guessed from the context than ascertained from authority.

CHORUS.

O demon, who art perching on the mansion   *Ant.* 1.
and double-raced Tantalidae,
and power of equal spirit
through women stablishest, to me heart-stinging,
behold, where on the body stationed   1460 (1402)
she boasteth, like some odious crow,
to chant a strain unmusical.

CLYTAEMNESTRA.

Thy mouth's intent thou now correctest,   *Ant.* 4.
that thrice-huge monster
the demon of this race invoking.   1465
yea, 'tis from him a thirst blood-lapping
preys on the belly, gore renewing
ere the old grief is ended.

CHORUS.

Ay, thou art citing a great demon,   *Str.* 5.
whose home is this, whose wrath is heavy: 1470 (1412)
alas, alas! an ill citation
of fortune cursèd and insatiate,
woe, woe! through Zeus all-causing, all-effecting:

1457. *double-raced*, δίφυιος, Hermann's reading. The word is a rare one.

1458. *of equal spirit*, ἰσόψυχος, i.e. with that of men. See ἀνδρόβουλον, 11.

1460. σταθεῖσ' (Herm. Dind. Blomf.), applied to Clytaemnestra, seems a more probable reading here than σταθεὶς applied to the demon. In support of this it may be observed that she first adopts a strain not iambic in her speech at 1450 (1392), to which the Chorus probably allude.

1464. *thrice-huge*, τριπάχυιος, another ἅπαξ λεγόμενον. Peile explains, *over-gorged* or *overgrown*, which Mr Paley approves.

1467. *belly*, νείρᾳ, Casaubon's restoration for codd. νείρει. It is for νείειρα = νεάτη (γαστήρ).

1470. *whose home is this*, ἐν μελάθροις, an emendation for the corrupt οἴκοις τοῖσδε of codd.

for what without Zeus is fulfilled
to mortals? which of these things is not   1475
by rule divine accomplished?
      Alas, alas!   *Str.* 6.
o king, o king, how shall I weep thee?
what can I say with friendly spirit?
within this spider's web thou liest,   1480 (1422)
by impious death thy life exhaling,
(o me, me for this couch illiberal!)   *Str.* 7.
by treacherous fate laid low
with two-edged wielded weapon.

CLYTAEMNESTRA.

That this is my deed thou maintainest: *Str.* 8. 1485
but ne'er imagine
that I'm the wife of Agamemnon:
not so! this dead man's spouse resembling
the old and bitter evil genius
of Atreus, cruel feast-provider,   1490 (1432)
paid this man off by sacrificing
his full-grown life to infants.

CHORUS.

That of this murder thou art guiltless   *Ant.* 5.
who is it that shall bear thee witness?
ah, who? but from thy sires might come   1495
an evil spirit thine abettor.
by streaming gore of kindred is black Ares
forc'd thither, where advancing he
to blood congealed of eaten children
shall grant a righteous vengeance.   1500 (1442)
      Alas, alas!   *Ant.* 6.
o king, o king, how shall I weep thee?

1486. *imagine*, ἐπιλέχθης (=ἐπιλόγισαι) a rare aorist form from ἐπιλέ-
γομαι, *to calculate, assume*.

1489. *evil genius*, ἀλάστωρ. See Introduction.

what can I say with friendly spirit?
within this spider's web thou liest,
by impious death thy life exhaling   1505
(o me, me for this couch illiberal!)   *Ant.* 7.
by treacherous fate laid low
with two-edged wielded weapon.

     [*Two spurious verses are here omitted.*]

CLYTAEMNESTRA.

And brought not this man to the dwelling   *Ant.* 8.
deceitful mischief?   1510 (1452)
suffering the worthy fruit of acts unworthy
done to a scion that from him I nurtured,
the much-bewailed Iphigeneia,
let him not highly vaunt in Hades,
by sword-inflicted death atoning   1515
the deeds he first ensampled.

CHORUS.

Perplexed am I—bereft of thought's   *Str.* 9.
ingenious speculations—
which way to turn myself, while sinks the dwelling.
I shudder at the bloody clattering shower   1520 (1462)
that shaketh the foundation:
for now the soft drip ceaseth;
and for another deed of mischief
on other whetstones Fate is sharpening Justice.
o earth, earth, would thou hadst received me   *Ant.* 2.
before I saw this *prince* possessing
a silver-sided bath for mattress!
who is to bury, who to mourn him?
wilt thou have hardihood to do it,
to kill thy spouse, and then bewail him?   1530 (1471)
unto his spirit to perform
a thankless favour,
unjust return for mighty actions?

*   *   *   *   *

who for a godlike man upon his tomb   [*Ant.* 3.]
the praise with tears proclaiming   1535
in truthfulness of heart shall labour?

CLYTAEMNESTRA.

'Tis no concern of thine to mention   *Str.* 10.
this *solemn* duty:
by us he fell, and we shall bury,
not with domestic lamentation: 1540 (1482)

*   *   *   *   *
*   *   *   *   *

but him his daughter, as befitteth,
with loving looks, Iphigeneia,
greeting her father at the ferry
of woes swift-travers'd,
shall *fondly* fling her arms around, and kiss him.   1545

CHORUS.

Reproach is answered by reproach,   *Ant.* 9.
and hard the interpretation.
she spoils the spoiler, he who slew pays forfeit;
while Zeus abides, the rule abideth always,
that one who wrought must suffer: 1550 (1492)
'tis lawful: from a dwelling
the brood of curses who can banish?
the race is *firmly* glued to cursèd evil.

CLYTAEMNESTRA.

This oracle with truth thou touchest,   *Ant.* 10.
and I am willing—   1555
oaths interchanging with the demon
of the Pleisthenid race—in these things
to rest content, though hard to suffer:
but that hereafter,

1544. *of woes*, ἀχέων, i.e. Ἀχέροντος.

departing from this house, he harass
another clan with kindred murders.   1560 (1501)
me a small share of wealth sufficeth,
if deeds infuriate
of mutual bloodshed from our halls I banish.

EXODOS.

[*Aegisthus, the accomplice and paramour of Clytaemnestra, now enters the
proscenium by the door on the (spectator's) right hand of the central one,
leading from the city. Whether he is accompanied by guards cannot be
certainly determined: but his words at line 1636 imply that he has an
armed force within call.*]

AEGISTHUS.

O cheerful sunlight of a day that brings redress!

Exodos. Aegisthus begins and ends his first and longest speech with
language of fierce exultation over the slain Agamemnon. He recounts the
wrongs and cruelties which his father Thyestes and himself had received
from Atreus, the father of Agamemnon, and relies on these as justifying the
plot, of which he avows himself the author, to circumvent and kill the
son of Atreus, Agamemnon himself. The Chorus threaten him with a
public sentence of stoning to death. He replies in language of defiance
and counter-menace. The Chorus renew their upbraiding, and are again
met by threatening words from Aegisthus. When they taunt him with
cowardice in not executing the deed himself, he tells them that circumven-
tion was evidently the woman's part: and once more he threatens them
with bonds and starvation. They continue their reproaches, and anticipate
the return of Orestes to take vengeance for his father's murder. The calmer
iambic metre is now superseded,—to the end of the drama—by the more
vehement and rapid rhythm of the Trochaic Tetrameter. Aegisthus calls
to his guards: the Chorus to the citizens of their party: but Clytaemnestra
interferes, and forbidding further bloodshed, advises a pacific compromise.
Nevertheless Aegisthus and the Chorus do not at once desist from mutual
recriminations: and the play ends with two lines, in which the queen entreats
Aegisthus to disregard the anger of the old men, for that they themselves, as
sovereigns, would have the entire management of affairs.

Mr Paley justly remarks that the cowardly selfishness of Aegisthus, with
his invectives and threats, places his character on a lower level than that
of the ruthlessly revengeful, but deeply injured Clytaemnestra.

now can I say at last that gods avenging men   1565
from realms supernal look upon the woes of earth,
since in the woven robes of the Erinyes
this man laid prostrate I behold to my delight,
atoning of his father's hand the subtle deeds.
for Atreus this man's sire, when ruler of this land,   1570 (1512)
drove from his country and his home to banishment
Thyestes (to relate the simple fact) my sire
and his own brother, wrangling with him for the sway.
but coming back again a suppliant of the hearth,
the poor Thyestes earned a lot *so far* secure   1575
as with his own blood not to stain his native ground:
but Atreus, this man's godless father, to my sire
professing hospitable acts more prompt than kind,
a joyous feast-day celebrating seemingly,
served up to him a banquet of his children's flesh.   1580 (1522)
seated himself in higher place apart, the toes
and fingers he was hiding; †*to that hapless one*†
the undistinguishable †*parts he sent to eat*,
which he† forthwith received in ignorance, and ate
a meal destructive to his race, as you behold.
soon as he learned the abominable truth, aloud   1585
he shrieked, and fell back sickened from the murder-feast;
then on the sons of Pelops calling down a fate
unbearable, the spurnèd board he justly made

1573 (20). *wrangling.* Aegisthus suppresses the graver charge against
his father Thyestes. See 1177.

1576 (23). We prefer Blomfield's reading αὐτός, *himself*, to the vulg.
αὐτοῦ, on the spot.

1579 (26). *feast-day*, κρεουργὸν ἦμαρ, " a day on which meat (κρέας) was
distributed after a solemn sacrifice." Pal.

1582 (29). *he was hiding*, ἔκρυπτε. We have fully concurred with Mr
Paley and other editors in adopting this emendation of Casaubon for ἔθρυπτε,
the reading of Codd.

1588 (35). *the spurnèd board*, λάκτισμα δείπνου, kicking-over of the
banquet (i.e. of the table on which it was laid). We follow Hermann and
Mr Paley in adopting ἀρὰν for ἀρᾷ.

his curse—'thus perish all the race of Pleisthenes!'
from hence it cometh that you see this man laid low: 1590(1532)
and I with justice am the planner of his death.
for with my wretched father me, third after these,
an infant in my cradle, drove he forth from home;
but justice brought me back again, to manhood grown.
so, while I dwelt at distance, yet I reached this man,
contriving a full scheme of mischievous intent: 1596
and now were even death to me a glorious thing,
looking on this man in the snares of justice *caught.*

CHORUS.

Aegisthus, I respect not insult after ill:
this man thou slewest (such thy tale) with full intent, 1600 (1542)
and singly didst contrive this piteous deed of blood.
I ween thou canst not righteously (be sure) escape
the execrations of a people stoning thee.

AEGISTHUS.

These words dost thou speak, sitting at the lowest oar,
while those upon the middle bench control the ship?   1605
old as thou art, thou'lt find how painful 'tis to learn
such lessons at that age, when told to be discreet.
best mediciners of wisdom e'en to teach the old

1589. *race of Pleisthenes.* Mr Paley says: "the commentators have remarked that the Pelopidae, Tantalidae, and Pleisthenidae are synonyms by which the poet describes the family of the Atreidae: but who Pleisthenes was, is not recorded." The conjectures are so baseless that we give it up as one of the unsolved problems of history.

1592. *third after these, τρίτον ἐπὶ τοῖνδε.* We adopt this reading for ἐπὶ δέκα, because the notion of twelve children served up seems too monstrous for even Greek fable.

1604—5. In a Greek trireme, the lowest of the three ranks of rowers were called θαλαμῖται, those above them ζυγῖται, the highest θρανῖται. We know that the θαλαμῖται had the poorest pay: and this place seems to prove that the ζυγῖται were the most dignified class. See Boeckh's *Public Econ. of Athens,* p. 383 &c. (Transl.).

are bonds and hunger: see'st not, having eyes, this truth—
'kick not against the goads, lest striking cost thee woe?'
1610 (1553)

CHORUS.

Thou, keeping this man's dwelling, didst defile his bed,
and with his wife, in dread of those from war returned,
for husband and for army-chief foul murder plan.

AEGISTHUS.

These words again will gender bitter penalties:
the tongue of Orpheus was the opposite of thine :   1615
he all things dragged behind his voice for very joy;
thou rousing us with silly barkings wilt be dragged :
a tamer creature, *thus* o'erpowered, thou'lt show thyself.

CHORUS.

As if forsooth our Argive sovereign thou shalt be,
who hadst not, even after scheming this man's death,
courage to do the deed by killing him thyself! 1621 (1564)

AEGISTHUS.

No: to deceive him plainly was a woman's part:
I stood suspected as an old familiar foe.
but I'll endeavour with the aid of this man's wealth
the citizens to rule : and one that hearkeneth not   1625
I'll yoke with heavy collar, not a high-fed colt,
nor by light traces pulling : him to mildness tamed
shall hateful hunger, that with darkness dwells, behold.

CHORUS.

'Twas from thy base soul'd cowardice thou didst not kill
this man thyself, but him a woman with thee slew, 1630 (1573)
pollution of her country and her country's gods.
doth not Orestes somewhere see the light *of day*,
that hither he with favouring fortune may return,
and of this pair become the slaying conqueror?

AEGISTHUS

Since not words but acts thou meanest, speedy shall thy
 lesson be.   1635

CHORUS.

†*Aged as we are, yet will we to the wicked ne'er submit.*†

AEGISTHUS.

Ho! what ho! my friendly guardsmen; not far off this work
 of ours.

CHORUS.

Ho! what ho! let each have ready to his hand the hilted
 sword.

AEGISTHUS.

I too verily refuse not hand upon the hilt to die.

CHORUS.

'Die' thou say'st: we take the omen; fortune's doom it is
 we choose.   1640 (1583)

CLYTAEMNESTRA.

Let us not, o my belovèd, further evils execute:
surely to have reaped so many makes a doleful harvest now.
large enough our crop of mischief; let us keep ourselves from
 blood.
go thyself, and ye too, elders, unto your appointed homes,
ere ye suffer for your actions: what is done should satisfy: 1645
if your share of these afflictions be sufficient, we're content,
thus unfortunately smitten by the heavy hoof of fate.
such the counsels of a woman, if there be that deign to
 learn.

AEGISTHUS.

And are these to fling upon me flowers of an unbridled tongue,
language of this sort to sputter, putting fortune to the test,
and from wise discretion erring, offer insult to the prince?
                                          1651 (1594)

CHORUS.

This were not the mood of Argives, on a wicked man to fawn.

AEGISTHUS.

Yet will I o'ertake thee with my vengeance in the days to come.

CHORUS.

Not if fate direct Orestes hither safely to arrive.

AEGISTHUS.

Well I know that men in exile feed upon the fare of hope.

CHORUS.

Play thy part: grow fat, polluting justice, since thou hast the
power.   1656

AEGISTHUS.

Of this folly thou shalt pay me—be assured—the penalty.

CHORUS.

Vaunt with confident defiance, as a cock beside his hen.

CLYTAEMNESTRA.

Of these senseless howlings take not any notice : you and I,
being rulers of this palace, shall arrange its duties well.

1660 (1603)

1654. Aegisthus speaks from his own experience : see ll. 1592—4.

1658. A Greek tragedy usually concludes with a gnomic speech of the
Chorus, as the moderating party: but their quarrel with Aegisthus gives that
character and office here to Clytaemnestra.

On the corrections in Epeisodion v. and Exodos see *Consp. Lect.* and
Notes on Lection.

CONSPECTUS LECTIONUM.

De Conspectus usu quae sequuntur animadvertenda sunt

i. (α) codicum textum designat, qui, si siglis caret, vol-
gatus est, i.e. communis omnium in quibus exstat locus
codicum :

(β) lectionem designat, quae in nostrae editionis textum
recepta est. Post lectionem ipsam sequitur fontis, unde prodiit,
sive codicis, sive critici, nomen vel siglum.

ii. Sigla codicum sunt :

B.	Bessarionis.	G.	Guelpherbytanus.
F.	Farnesianus.	M.	Mediceus.
Fl.	Florentinus.	V.	Venetus.

iii. Sigla virorum, qui Aeschyli fabulas vel ediderunt, vel
notis illustrarunt, haec sunt :

Abr.	Abresch.	Dind.	Dindorf.
Ahr.	Ahrens (H. L.)	Do.	Dobree.
Ald.	Aldi.	Ed.	Editor.
Aur.	Auratus.	Elm.	Elmsley.
Bam.	Bamberger.	Eng.	Enger.
Bl.	Blomfield.	Erf.	Erfurdt.
Bo.	Bothe.	Fr.	Franz.
Bu.	Butler.	Gro.	Grotius.
Can.	Canter.	Halm.	
Cas.	Casaubon.	Hart.	Hartung.
Con.	Conington.	Haupt.	
Dav.	Davies.	Heath.	

Heim.	Heimsoeth.	Schn.	Schneidewin.
Herm.	Hermann.	Schol.	Scholiastae.
Jac.	Jacob.	Scholef.	Scholefield.
Kar.	Karsten.	Schü.	Schütz.
Keck.		Seid.	Seidler.
Kl.	Klausen.	Sp.	Spanheim.
Madv.	Madvig.	St.	Stanley.
Mar.	Martin.	T.	Turnèbe.
Mül.	Müller (K. O.)	Tyr	Tyrwhitt.
Mus.	Musgrave.	Val.	Valckenaer.
Pal.	Paley.	V. H	Van Heusde.
Pauw.		Vict.	Vettori.
Pea.	Pearson.	Voss.	
Pei.	Peile.	Weil.	
Pors.	Porson.	Weise.	
R.	Robortello.	Well.	Wellauer.
Salm.	Salmasius.	Wies.	Wieseler.
Scal.	Jos. Scaliger.		

7 (a) ἀστέρας (β) ἀθρῶν Ed.
   (a) ἀντολάς τε τῶν (β) ἀντέλλωσί τ' αὖ Ed.
17 (a) ἐντέμνων M. F., ἐκτέμνων V. Fl. (β) ἐν τέμνων Ed.

NOTES ON LECTION.

7. Val. and after him Pors. Bl. Pal. have judged this v. spurious. Herm. keeps it. We deem it not spurious but corrupt. Ἀστέρας here is certainly a gloss, probably also the inelegant ἀντολάς τε τῶν. Our corrections ἀθρῶν…ἀντέλλωσι τ' αὖ give a suitable sense, and are not too far removed from the vulg.

14. Hermann's conj. τί μήν; for ἐμήν is neither good nor required. The emphatic position of ἐμήν, followed by γάρ, is quite defensible: compare 1150—1, οἰκουρόν, εἴμοι, τῷ μολόντι δεσπότῃ | ἐμῷ· φέρειν γὰρ χρὴ τὸ δούλιον ζυγόν.

17. In estimating the value of the reading ἐν τέμνων for vulg. ἐντέμνων, it must be observed: (1) In an uncial cod. the verses appear without break between the words: and this line would be

ΥΠΝΟΥΤΟΔΑΝΤΙΜΟΛΠΟΝΕΝΤΕΜΝΩΝΑΚΟϹ.

25 (a) ἰοὺ ἰού (β) ἰοῦ ἰού Herm.
26 (a) σημανῶ V. Fl. F. B. Herm. (β) σημαίνω M.

The division of words made by a scribe copying them in cursive letters would be at the mercy of that scribe. And the oldest Cod. M. gives the line thus

ὕπν ο υτοδ᾽ ἀντί μολπον ἐντέμν ων ἄκο ς.

The accents and breathings are, it will be seen, correct, on the assumption of ἐντέμνων being the right division: but whether these are by the first copier or by a later, there is nothing to prove: and, while we doubt not that scribes believed in the participle, we cannot trust the judgment of any. It was their habit to join ἐν with the following word. Having thus got ἐντεμνων, which happens to be a Greek word, they, in their ignorance of critical interpretation, received it as the participle of ἐντέμνω. The other scribes of the Medicean group naturally followed in the wake. But those of codd. Fl. and Ven. appear to have seen that the compound ἐντέμνων has no just meaning here, and they adopted a various reading ἐκτέμνων, which does not, however, improve the sense. This reading Mr Paley has not cited. It will be found in our Conspectus Lectionum: and it proves that those who introduced it, saw no sense in ἐντέμνων. Thus ἐντέμνων has no true support from ms. authority.

(2) Mr Paley says in his note 'the compound ἐντέμνων *properly refers* to the shredding in of herbs in preparing a potion &c. But this cannot be proved from any passage of any author. The verb ἐντέμνω has two classical senses, (a) *to carve on, to engrave, to make incision*, whence ἔντομον, insectum, *an insect*: (b) *to sacrifice a victim* by bending its head to the ground and decapitating it, in offerings to the *di inferi*, or to heroes (*inferiae*). See Thuc. v. 11, Herod. ii. 119, vii. 191, Arr. Ind. 20. 'Shredding in' is a mere guess invented to account for the word in this place.

(3) On the other hand, τέμνειν φάρμακον (or ἄκος) *to prepare a medicine by chopping its ingredients*, is a recognised medical term, used also metaphorically in the sense of *providing a remedy* for any evil. It occurs in Plato several times in this sense. *Leg.* VIII. 836, τί τεμὼν φάρμακον τούτοις ἑκάστοις τοῦ τοιούτου κινδύνου διαφυγὴν εὑρήσει; XI. 919, τούτων...χρὴ φάρμακον ἀεὶ τέμνειν τὸν νομοθέτην. *Epist.* VIII. 353, τούτων δὴ χρὴ πάσῃ προθυμίᾳ πάντας τοὺς Ἕλληνας τέμνειν φάρμακον. See Eurip. *Andr.* 121 ἄκος τῶν δυσλύτων πόνων τεμεῖν, where Schol. ἀπὸ τῶν ῥιζοτομούντων ἡ μεταφορά· τεμεῖν οὖν ἀντὶ τοῦ εὑρέσθαι· and in Pindar *Pyth.* IV. 394, we find φαρμακώσαισ᾽—ἀντίτομα στερεᾶν ὀδυνᾶν. The use of ἐν is a well-known idiom. The two modes of chanting (ἀείδειν ἢ μινύρεσθαι) form *one music-antidote to sleep* (ἐν ἄκος ἀντίμολπον ὕπνου), distinguished from others not

40 (a)   Πριάμω M.   (β) Πριάμου V. Fl. F.
61 (a)   ἐπ' Ἀλεξάνδρῳ   (β) omisit ut glossema (vid.
341) Ed.

musical, such as walking up and down.   See *Eum.* 559, ἓν μὲν τόδ' ἤδη
τῶν τριῶν παλαισμάτων.

25. τὸ ἰοῦ ἰοῦ ἐπὶ χαρᾶς, Suidas, citatus ab Herm. qui hunc v. post 21
ponit.

40—106 (Anapaests of the Parodos).   In criticising the text of anapaests,
it must be kept in mind that, on account of their peculiar and easy rhythm
(consisting, in the main, of a series of monometers, chiefly in pairs, but
sometimes single; composed of anapaests, dactyls and spondees, which
may be combined anyhow, except that anapaest must not follow dactyl),
they are specially liable to be corrupted by omission or intrusion of such
monometers.   Again, as an anapaestic system, closed by a dimeter cata-
lectic (called 'versus paroemiacus'), has no defined length, but consists of
any number of lines, more or fewer, we sometimes find mss. trying to
lessen the number of systems by changing paroemiac lines into dimeters.
Further: it is an ordinary practice, but not a necessary rule, that a
paroemiac is preceded by a monometer, and this variable custom also leads
to corruption, oftener shown, it would seem, in neglecting the monometer,
than in maintaining it, though the latter mistake is not impossible : and, on
this point, it must be owned that modern criticism finds difficulty, and may
sometimes err.   The anapaests before us contain 9 systems, keeping
θυοσκινεῖς 89.   Long and oft-resumed consideration has finally led us to
believe (1) that each of these 9 systems should have a monometric base
before its paroemiac; (2) that in the ms. text of these lines occur 3 spurious
monometers at 61, 71, 92, possibly another at 57; (3) that two monometers
have fallen out, one at 69, supplying a subject to παραθέλξει 72, another at
101, filling up the grammatical lacuna between λέξασ' 98 and παιών τε
γενοῦ 101.

57. τῶνδε μετοίκων.   Pauw, Schü. Bl. make this gen. depend on
Ἐρινύν, not on γόον, referring the phrase to the captured nestlings.
Such was our former view also.   We now refer it, if genuine, to the old
birds, joining it to γόον.   It may be spurious; and in that case it must
have been added by some one who wished to join a gen. to Ἐρινύς, but
without necessity.   Were it removed, we should arrange vv. 56—7 as
monom. and dim. ἢ Πᾶν ἢ Ζεὺς | οἱ. γ. ὀξ.

61. ἐπ' Ἀλεξάνδρῳ, mss.   In our intimate conviction, this is a spurious
gloss here, borrowed from 339—41, Δία τοι ξένιον μέγαν αἰδοῦμαι | τὸν
τάδε πράξαντ' | ἐπ' Ἀλεξάνδρῳ τείνοντα πάλαι τόξον.   This recurrence

64 (a) ἐριδομένου M , ἐρειπομένου Fl. pr. m. F.

(β) ἐρειδομένου B. G. Fl. sec. m.

67 (a) Δαναοῖσιν | Τρωσί θ' ὁμοίως.

(β) Τρωσὶν Δαναοῖσί θ' ὁμοίως ut Hom. Il. II. 39 Ed.

alone is a presumptive argument for our opinion; but scholars of taste who examine the question will find it strengthened by the consideration that the mention of Paris here is, aesthetically, premature and uncalled for.   His guilt and that of his countrymen (συντελὴς πόλις), with the dire consequences, are a theme reserved for Stasimon I.   The mustering of the Grecian host under the Atreidae, the events on its march, the prophecy of Calchas, the sacrifice of Iphigeneia, the dark forecast of their issues—these are the topics of the Parodos.   Evidently, in our view, the ms. commentator who suggested the addition ἐπ' Ἀλεξάνδρῳ after πέμπει here was stimulated to do so by πέμπει παραβᾶσιν in 59.   We do not draw any argument on our side from the difference between the pure dative after πέμπει and the dative with ἐπί, for, though we know of one only parallel, viz. Hom. *Il.* ii. 6 πέμψαι ἐπ' Ἀτρείδῃ Ἀγαμέμνονι οὖλον ὄνειρον, we think this—added to the places where, as in 341, ἐπὶ with dat. means *against, to the damage of*—sufficient to sustain ἐπ' Ἀλεξάνδρῳ grammatically.   Therefore we condemn it on aesthetical grounds alone.   See 69.

65—67.   Codd. write here:

> διακναιομένης τ' ἐν προτελείοις
> κάμακος θήσων Δαναοῖσιν
> Τρωσί θ' ὁμοίως.

Hermann, in his Treatise on Metres (Lib. II. Cap. xxxii., II.) states the general rule, that a paroemiac verse, in concluding an anapaestic system, concludes at the same time a sentence and a thought.   After noticing some rare instances to the contrary in the *Supplices*, the earliest and most corrupt Aeschylean drama, he calls special attention to the place before us, defending the vulgate text as follows:

'Plena est et absoluta sententia versu paroemiaco, sed egregie, *quasi nunc demum Trojani in mentem veniant,* hi in principio novi systematis commemorantur.   *Est enim praecipua quaedam vis in horum commemoratione.*   Perderet omnem hujus loci virtutem, qui versus sic vellet distingui:

> κάμακος θήσων
> Δαναοῖσιν Τρωσί θ' ὁμοίως.'

Being at issue with this view, we have noted by italics the logical con tradiction existing in it.   The 'chief force' of the passage, says Herm.

69 (a) πεπρωμένον οὔθ᾿   (β) intercidisse videtur (post πεπρωμένον) οὐδέ τις ἀνδρῶν Ed.

'lies in the mention of the Trojans.' Yet he says just above that the poet superadds this mention of the Trojans, 'as if they were not in his mind before,' as if it were a mere afterthought. Which of these counter-statements are we to accept? That the Trojans are a mere afterthought, or that the chief force lies in the mention of them? Doubtless the latter rather than the former; yet not quite so decisively as Hermann suggests. The Trojans are the 'παραβάντες, the transgressors,' in the simile of the foregoing system, 58, as the Atreidae and their host are 'the after-punishing Erinys,' 59. In the 'παλαίσματα, the struggles' waged 'for a many-suitored woman,' no 'praecipua vis, chief force,' can be ascribed to either party of equally matched combatants; but perhaps the Hellenic poet, speaking by an Hellenic chorus, may be supposed to dwell most on the retribution suffered by the wrong-doers, that is, to think more of 'the dust-biting knees and snapping spears' of the Trojans than of the same trials endured by his own people; and if so, surely this would cause him to name *the Trojans first* as sufferers by the will of Zeus, and to superadd, as a sighing afterthought—'*ay and for Danaans also.*' If the argument rested here, we should consider it proved; but the lines of Homer, which Pal. cites and which Herm. had overlooked, being manifestly followed by Aeschylus, come in to place it beyond the reach of doubt. These are, *Il.* ii. 39

> θήσειν γὰρ ἔτ᾿ ἔμελλεν ἐπ᾿ ἄλγεά τε στοναχάς τε
> Τρωσί τε καὶ Δαναοῖσι διὰ κρατερὰς ὑσμίνας.

Here is Zeus, the same agent, θήσειν, the same verb, Τρωσί τε καὶ Δαναοῖσι, the same sufferers, ἄλγεά τε στοναχάς τε διὰ κρατερὰς ὑσμίνας parallel to the παλαίσματα γυιοβαρῆ described by Aeschylus. All this proves decisively that Τρωσὶν Δαναοῖσί θ᾿ ὁμοίως is the true reading in this system, and that this paroemiac has κάμακος θήσων for its antecedent base. Erroneous inversion of words is a frequent error in the codd. Thus we find 5 βροτοῖς θέρος, 1077 ἀηδόνος μόρον, and other instances. Finally, by this change the solemn words ἔστι δ᾿ ὅπη νῦν ἔστι, τελεῖται δ᾿ | ἐς τὸ πεπρωμένον begin with far more power the next system, which now stands alone in its religious grandeur.

69—72. We have suggested here the insertion in 69 of a monometer οὐδέ τις ἀνδρῶν, containing a suitable subject for the verb παραθέλξει in 72. Agamemnon cannot be the subject meant; for we see, looking back, that since the chorus came to its platform, it has said nothing of Agamemnon, beyond naming him as one of the two Atreidae (Μενέλαος ἄναξ ἠδ᾿ Ἀγα-

70 (a)   ὑποκλαίων   (β) ὑποκαίων Cas.
71 (a)   οὔτε δακρύων   (β) omisit ut glossema Herm.
78 (a)   ἀνάσσων   (β) ἀνᾴσσων Herm.
80 (a)   τιθιπεργήρως M., τόθιπερ γήρως Fl., τόθ᾽ ὑπέργηρων
F. (β)   τό θ᾽ ὑπέργηρων Vict.
83 (a)   οὐδὲν   (β) οὔ τις Ed.

μέμνων); and we see, looking onward through the tragedy to the place
where Clytaemnestra speaks her mind (1342) that the chorus nowhere
indicates any knowledge of the resentment felt by the queen against her
husband (which Pal. understands by ὀργὰς ἀτενεῖς here). And though
they report the prophetic words of Calchas respecting it (144—6), they are
not supposed to interpret them (226—30). Nor is it much more reasonable
to make Paris the unnamed subject of παραθέλξει. The Schol. and Herm.
undoubtedly have truth in view, when they call τις (understood) the subject
here. The sentiment is general, though Aesch. meant to glance at the
special cases of Agamemnon and his unholy sacrifice, of Paris and his
unlawful marriage rites, the ὀργαί ἀτενεῖς of which imply the wrath of deities
injured by the neglect of their just dues, and the adoption of impious sub-
stitutes. But the ellipsis of τις as subject of a verb is a grammatical *tour de
force*, which we would not admit in Aeschylus except upon the strength of
examples adduced from other parts of his writings. We are therefore glad
to obviate it by supplying a good subject in a place where it is very satisfactory, by the οὐδὲ before the double οὔτε, and by the support given to
the metre after casting out, as we do with Herm. and Pal., the idle gloss
οὔτε δακρύων. These things being done, the five anapaestic lines stand
forth distinct and complete, a fine specimen of Greek religious sentiment.

70, 71. Recte censuit Cas., ὑποκαίων legens, victimarum mentionem
omitti non posse : Herm. autem illud οὔτε δακρύων delevit, ut glossema
ad lectionem ὑποκλαίων.

80. Ex colluvie codicum sunt qui eliciunt ὅ θ᾽ ὑπέργηρως, ut Fr.
et Pal. Nos malumus cum cod. F. Vict. Bl. Pei. τό θ᾽ ὑπέργηρων.

83. For οὐδὲν we venture to read οὔ τις, thus escaping the disagreeable
synesis of masc. ἀρείων, referred to τὸ ὑπέργηρων. Οὔ τις ἀρείων παιδὸς
is a well-known brachylogy=τις (i.e. πᾶς τις γέρων) οὐκ ἀρείων παιδός, *any*
(or *every*) *old man, no stronger than a child*. For an analogous brachylogy,
see 370—372. λιτᾶν δ᾽ ἀκούει μὲν οὔτις θεῶν, τὸν δ᾽ ἐπίστροφον τῶνδε φῶτ᾽
ἄδικον καθαιρεῖ (i.e. πᾶς τις). In this place we may say that οὐ is confined
to a single word in the sentence, i.e. ἀρείων, the boldness lying in the fact
that for this purpose it is sundered from its natural companion τις.

89 (*a*) πυθοῖ Fl. (β) codd. cet. πειθοῖ.

91 (*a*) τῶν ἀστυνόμων (β) τῶν τ᾿ ἀστυνόμων Ed.

92 (*a*) τῶν τ᾿ οὐρανίων (β) omisit ut glossema Ed.

97 (*a*) φαρμασσομένη (β) traiecit a v. 94 Ed.

100 (*a*) αἰνεῖν (β) aliquid excidisse videtur, quale δεῖξόν τι σαφές, Ed.

104 (*a*) ἀγανὰ φαίνεις M. (β) ἀγανὰ φαίνουσ᾿ Fl. F. Herm.

106 (*a*) τὴν θυμοφθόρον λύπης φρένα M. B., τὴν θυμοβόρον λύπης φρένα Fl., τὴν θυμοβόρον λυπόφρενα F.

(β) λύπης, θυμοφθόρον ἄτην Ahr.

89. Dind. Blomf. Pal. ex. cod. Fl. lectione πυθοῖ eliciunt πευθοῖ, satis illam probabilem : sed nihilo deterior est πειθοῖ, quam plurimi codd. ostendunt.

θυοσκινεῖς habent codd., pro quo sunt quibus θυοσκεῖς placet, aliis θυοσκνεῖς. In re incerta nihil mutandum est.

92. We have expunged τῶν τ᾿ οὐρανίων, as a superfluous gloss on ὑπάτων, reading τῶν τ᾿ ἀστυνόμων alone, of which ὑπάτων, χθονίων are subdivisions. Weil's conj. ἀγρονόμων for οὐρανίων, adopted by Mr Paley, we cannot receive, as we consider the rural deities out of place here.

97. We have transposed φαρμασσομένη from 94, to form a monometric base here, where we think it stands better in all respects.

99—101. The lacuna in grammar here is defended by several scholars, as Herm. and Pal. : but not so as to satisfy us. Bl. for λέξασ᾿ reads λέξον θ᾿, Hartung λέξαις, which we formerly received. Now we believe that the loss of a monometer should be assumed. This cannot be supplied with assurance that the lost words are found. We suggest the most simple phrase, δεῖξόν τι σαφές, though such words as δὸς χάριν ἡμῖν are quite possible.

106. We now, without a shade of doubt, read, with H. L. Ahrens,

λύπης, θυμοφθόρον ἄτην.

We had hit upon this correction before we discovered (from Mr Paley's note) that Ahr. had anticipated us. We elicited it (as probably he did) from the Medicean distortion τὴν θυμοφθόρον λύπης φρένα. As φρένα now appears to us a manifest gloss, growing out of κακόφρων and φροντίς, and contained in a marginal explanation of θυμοφθόρον, we find that, after removing the syllable φρεν from the Medicean line, there remain exactly all the letters (disjecta membra) which make up the excellent reading above

108 (a) ἐκτελέων (β) ἐντελέων Aur.
— (a) καταπνέει M. T., καταπνεύει Fl. F.
     (β) καταπνείει A.
110 (a) ἀλκὰν (β) ἀλκᾷ Herm.
111 (a) ἥβαν (β) ἥβας (ex Aristoph. Ran. 1284).
112 (a) τὰν γᾶν M., ταγάν Fl. (β) τάγαν Herm.
113 (a) δίκας (β) καὶ χερὶ (ex Aristoph. Ran. 1289).
115 (a) ἀργίας (β) ἀργᾷς Dind.
117 (a) παμπρέποις M. (β) παμπρέπτοις B.
118 (a) ἐρικύματα φέρματι M., ἐρικύμονα φέρβοντι Fl. F.
     (β) ἐρικύμονα φέρματι Herm.
121 (a) κεδνὸς δὲ (β) τὼ δ' ἀγαθὸς Ed.
     (a) δισσοὺς (β) δισσοῖς Aur.

given, and first discerned by Ahr. Quid apertius? Thus the version
becomes 'hope...dispels thought insatiate of sorrow, a soul-consuming
curse.' It may be observed that the dislocation of τὴν in Cod. M. led later
scribes (Fl. F.) to conj. θυμοβόρον, as favouring anapaestic rhythm, just as
in 1017 (1059) αὐτοφόνα was substituted for αὐτοκτόνα.

108. We adopt the conj. of Aur., ἐντελέων, as perhaps, more probable than the vulg. ἐκτελέων. If ἐντελεῖς can be accepted as=οἱ ἐν τέλει
(of which we lack adequate proof) then ἄνδρες ἐντελεῖς will mean *chieftains*
or *captains*. If not, it (or ἀ. ἐκτελεῖς) may be taken for 'those who have
attained the full strength of manhood,' *stalwart heroes*, as we have rendered
the phrase. Mr Paley would make ἐκτελέων a participle, 'declaring the full
purport of,' but he adduces nothing which can justify such an extension of
sense in the verb ἐκτελεῖν. to *fulfil, complete*. The reading ἐκ τελέων,
favoured by Herm. and Kl., has no probability.

121—123. The spondee κεδνὸς in 121, answering to the dactyl κύριος in
the strophe 107, violates that law of metrical agreement, which we firmly
believe to be maintained in this drama (see Preface). We therefore
deem it highly probable that Aeschylus wrote τὼ δὲ (referred to the δύο
following) with an epithet for στρατόμαντις, such as ἀγαθὸς or σοφός, and
that the change was afterwards made by a scribe who did not recognize the
use of τώ, which improves the emphasis, and so substituted the epithet
κεδνός, which seemed to him suitable and sufficient. For κεδνὸς the fitter
substitute of the two adjectives named would be ἀγαθός: comp. ἀγαθὸς
προβατογνώμων 723. We therefore read τὼ δ' ἀγαθὸς στρατόμαντις. This
suggests a pause after ἰδών, "them twain when the good army-seer beheld,
two sons of Atreus, warriors of diverse tempers." Plato (*Conviv.* p. 274),

123 (a) πομπούς τ' (β) πομπᾶς Ed.

     (a) ἀρχάς M. (β) ἀρχούς Fl. F.

124 (a) τεράζων (β) τεράζων Herm. (ex Etymol. M.)

125 (a) ἀγρεῖ (β) αἱρεῖ Elm.

127 (a) δημιοπληθῆ (β) δημιοπληθέα Mül.

128 (a) μοῖρ' ἀλαπάξει M. Fl. Pal.

     (β) μοῖρα λαπάξει F. Herm.

129 (a) ἄτα ⟨β⟩ ἄγα Herm.

135 (a) τόσσων M. R., τόσον Fl. F. (β) τόσσον Vict.

— (a) εὔφρων καλὰ M. R. (β) εὔφρων ἁ καλὰ Fl. F.

136 (a) δρόσοισιν ἀέλπτοις M.

     (β) δρόσοις ἀέπτοις Fl. Herm.

alluding to Hom. *Il.* II. 579, XVII. 588, says ποιήσας γὰρ τὸν Ἀγαμέμνονα διαφερόντως ἀγαθὸν ἄνδρα τὰ πολεμικά, τὸν δὲ Μενέλαον μαλθακὸν αἰχμητήν ...ἄκλητον ἐποίησεν ἐλθόντα τὸν Μενέλαον ἐπὶ τὴν θοίνην, χείρω ὄντα ἐπὶ τὴν τοῦ ἀμείνονος. Δισσοὺς and δισσοῖς would be equivalent in sense, but perhaps δισσοῖς is preferable on account of the accus. μαχίμους.

Admitting the correction τὼ δ' ἀγαθὸς above, and δημιοπληθέα in 127, comparison of the strophe at 104 with its antistrophe will happily illustrate the fact on which so much of our criticism is based—that in this play an exact correspondence of syllables between str. and antistr. is maintained, with a few definite exceptions. Even final short syllables correspond to short finals, as 114 αἰᾶν to 128 βίαιον; 117 ἕδραισΐ to 131 πατρὸς, after each of which final consonants the next line begins with a vowel. Herm. and Pal. have been so inattentive to this circumstance that they read ἕδραισιν with Cod. M.; but Cod. B. ἕδραισι, and this cod. shews metrical knowledge by having θυομένοισΐ before στ, while the rest add an unnecessary ν.

123. We have never felt satisfied with the version given to the prevalent reading ἐδάη λαγοδαίτας πομπούς τ' ἀρχάς, 'he understood the hare-devouring eagles and the conducting chieftains (to be identified).' We have now adopted ἀρχοὺς from Fl. F. Vict. and ventured, for πομπούς τ', to read πομπᾶς, the sense being: 'he understood the hare-devouring leaders of the escort' (the two eagles who first appeared and escorted, as it were, the marching host) : in other words, he understood the omen which they conveyed as representing the Atreidae.

136. If the difficulty of gender could be overcome, we would gladly read δρόσοισι λεπτοῖς with Wellauer, rather than accept the doubtful ἀέπτοις which Herm. and Dind. receive from Cod. Fl.

CONSPECTUS LECTIONUM.   155

136 (a) μαλερῶν ὄντων M., μαλερῶν Fl.
    (β) μαλερῶν λεόντων St.
139, 140 (a) τούτων αἰτεῖ ξύμβολα κρᾶναι,
            δεξιὰ μὲν κατάμομφα δὲ φάσματα στρουθῶν.
    (β) στρουθῶν αἱ. ξ. τούτων δ. μ. κ. δὲ φ. κρᾶναι. Ed.
141 (a) δὲ καλέω (β) δ' ἐκκαλέω Keck.
153 (a) προσεννέπω. (β) punctum delevit Ed.
154 (a) οὐκ ἔχω προσεικάσαι
    (β) τοὔνομ᾽· ἄλλο δ' οὐκ ἔχω Ed.
157 (a) οὐδ' ὅστις (β) εἰ δ' εἷς τις Ed.
159 (a) οὐδὲν λέξαι (β) οὐδ' ἐλέγξεται Ed.

138—140. The corruption in this epode has been for the most part
successfully corrected by scholars, though without antistrophic lines to aid
them. Τερπνά cannot, we think, be referred as fem. to Artemis.   We
therefore take it, as neuter, with ξύμβολα. That φάσματα στρουθῶν is corrupt, there can be no doubt. We have adopted transposition as the least
violent correction.

153. 154. We think corruption here certain for three reasons : one,
the use of προσεικάσαι for εἰκάσαι or ἐπεικάσαι; another, that, although the
preceding line τοῦτό νιν προσεννέπω, and τόδε before, can dispense with
τοὔνομα, yet what follows, πάντ᾽ ἐπισταθμώμενος πλὴν Διός, cannot do
without it; thirdly, the hiatus of -ω | οὐκ is not pleasing. We therefore
believe that Aesch. wrote in 154 τοὔνομ᾽· ἄλλο δ' οὐκ ἔχω κ.τ.λ., without
stop at προσεννέπω. Προσεικάσαι cannot mean 'to refer ': it means 'to
liken' or 'compare;' and is evidently the gloss of a scribe, who thought
ἔχω required a following infinitive. Mr Paley seems to mistake the
tenour, of this digressive passage from Ζεὺς to ἠμένων. As far as the
words κυρίως ἔχειν the poet pursues one sole inquiry: Is Ζεὺς the true name
of the reigning king of heaven? This question is the ἄχθος φροντίδος,
the weight on the mind. Yes, he says, Ζεὺς is the true name. There
were two before him: but one is obsolete and forgotten, the other de-
feated and expelled. All who covet wisdom must glorify Ζεύς. He gives
wisdom by the way of suffering. Criminality brings painful remorse, and
with it repentant discretion (σωφροσύνη), which must be regarded as a
blessing (χάρις), from the deities who sit on the sacred bench. These are
general maxims of religion and morality, which the poet brings forward
as applicable to the whole history of the Pelopidae, from Tantalus to
Orestes.

157. 159. That οὐδ' ὅστις and οὐδὲν λέξαι are corrupt, is not doubtful.

163 (a)   τῷ (β) τὸν Schü.
167 (a)   βιαίως (β) τοιάδε Ed.
178 (a)   ναῶν καὶ (β) νεῶν τε καὶ Pors.
180 (a)   τρίβῳ κατέξαινον ἄνθος Ἀργείων·
      (β) κατέξαινον ἄνθος Ἀργείων τρίβῳ·   Ed.

But the right corrections cannot be certainly determined. We feel no hesitation in refusing to accept Hermann's οὐ λελέξεται in 159, for which Mr Paley writes νῦν λελέξεται. We prefer our own suggestions εἰ δ' εἶς τις in 157, followed by οὐδ' ἐλέγξεται in 159 '*if some one was* &c., *he will not be even proved to have once existed.*' i. e. the pre-antique Uranus.

167. βιαίως does not correspond metrically with the antistrophic παλιρρο.—Hence Ahr. conjectured παλιρρόχθοις 173 for παλιρρόθοις. In our view the corruption lies in the word βιαίως here, which we regard as a spurious gloss founded on ἄκοντας above. We have ventured to substitute for it τοιάδε, 'such is the favour of the deities:' i.e. they send in mercy this reminiscence of evil, which leads to repentant discretion (σωφρονεῖν). Herm. condemns the view of Bl. and Pal. that χάρις δαιμόνων here means 'reverence of the gods.' We agree with him. To our mind the Greek use of χάρις is comprised in the line χάρις χάριν γάρ ἐστιν ἡ τίκτουσ' ἀεί. It means (1) '*favour* or *kindness* graciously conferred (hence in secondary sense, *kindness, joy, blessing*) (2) *favour* or *kindness* due in return for that received, or returned as due (hence in secondary sense, *grateful return, grateful feeling, gratitude*). The idea of reverence which appears in a few passages, as ἀθίκτων χάρις is only a particular modification of this latter meaning, *grateful respect* due for blessings received. This is illustrated by the words at 540, χὴ χάρις τιμήσεται Διὸς τάδ' ἐκπράξασα, where it would be possible to regard χάρις as possessing sense 2 but for τάδ' ἐκπράξασα which determines it to sense 1. And what χάρις Διὸς is there, we believe χάρις δαιμόνων to be here; therefore we treat βιαίως as the gloss of a misjudging scribe substituted for τοιάδε.

178—180. 189—191. In order that our corrections may be fully and fairly estimated, we exhibit here the 3 strophic lines 178—180 in comparison with the antistrophic 189—191 (a) as they stand in codd. (β) as they are emended in our text.

(a) The lines in codd. stand thus:

Stroph. 178 ναῶν καὶ πεισμάτων ἀφειδεῖς
          παλιμμήκη χρόνον τιθεῖσαι
          τρίβῳ κατέξαινον ἄνθος Ἀργείων.

190 (a) μιαίνων (β) ῥεέθροις Ed.
191 (a) ῥεέθροις (β) μιαίνων Ed.
— (a) πατρῴους (β) πατρὸς Ed.
201 (a) βροτοῖς (β) βροτοὺς Schü. Bl. Herm. Dind.
207 (a) παρθένειον (β) παρθένειόν τ᾽ Pea.
216 (a) χέουσα (β) χέουσ᾽ εἶτ᾽ Ed.

Antistr. 189 τέκνον δαῖξω δόμων ἄγαλμᾰ
μιαίνων παρθενοσφάγοισιν
ῥεέθροις πατρῴους χέρας βωμοῦ πέλας.

(β) In our edition they are printed as follows:

Stroph. νεῶν τε καὶ πεισμάτων ἀφειδεῖς
παλιμμήκη χρόνον τιθεῖσαι
κατέξαινον ἄνθος Ἀργείων τρίβῳ·
Antistr. τέκνον δαῖξω δόμων ἄγαλμα
ῥεέθροις παρθενοσφάγοισιν
μιαίνων πατρὸς χέρας βωμοῦ πέλας.

Νεῶν τε is Porson's correction for ναῶν in 178. In 180 Ἀργείων is both
unmetrical in itself, and at variance with the antistrophic βωμοῦ πέλας.
This blot is obviously removed by transposing τρίβῳ to the end of the verse,
whence it had been displaced by a scribe who mistook its construction.
In the antistrophic lines three blots exist, (a) the short final in ἄγαλμα,
compared with the strophic ἀφειδεῖς; (β) the presence of 12 syllables
in 191, as compared with 180 which has only 11; (γ) the use of πατρῷος
in a sense for which no authority can be found in Greek literature,
of me a father. The first blot is removed by transposing μιαίνων and
ῥεέθροις, for thus the final a of ἄγαλμα obtains long quantity. Blots
β and γ are both removed by simply reading πατρὸς for πατρῴους. And
these effective changes make absolutely no difference in the sense of the
passage, nor even in its translation. Mr Paley, indifferent to blots a and γ,
seeks to remove β by reading with Kl. and Pei. ῥείθροις for ῥεέθροις,
thus introducing a new metrical discrepancy, and a contracted form which
would not be used in lyrics by Aesch. who has adopted the form ῥέεθρον
even in dialogue, *Pers.* 489 ῥέεθρον ἀγνοῦ Στρύμονος. It may be added
that the passage is grammatically and poetically improved by the transposition of ῥεέθροις aud μιαίνων.

216. Herm. justly refuses to believe that Aesch. would write χέουσα
at the close of a verse before a vowel beginning the next. He therefore
reads χέουσ᾽ ὧδ᾽. We read χέουσ᾽ εἶτ᾽ which is in effect the same. But

222 (a) ἀγνὰ (β) ἀγνᾷ Schü.
223 (a) αἰῶνα (β) παιᾶνα Hart.
228—9 (a) corrupti sunt codd. vid. infra.
    (β) τὸ μέλλον δ' | ἐπεὶ γένοιτ' ἂν κλύοις· Bam.
231 (a) σύνορθον M., σύναρθρον Fl. F.
    (β) ξύνορθρον Well.
— (a) αὐταῖς (β) αὐγαῖς Herm.
232 (a) τἀπὶ (β) ἡ 'πὶ Ed.
— (a) εὔπραξις (β) εὖ πρᾶξις Eng.
238 (a) εἴτε (β) εἴ τι Aur.
249 (a) τί γὰρ τὸ πιστόν ἐστι τῶνδέ σοι τέκμαρ ;
    (β) τί γὰρ τὸ πιστόν ; ἔστι τῶνδέ σοι τέκμαρ ; Ed.
259 (a) ἀγγέλου (β) ἀγγάρου Schü. ex Etym. M.
261 (a) φανὸν (β) πανὸν Cas. ex Athenaeo.
265 (a) πεύκη τὸ (β) προὔκειτο Ed.

we think it not improbable that the poet wrote μεθιεῖσ', and that χέουσα
is the gloss of some annotator who fancied κρόκου βαφὰς meant blood.

228—9. μαθεῖν ἐπιρρέπει τὸ μέλλον· τὸ δὲ προκλύειν (tria haec alia
manu) ἐπιγένοιτ' ἂν κλύοις προχαιρέτω. M. Ita fere Fl., sed ἐπεὶ γένοιτ'.
F. omittit τὸ δὲ προκλύειν. Ald. pro ἂν κλύοις scrib. ἀνηλύοις. F. Vict.
hab. ἂν ἡ λύσις. Edd. plur. interpungunt post ἐπιρρέπει, recte, ut videtur.
(1) τὸ μέλλον δ' ἐπεὶ οὐ γένοιτ' ἂν λύσις προχαιρέτω Elm. Bl. Pal. (2) τὸ
μέλλον· τὸ προκλύειν δ' ἥλυσιν προχαιρέτω Herm. Kl. al. (3) τὸ μέλλον· τὸ
δὲ προκλύειν πρὶν γένοιτο χαιρέτω, Heim. Dav., quod veremur ut bene
graecum sit. (4) Bambergeri lect , quam edidimus, recipiunt etiam Dind.
Weil. Schn. Ahr. Eng.

232. It seems to us that the reading ἡ 'πὶ justifies πρᾶξις, which after
τἀπὶ is utterly superfluous. Ἡ ἐπὶ τούτοισι πρᾶξις πέλοιτο εὖ=τὸ δ' εὖ
νικάτω above, and τὸ δ' εὖ κρατοίη 326. See also 464.

265. By the easy substitution of ΠΡΟΥΚΕΙΤΟ for ΠΕΥΚΗΤΟ these
bald, unconstructed words immediately become lucid and beautiful.

(1) The place (263—265) is manifestly in want of a finite verb, and
deformed by the presence of the worse than useless noun πεύκη. Here then
a verb must take the place of the noun, clearing up the sense, and supported
by the adverbial phrase πρὸς ἡδονήν. We had thought of προὔβη, but further
consideration showed the idleness of the article τό, and led to the perception
of προὔκειτο, as the true word. (2) Palaeographic critics will at once see
that the 'ductus litterarum' in uncial writing shows almost exact corre-

266 (a) σκοπὰς (β) σκοπαῖς T. Vict.

281 (a) μὴ χαρίζεσθαι M. Fl., δὴ χαρίζεσθαι F.

(β) μηχαρίζεσθαι Well. Pei.

spondence. (3) Mr Paley objects, without a shadow of reason, that a verb of motion is wanted. Let us translate the lines. *High-reaching, so as to skim the sea, the strength of the travelling torch lay forth to full delight, and transmitted, like some sun, a blaze of golden light to the watchmen of Makistus.* A torch which travels in its strength, skimming the sea, and transmitting light, needs no other verb of motion, while the simile ὥς τις ἥλιος amply proves that the verb required is one which, as προὔκειτο, shall express the *continuous stream* of radiated light between the beacon on Athos and the watchmen on Makistus. And what business has the noun πεύκη here when its synonym λαμπάδος stands just before it? The site of the Euboean mountain Makistus is not clearly known: but it must have been somewhere near Cape Koumi, from which point a great beacon lighted on Mt. Athos (Monte Santo) might possibly be descried in a direction due north, at a distance of 90 miles. The word ὑπερτελής, and still more the simile ὥς τις ἥλιος, distinctly prove that in the ἰσχὺς πορευτοῦ λαμπάδος Aesch. meant to include the source of light, the beacon on Athos itself. Whoever, like ourselves, has spent the autumn and winter months on an eastward-looking beach, and faced, morning after morning, the golden path of rays streaming over the sea between his own eyes and the newly risen sun, will understand the perfect fitness and beauty of the verb προὔκειτο here. The fitness derives further force from the application of the verb προκεῖσθαι to headlands such as Athos (ἐν τῇ θαλάττῃ προκείμενον χωρίον, Xen. *An.* VI. 4), and to arranged signals, as προκείμενα σημήια in Herod. (See Soph. *O.T.* 865, νόμοι πρόκεινται.) ' *To full delight*' is a neutral rendering of πρὸς ἡδονήν. It is open to question whether this phrase refers to the light itself (*at its own sweet will*) or means (as we suggest) *to the delight of beholders*, especially the watchmen of Makistus. So *Prom.* 503, δαίμοσιν πρὸς ἡδονήν.

281. This is one of the places in which all we can do is to choose that reading which seems, on the whole, to have the fewest disadvantages, though we cannot be satisfied, as we were in the preceding note, that it restores the original. On one point we feel confidence: viz.: that the duty urgently suggested to the watchmen of Aegiplanctus is, to enlarge and strengthen their beacon blaze, in order to surmount a headland on the opposite coast of the Sinus Saronicus. This premise excludes the conjecture (of Martin) μὴ χρονίζεσθαι which Mr Paley edits, and implies the inadequacy of all which keep the vulgate χαρίζεσθαι. Μὴ χατίζεσθαι

283 (a)   πωγῶνα   (β) excidisse videtur aliquid quale
   καὶ κεκτημένον | ἰσχὺν τοσαύτην ὥστε Ed.
284 (a)   κάτοπτρον   (β) κάτοπτον Can.
285 (a)   εἶτ’ ἀφίκετο   (β) ἔς τ’ ἀφίκετο Ct.
299 (a)   ἐκχέας   (β) ἐγχέας Can.
300 (a)   φίλως   (β) φίλω St.
308 (a)   νῆστις Fl.   (β) νήστεις F.

(Heath), is a reading which tends to convey (though hardly with enough strength) the sense required; but we doubt its fitness as Greek. Kl. with St. reads μῆχαρ ἵξεσθαι, and supposes θεσμὸν to mean the watchmen, which we cannot admit, because the translation resulting appears to us impossible. We have no doubt that θεσμὸν πυρὸς (if indeed πυρὸς is certainly genuine) means τὸ τεθειμένον πῦρ 'the stablished fire-supply' = τὸν φρυκτόν as at present laid down. This view has naturally led us to accept Wellauer's conjecture, adopted by Scholef. and Pei., μηχαρί-ζεσθαι, a supposed derivative of μῆχαρ a remedy. This gives the meaning shewn in our version 'it urged the improvement (or enlargement) of the stablished fire-supply.' With θεσμὸν πυρὸς compare σφαγὰς πυρὸς 978. As here the fuel laid down to be fired is called 'the constitution of fire,' so the slaughter of sheep to be burnt is called 'the slaughter of fire.' If we were disposed to adopt any conjecture less near to the ms. text, it would be μεῖζον’ αἴθεσθαι for μὴ χαρίζεσθαι, or θεσμοῦ μῆχαρ αἴθεσθαι.

283—285. Abandoning our former conjectures and that of Schü. (ὑπερβάλλει) in this passage, we now avoid the ugly construction of the vulgate text by assuming a loss of words, such as we have printed, after πωγῶνα. The recurrence of καὶ in the same foot would help to account for the omission.

296. We maintain the ms. reading λέγοις, which must not be changed to λέγεις. The chorus cannot possibly say they wish Clyt. to repeat what she has said. They do say they wish to hear her tale continued to the very close (διηνεκῶς). We think with Mr Paley that ὡς is not to be rendered *as,* but to be taken in its rarer yet well-established sense, for ὅπως *how.* Herod. VII. 161. ὡς δὲ στρατηγήσεις γλίχεαι. Xen. *Cyr.* 1, 2, 3 ὡς καλῶς ἕξει τὰ ὑμέτερα, ἢν φίλοι γένησθε, ἐμοὶ μελήσει. The mood of λέγοις (for λέξεις) we refer to the attraction of θέλοιμ’ ἄν. Πάλιν is not bound to λέγοις, but free to modify the infinitive ἀκοῦσαι. The meaning of the compound verb ἀποθαυμάσαι is given in the following translation:

'But I should like to hear again and so crown my wonder, how you tell this story to its close.'

313 (α) ὡς δυσδαίμονες   (β) ὡς δ' εὐδαίμονες St. Ed.

317 (α) οὐκ ἄν γ'   (β) οὐτᾶν Herm.

— (α) αὖ θάνοιεν Fl. F. Vict., ἂν θάνοιεν B.

   (β) ἀνθαλοῖεν Aur.

322 (α) θεοῖς δ' ἀναμπλάκητος B. F. Vict.

   (β) θεοῖς δ' ἂν ἀμπλάκητος Fl.

323 (α) ἐγρήγορον   (β) ἐγρηγορὸς Pors.

325 (α) κλύοις   (β) κλύεις B.

345 (α) ἔχουσιν εἰπεῖν   (β) ἔχουσιν· εἰπεῖν Bl.

313. Receiving Stanley's emendation for the unsuitable ὡς δυσδαίμονες of codd., we are disposed to modify it by accentuating the particle, ὡς δ' εὐδαίμονες 'and thus blest of heaven,' &c. So 858, εἰ πάντα δ' ὡς πράσσοιμεν. Hermann's suggestion, ὡς δὲ δαίμονες, may possibly be true.

345—359. In this Stasimon, strophe α', Str. β', and antistr. β' are full of corruption, the rest is comparatively pure.

In the first two lines of Str. α', we do not hesitate to place a colon after ἔχουσιν, connecting εἰπεῖν with πάρεστιν, and adding τ' after ἐξιχνεῦσαι. We then take Hermann's readings to 354 ὑπέρφευ. The next three lines are manifestly corrupt, and corruption continues, we doubt not, to the close of the Strophe (ἀφάνειαν). The text of Codd. is

> ὑπὲρ τὸ βέλτιστον· ἔστω δ' ἀπή-
> μαντον, ὥστ' ἀπαρκεῖν   (F. ὥστε κἀπαρκεῖν)
> εὖ πραπίδων λαχόντα·
> οὐ γάρ ἐστιν ἔπαλξις
> πλούτου πρὸς κόρον ἀνδρὶ
> λακτίσαντι μεγάλα Δίκας βωμὸν εἰς ἀφάνειαν.
>
>   F. has ἐκλακτίσαντι.

which becomes, with our emendations,

> τὸ δ' οὔ τι βέλτιστόν ἐστ', οὐδ' ἀπή-
> μαντον, ὥστ' ἀπαρκεῖν ἂν εὖ πραπίδων λαχόντι·
> πλούτου γὰρ τίς ἔπαλξις
> φωτὶ πρὸς κόρον ἔξω
> λακτίζοντι μέγαν Δίκας βωμὸν εἰς ἀφάνειαν;

the corresponding antistrophic lines are,

> λιτᾶν δ' ἀκούει μὲν οὔτις θεῶν,
> τὸν δ' ἐπίστροφον τῶνδε φῶτ' ἄδικον καθαιρεῖ.
> οἷος καὶ Πάρις ἐλθὼν

346 (a)   πάρεστι τοῦτ' ἐξιχνεῦσαι Fl., π. τοῦτό γ' ἐ. F.

    (β)   πάρεστιν τοῦτό γ' ἐξιχνεῦσαί τ'. Ed.

347 (a)   ὡς ἔπραξεν   (β) ἔπραξαν (eiecto ὡς) Herm.

351 (a)   ἐγγόνους   (β) ἐκγόνοις Herm.

352 (a)   ἀτολμήτων   (β) ἀτολμήτως Bam. Herm.

355 (a)   ὑπὲρ τὸ   (β) τὸ δ' οὔ τι Ed.

— (a)   ἔστω δ'   (β) ἐστ' οὐδ' Ed.

356 (a)   ὥστ' ἀπαρκεῖν Fl., ὥστε κἀπαρκεῖν F.

    (β)   ὥστ' ἀπαρκεῖν ἂν Weil.

— (a)   λαχόντα   (β) λαχόντι Schü.

357 (a)   οὐ γάρ ἐστιν   (β) πλούτου γὰρ τίς Ed.

358 (a)   πλούτου   (β) φωτὶ Ed.

— (a)   ἀνδρὶ   (β) ἔξω Ed.

εἰς δόμον τὸν Ἀτρειδᾶν
ᾔσχυνε ξενίαν τράπεζαν κλοπαῖσι γυναικός.

(a) ὑπὲρ τὸ β. in codd. is a manifest gloss interpreting the adv. ὑπέρφευ (*over-well*) which immediately precedes, but βέλτιστον is probably genuine. Τὸ δ' οὔ τι is a guess, suiting the sense of the place. (β) Ἀπήμαντον is certainly genuine, and, as the context shews, it means *free from wrong*, or *harmless*. (γ) After ὥστ' ἀπαρκεῖν we supply, with Weil, the syllable wanted, ἄν. Triclinius, seeing that want, wrote κἀπαρκε͡ν badly in F. Λαχόντι seems a little better Greek than the accus. λαχόντα. (δ) In the three next lines corruption appears in οὐ following final ἄ of preceding line; in οὐ γάρ, πλούτου, and ἀνδρί, which do not agree with antistr.; in λακτίσαντι which does not correspond with antistr. (ᾔσχῦνε ξε.); and in μεγάλα. The reading of F. ἐκλακτίσαντι hints the omission of such a word as ἔξω. As to correction—μέγαν is the obvious and accepted substitute for μεγάλα, φωτὶ for ἀνδρὶ is a good exchange: the substitution of τίς for οὔκ ἐστιν leaves the general sense unimpaired, and the transposition of πλούτου not only supports the final ι of λαχόντι, but adds much to the vigour of the sentence.

The translation of the lines becomes:

'But this is not the best thing, nor even free from wrong, so that it can suffice one who is wise of heart; for what defence is wealth to a man who insolently spurns into outer darkness the mighty altar of Justice?'

That everything here is exactly what Aeschylus wrote, we dare not affirm: that the general sense is that of Aeschylus we are sure: we think also that it is good poetic Greek.

359 (a) λακτίσαντι Fl., ἐκλακτίσαντι F.

    (β) λακτίζαντι Ed.

— (a) μεγάλα (β) μέγαν Can.

361 (a) προβουλόπαις (β) πρόβουλος, παῖς Weil.

362 (a) παμμάταιον (β) πᾶν μάταιον Well.

368 (a) πτανὸν (β) ποτανὸν Pors. Schü.

376 (a) λογχίμους τε καὶ (β) τε καὶ λογχίμους Ahr.

377 Post φθοράν, intercidisse videtur versus, qualis

    δυοῖν μἷ᾽ Ἄτα πολέοιν μέτοικος Ed.

378 (a) βέβακεν F. Vict. (β) βέβακε Fl. Pors. Bl. Herm.

379 (a) πολὺ δ᾽ ἀνέστενον Fl.

    (β) πολλὰ δ᾽ ἔστενον F. Pauw, Herm.

383 (a) σιγᾶς ἄτιμος ἀλοίδορος

    (β) σῖγ᾽ ἀτίμως ἀλοιδόρως Ed.

384 (a) ἄδιστος ἀφεμένων ἰδεῖν.

    (β) ἄδισθ᾽ ὅσ᾽ ἦν ἀφειμένων. Ed.

---

377. Our suggestion of assuming a verse lost after φθοράν grows out of the necessity we find of supposing a similar loss in the antistrophe after ὁρᾶν 392. When we became convinced of this necessity, we looked back to the strophe to see what would happen there if the antistrophe were increased by a verse. On seeing this place, the words in Virgil concerning Helen, 'Troiae et patriae communis Erinys' sprang to our mind, and we said to ourselves 'here was the original of that clause.' The form of rendering it was not far to seek : for, remembering that in another place Aesch. had called Helen νυμφόκλαυτος 'Ερινὺς (688), we felt sure he would not repeat this term ; while Virgil not having latinised Ἄτη, would naturally render it here by the term he had latinised, Erinys. We have therefore suggested δυοῖν μἷ᾽ Ἄτα πολέοιν μέτοικος. Helen, having come from Sparta to Argos, afterwards flying from Argos to Troy, might well be called a μέτοικος of the two cities, and of both μἷ᾽ Ἄτα, 'communis Erinys.'

383, 384. No scholar can be sure that he has restored these two corrupt lines as Aesch. wrote them. We had written the former thus πάρεστι σῖγ᾽ ἄτιμος ὡς ἀλοίδορος δ᾽ and the antistrophic, τὸ πᾶν δὲ γᾶς ἀφ᾽ 'Ελλάδος ξυνορμένοις, but we now think the following more probable: str. πάρεστι σῖγ᾽ ἀτίμως, ἀλοιδόρως antistr. τὸ πᾶν δ᾽ ἀφ᾽ 'Ελλάδος γᾶς ξυνορμένοις, the metre being anacrusis † bini troch. trihem. Cf. *Choeph.* 90, σῖγ᾽ ἀτίμως.

388 (a)   ἀνδρί,   (β) ἔρρει δ᾽ Ed.
389 (a)   ὀμμάτων δ᾽   (β) ὀφθαλμῶν Ed.
—   (a)   ἔρρει   (β) ἀνδρὶ Ed.
392 Post ὁρᾶν intercidisse videtur versus, qualis
   φίλοισιν εὕδῃ ξυνὼν ὀνείροις, Ed.

The restoration of 384 is still more uncertain, on account of ἰδεῖν, which may be a gloss, or may not be. We have now adopted a correction which excludes it, ἄδισθ᾽ ὅσ᾽ ἦν ἀφειμένων, ' all that was sweetest being gone.' Mr Paley reads ἄλγιστ᾽ ἀφειμέναν ἰδών, each word being an emendation. But we want examples of the form ἄλγιστα, and ἀφ. ἰδὼν we little like here, though not unexampled.

 388, 389. These lines are in Fl. and F.

    ἔχθεται χάρις ἀνδρί·
  ὀμμάτων δ᾽ ἐν ἀχηνίαις ἔρρει πᾶσ᾽ Ἀφροδίτα.

We restore agreement by facile corrections, which in every way improve the place without any change of sense.

 The antistrophic lines are (402)

    οἶδεν, ἀντὶ δὲ φωτῶν
  τεύχη καὶ σποδὸς εἰς ἑκάστου δόμους ἀφικνεῖται.

 392. εὖτ᾽ ἂν—δοκῶν ὁρᾶν. Hermann's attempt to explain this Greek by an ellipse of ὁρᾷ, though adopted by Mr Paley, seems to us futile. What is the sense of ' When one seeming to see (or, thinking he sees) sees?' Our own conjecture δοκῶν ὁρᾷ 'in fancy sees,' is a better resource in point of sense, but, as a Greek idiom, it lacks support. We therefore think a line is here lost, the nature of which we have ventured to suggest. If our conjecture is just, we surmise that the strophic line at 377 was the first loss, and the removal of the antistrophic a later consequence.

 393. Herm. reads παραλλαγαῖσι for παραλλάξασα, to preserve correspondence with the strophic βέβακε ῥίμφα. Conversely F. Vict. and Mr Paley read βέβακεν to make the strophe harmonize with the antistr. Neither expedient pleases us. The rapid rhythm βέβακε | ῥίμφα διὰ πυλᾶν (παραλλάξ | ασα διὰ χερῶν) ought certainly not to be clogged by the added ν, while on the other hand Hermann's substantive is clumsy and improbable. We had almost adopted παραλλαγεῖσα, in spite of the want of authority for the passive forms of παραλλάσσω in *earlier* Greek; but we now keep both βέβακε and παραλλάξασα, because the initial ῥ in ῥίμφα seems to satisfy correspondence, and to give the rhythm βεβακέυριμφα answering to παραλλάξασα, the voice in each verse laying stress on the second syllable, and gliding over the third as if it were a short one.

CONSPECTUS LECTIONUM. 165

395 (a) ὀπαδοῖς (β) ὀπαδοῦσ' Do. Herm.
396 (a) ἐφ' ἑστίας (β) ἐφεστίους St.
397 (a) ὑπερβατώτερα. (β) ὑπερβολὴν ἔχει. Ed.
398 (a) αἴας (β) γᾶς Ed.
402 (a) οὓς μὲν γὰρ πέμψεν F.
    (β) τοὺς μὲν γάρ ποτε πέμψας Ed.
404 (a) εἰσαφικνεῖται (β) ἀφικνεῖται Pors. Herm.
413 (a) διὰ (β) διαὶ Herm.
414 (a) τάδε (β) τὰ δὲ Herm.
419 (a) εὔμορφοι (β) ἔμμορφοι innuente Herm. Ed.
421 (a) δημοκράτου (β) δημοκράντου Pors.
426 (a) παλιντυχῆ (β) παλιντυχεῖ Scal. Pors.
427 (a) τιθεῖσ' (β) κτίζουσ' Ed.

395. We receive without hesitation Dobree's emendation ὀπαδοῦσ' for ὀπαδοῖς, as Hermann does. We think that Mr Paley errs in translating οὐ μεθύστερον *forthwith*, and joining it with βέβακε. Good taste as well as the Greek language forbids this. Οὐ μεθύστερον means *at no later time*, i. e. *never again*, and belongs to ὀπαδοῦσ'. The vision is gone, never to return.

397. Ὑπερβατώτερα is spurious, as appears not merely from the final α, which does not correspond with the strophe, but also from the fact that ὑπέρβατος means *what is*, or *can be, transcended*, not *what transcends*.

402. It is evident that οὓς μὲν γὰρ πέμψεν F. is corrupt: and all editors have written ἔπεμψεν, inserting before it, with Porson, τις. But to the disagreement of ἦπἄρ with strophic ἀνάσσειν, and of ἔπεμψέν with κολοσσῶν they have remained callous. That οὓς μὲν ought to be τοὺς μὲν is manifest from its antithesis οἱ δὲ 417. The τοὺς μὲν are those whose bodies were burnt, and the dust sent home, the οἱ δὲ are those buried before Troy. This correction involves πέμψας for πέμψεν, and τίς ποτε or γάρ ποτε, for perhaps, after ἑκάστου, τις is not essential.

419. We have ventured, somewhat boldly, to edit ἔμμορφοι (as suggested by Herm.), for vulg. εὔμορφοι, not being able to believe that Aesch. would describe buried corpses by this latter epithet. Ἔμμορφος is not cited earlier than Plutarch, but the analogical words ἔμμετρος, ἔμμηνος, ἔμμισθος, ἔμμοχθος, are classical; and in Aesch. ἅπαξ λεγόμενα are frequent. A scribe would very glibly change the form for one with which he was familiar.

427. We venture to edit κτίζουσ' here for τιθεῖσ', thus preserving corre-

429 (a) ὑπερκότως (β) ὑπερκόπως Gro.
438 (a) ἤτοι (β) εἴτε Ahr.
— (a) μὴ (β) τι Ed.
440 (a) παραγγέλμασι (β) παραγγέλμασιν Pors.
470 (a) ἦλθες (ἦλθ᾿ Fl. pr. m.)
    (β) ἦσθ᾿ Bl. ex marg. Askev.
471 (a) καὶ παγώνιος Fl., κἀπαγώνιος F.
    (β) καὶ παιώνιος Do.
479 (a) ἦ που (β) εἴ που Aur.
502 (a) πῶς δὴ διδαχθεὶς (β) πῶς δή; διδαχθεὶς Schü.
503 (a) πεπληγμένος (β) πεπληγμένοι Tyr.
505 (a) ἀναστένειν (β) μ᾿ ἀναστένειν Scal.
506 (a) στρατῷ (β) πόλει Ed.
508 (a) καὶ πῶς ἀπόντων (β) καὶ πῶς; ἀπόντων St.
— (a) τυράννων Fl. Vict. (β) κοιράνων F. Can.
509 (a) ὧν (β) ὡς Scal.
511 (a) εὖ λέξειεν (β) ἂν λέξειεν Aur.
516 (a) λαχόντες (β) λάσκοντες Ed.
530 (a) παλιγκότου ;
    (β) hinc excidisse versum credimus, qualis sit
        τούτων ἐπαινῶ μηδὲ φροντίζειν ἔτι Ed.

spondence with the strophic τὸν δ᾿ ἐν 412. The verb κτίζειν is used by Aesch. in this sense (efficere) almost as often as τιθέναι.

506. We write πόλει here with full conviction that it is the word of Aesch., στρατῷ being either the blunder of a careless copier, or the gloss of a bungling commentator. Πόλει not only makes sense clear, but supplies to ἐπῆν the dative which is felt to be wanting.

531. We cannot doubt that a line is lost before καὶ πολλά, such in effect as we suggest.

556. It is possible that κινοῦντες for κοιμῶντες may be a true conjecture. See θυοσκινεῖς 89. But we have not adopted it, because it is also not impossible that, as Butler suggested, the ὀλολυγὴ took place when the lights were being extinguished, though we nowhere read of such a custom.

559. Retracting our former acceptance of ὅπως as a final conjunction, we render σπεύσω ὅπως ἄριστα δέξασθαι, *I will haste to receive with all possible honour.*

564 (a)   τάχιστ'   (β) μάλιστ'
dein post hunc versum intercidisse alterum putamus, qualis sit
   ὅστις κατ' Ἄργος πρῶτα μὲν μέλλοι λεὼν Ed.
565 (a)   γυναῖκα πιστὴν δ'   (β) πιστόν, γυναῖκα δ' Ed
   (a)   εὕροι   (β) εὑρεῖν Ed.
570 (a)   οὐδ'   (β) οὐκ Schü. Bl.
577 (a)   γε   (β) τε Herm.
581 (a)   τύχης   (β) τύχοις Pors.
583 (a)   ἀνὴρ   (β) ἀνὴρ Herm.
603 (a)   σεσαγμένων   (β) σεσαγμένον Schü.
608 (a)   Ἀχαιῶν...θεοῖς
   (β)   Ἀχαιοῖς...θεῶν Do. Herm. Pal.
615 (a)   τυφῶ   (β) , τυφῷ (a ξὺν pendens).
641 (a)   προνοίαις   (β) προνοίαισι Pauw.
645 (a)   ἑλένας   (β) ἑλέναυς Bl. Herm.
647 (a)   ἔπλευσεν   (β) ἔπλευσε Weil.
654 (a)   ἀτίμως F., ἀτίμως ἵν' Fl. Vict.   (β) ατίμωσιν Can.

564, 565. It is now manifest to us that ἥκειν ὅπως τάχιστα is sheer non-
sense. Ἥκειν can only mean 'is come' (for had come is not possible here).
We read above in the speech of the herald 481, 490, that Agamemnon
ἥκει, is come: i.e. he has landed on the Argive coast, and has sent the herald
forward to announce his approach. For ὡς τάχιστ' must be read therefore
ὡς μάλιστ' (or ὡς μέγιστ'): 'tell my lord, that he is come supremely dear to
the city.' As to εὕροι which follows in codd., Herm. supposes it to be
obliquely constructed : but this cannot be for two reasons ; first, it has no
conjunction or relative to connect it with ἥκειν ; next, it should be fut. opt.
not aorist. We therefore hold that a line must be lost here, in effect as
follows: ἐπεὶ (or ὅστις) κατ' Ἄργος πρῶτα μὲν μέλλοι λεὼν (reading then)
πιστόν, γυναῖκα δ' ἐν δόμοις εὑρεῖν μολών.

575. These two lines are somewhat obscure, perhaps by the poet's
design. We would now join no particle to τοροῖσιν. ' Thus indeed hath
she made a speech for you to learn, specious to the minds of thorough-
judging interpreters.' The Chorus seem to hint that they know the real
truth better than the herald was likely to discern it from the queen's
speech.

658 (a)   ὑμέναιον   (β) νέον ὑμέν' Ed.
—   (a)   ἐπέρρεπεν (β) ἐπέρρεπε Weil.
664 (a)   παμπρόσθη (β) πάμπροσθ' ἢ Herm.
—   (a)   αἰῶν' ἀμφὶ (β) αἰῶνα διαὶ Dav.
666 (a)   λέοντα σίνιν (β) λέοντος ἷνιν Con.

658. Our correction νέον ὑμέν' for ὑμέναιον is somewhat bold, but, in our view, required by the final syllable of τίοντας before it, as compared with the strophic word πρεπόντως.

664. Αἰῶν' ἀμφὶ in the two codd. is manifestly corrupt. We had formerly conjectured for ἀμφὶ, ἅμα καὶ, which we afterwards abandoned for αἰῶνα διαὶ, the correction of Mr Davies.

666—679. In this corrupt strophe and antistrophe we have edited several improvements of the text. First, Conington's excellent λέοντος ἷνιν for λέοντα σίνιν. In 667 we have added δ' after φιλόμαστον, not only sustaining the metre, but usefully contrasting that adj. with ἀγάλακτον, 'though weaned, yet fond of the teat,' still an infant lion. The addition of τε in 669 and of ἐν in 676 improve metre without injuring sense. In 673 the bad emendation πρόσθε and the untragic form τοκήων are removed: in 674 the excellent reading of F., τοκεῦσιν, is adopted. Mr Paley mentions our conjecture θανάτοισιν in 675, but with a qualifying doubt as to speaking of the deaths (θάνατοι) of sheep. He says : " the only objection seems to be the doubt whether θάνατοι 'violent death,' is ever applied to animals." The objection is futile. A few passages are cited in the Lexicon, where θάνατοι is supposed to imply 'violent death,' such as Eur. El. 485 σέ ποτ' οὐρανίδαι πέμψουσιν θανάτοισι, yet even here it may be suggested that the double deaths of Aegisthus and Clytaemnestra are implied. In Soph. El. 205 τοὺς ἐμὸς ἴδε πατὴρ θανάτους αἰκεῖς διδύμαιν χειροῖν, it is evident that one death by the hands of two murderers is named as if the death were double. In Agam. 1502 θανάτοις αὐθένταισιν, not merely violent death is meant, but many murders of various persons by various. In Plat. Rep. 399 εἰς τραύματα καὶ θανάτους may mean a scene of wounds and deaths (a battlefield). Thus it may be questioned whether θάνατοι (in itself) ever carries the sense of a violent death. On the other hand, it does frequently mean 'deaths' of various kinds, of various persons, of one person (rhetorically) as Dem. 521 πολλῶν ἄξιος θανάτων καὶ οὐχ ἑνός. Hence it is not necessary to reply that the death of sheep in the claws of a lion is 'a violent death :' we render with justice 'the deaths of slaughtered sheep.' We can cite no examples of θάνατος used of beasts : neither can we adduce one of φόνος applied to them : but we find no difficulty in joining θανάτοισιν τὸ μηλοφόνοις

667 (a) φιλόμαστον (β) φιλόμαστον δ' Ed.
669 (a) εὐφιλόπαιδα (β) εὐφιλόπαιδά τε Ed.
673 (a) ἔθος (β) ἦθος Con.
674 (a) τοκήων Fl. Vict. (β) τοκέων F.
— (a) γὰρ τροφᾶς Fl. Vict. (β) γὰρ τροφεῦσιν F.
675 (a) μηλοφόνοισιν ἄταις Fl., μηλοφόνοισιν ἄταισιν F.
    (β) μηλοφόνοις θανάτοισιν Ed.
676 (a) αἵματι (β) ἐν αἵματι Bothe, ἐν αἵμασι Ed.
679 (a) ἐκ θεοῦ δ' (β) θείας ὧδ' Ed.
— (a) προσετράφη (β) προσεθρέφθη Heath.
685 (a) παρακλίνουσ' F. (β) παρακλίνασ' Fl.
    (a) Πριαμίδαισι Fl. Vict. (β) Πριαμίδαισιν F.
695 (a) μετὰ (β) μέτα Herm.
699 (a) ἐν κακοῖς (β) ἔν γε τοῖς κακοῖς Ed.

(compare ἀντιφόνοις θανάτοις, Sept. 785) seeing that death (θάνατος) is a common necessity of beasts as well as of men. Σφάζειν, σφαγή, are applied to the sacrificial slaughter of animals; but also to the murder of human beings.

679. We have no doubt that ἐκ θεοῦ is corrupt, as it does not correspond with stroph. φαιδρωπός, and follows ὄν in 678. But, being without a certain clue to correction, we find no substitute more likely than θείας ὧδ', because ἐκ θεοῦ δ' may have crept into the text as a gloss on these words. In this play we have θεῖον ψύθος, in Sophocles θεία νόσος, θεία μανία. We adopt θείας ὧδ' therefore as exceedingly probable, and certainly a good tragic representation of the meaning which ἐκ θεοῦ contains.

699. In the corrupt strophe δ', comparing this line as it stands in codd. with the antistr. 705, we observe that they differ by two syllables. Viewing their contents, we consider that antistr. τὸν δ' ἐναίσιμον τίει βίον is unassailably genuine, and that βίον (which Mr Paley would obliterate) cannot be dispensed with. But in str. we are greatly dissatisfied with ἐν κακοῖς βροτῶν, which can only mean 'in human misfortunes,' a sense not suited to the place, which requires 'in bad men.' This at once suggests the insertion γε τοῖς, which gives the sense and the rhythm required. Mr Paley has left this emendation unnoticed, and deals with the words ἐν κακοῖς βροτῶν thus : "it is this ὕβρις which in turn generates a young ὕβρις of a still worse kind, that namely which wantons in the misfortunes of others (ὑβρίζειν ἐν κακοῖς inf, 1590, cf. Suppl. 96—7)." Here he refers his readers to places which tell against his teaching. To particularize this second Ὕβρις as that

700 (a)   ὅταν   (β) ὅτε Kl.
701 (a)   νεαρὰ φάους κότον   (β) νέα δ᾽ ἔφυσεν Κόρον Pal.
702 (a)   τε τὸν ἄμαχον   (β) τ᾽ ἄμαχον Pal.
704 (a)   εἰδομέναν   (β) εἰδομένας Ed.
707 (a)   ἐσθλὰ   (β) ἔδεθλα Aur.
708 (a)   παλιντρόποις   (β) παλιντρόποισιν Ed.
709 (a)   ὄμμασιν λιποῦσ᾽   (β) λιποῦσ᾽ ὄμμασιν Ed.
— (a)   προσέβα τοῦ   (β) προσέμολε Herm.

which insults the unfortunate is wide of the purpose of Aeschylus, whose design is general, namely, to show how excessive Prosperity (the first ῞Υβρις) engenders a second ῞Υβρις, which we may call Recklessness, growing up in evil natures (ἔν γε τοῖς κακοῖς βροτῶν), and how this second ῞Υβρις engenders two wicked children, Arrogance and Audacity, which resemble their progenitors, and prove fatal curses to the families in which they dwell. Now let us look at his citations. The first is Ag. 1590, ὑβρίζειν ἐν κακοῖς. But it is not ὑβρίζειν ἐν κακοῖς which we have here, but νεάζουσαν ἐν κακοῖς, 'youthfully growing in'—as the next citation distinctly shows: ἰδέσθω δ᾽ εἰς ὕβριν βρότειον οἷα νεάζει πυθμὴν...τεθαλώς, where Mr Paley himself writes, 'the old stock is here said to bud and blossom *anew in the insolence of his sons.*' Can any proof be more complete of the truth of our correction, and of the error committed by suppressing it?

700 (750). ῞Οτε, Klausen's correction, is manifestly right. In the next two lines we have adopted Mr Paley's excellent emendations; but we see nothing gained by Donaldson's suggestion μελαίνα ῎Ατα for μελαίνας ῎Ατας, which gives a needless hiatus at the close of the line. In the places cited from Sophocles the presence of δύο is an argument against the proposed reading here. Εἰδομένας for vulg. εἰδομέναν is quite as defensible as εἰδομένα. Hermann's endeavour to reform this strophe (by printing ἔς τ᾽ ἂν ἐπὶ τὸ κύριον μόλῃ νέᾳ ῥαφᾷ, and afterwards τὰν ἄμαχον referred to θράσος ῎Ατας as = θρασεῖαν ῎Αταν) seems a complete failure.

700—759. Codd. have corruptly

παλιντρόποις ὄμμασιν
λιποῦσ᾽ ὅσια προσέβα τοῦ.

For the two last words Herm. supplies προσέμολε, and an easy transposition of our own restores just agreement with the strophe by giving

παλιντρόποισιν λιποῦσ᾽
ὄμμασιν ὅσια προσέμολε.

712 (a) ἄγε (β) λέγε Ed.

714 (a) σε σεβίζω (β) δὲ σεβίζω Ed.

716 (a) πολλοὶ δὲ βροτῶν τὸ δοκεῖν εἶναι

    (β) τοῦ τε γὰρ εἶναι πολλοὶ τὸ δοκεῖν Ed.

717 (a) παραβάντες. (β) παραβάντες, Ed.

718 (a) δ' (β) τ' Herm.

722 (a) βιαζόμενοι (β) versus intercidit, qualis est

    τὸν μὴ καθορῶντ' ἀπατῶσιν. Ed.

728 (a) γὰρ ἐπικεύσω, (β) γάρ σ' ἐπικεύσω, Mus.

731 (a) ἑκούσιον (β) ἐκ θυσιῶν Fr.

733 (a) ἀφίλως (β) versum intercidisse credimus, qualis

    αἰνῶ σε λέγων Ed.

712. The difference between ΑΓΕ and ΛΕΓΕ in uncial writing is very slight: and we think λέγε with indirect question following is much better suited to this place than the interjectional ἄγε with direct question. In 713 we prefer πῶς δὲ σεβίζω to σε.

716. Deeming this place corrupt on account of τὸ δοκεῖν εἶναι, and also feeling the strongest conviction that προτίουσι must have a genitive dependent on it, we venture to read

τοῦ τε γὰρ εἶναι πολλοί τὸ δοκεῖν

a comma following after παραβάντες, and τῷ δυσπραγοῦντί τ' afterwards.

721. συγχαίρουσιν (particip. dat. pl.) ὁμοιοπρεπεῖς 'assuming the semblance of congratulators.'

722. The loss of a line after βιαζόμενοι is manifest, as Hermann says, from the want of συνάφεια when ὅστις follows. Evidently too the lost line is a paroemiac (dim. cat.) and may well be what we have suggested,

τὸν μὴ καθορῶντ' ἀπατῶσιν.

728. Not thinking a paroemiac probable here, we adopt Musgrave's insertion σ'.

731. We accept Franz's reading

θράσος ἐκ θυσιῶν for θράσος ἑκούσιον of codd.

732. We have not ventured to edit θρησκοῖσι (*superstitious*) for θνή-σκουσι, though the sense would be improved by doing so. The adj. θρησκὸς first appears in the Epistle of St James: but the subst. θρησκηίη (= Attic θρησκεία) is used by Herodotus.

734. That a line is lost after ἀφίλως such as αἰνῶ σε λέγων, we must inevitably believe, unless we read in the next line—

736 (a) ἀκαίρως (β) versum intercidisse credimus cum Herm., qui esse potuerit

σέθεν οἰχομένου Ed.

742 (a) κλύοντες (β) κρίνοντες Ed.

εὔφρων πόνος εὖ τελέσασιν, ἐρῶ.

i.e. but now, without simulation and without unfriendliness, I will say: 'all's well with toilers when their toil's well ended.'

736. Herm. marks a lacuna after ἀκαίρως suggesting σου ἀφεστῶτος badly. We prefer σέθεν οἰχομένου.

The constitution of these concluding anapaests (731—737) is to us one of the most doubtful questions in this drama. Our difficulty turns mainly on the monometric base θράσος ἐκ θυσιῶν, which seems to be the only one in the 7 systems. The first four have the paroemiac (including that supplied after βιαζόμενοι) without a base; and the two last are also without base in codices; but these have indications of a lost base. We do not believe that the base of system 5 can have been the only one placed in these anapaests by Aeschylus. But correction has before it two alternatives. (1) Has a monometer been lost, which made that base a dimeter? If so, it could only be an epithet of θυσιῶν (which certainly seems somewhat naked without one), but in that case such epithet must have been one of a strongly marked kind, such as αἱμορράντων; and we shrink from suggesting this addition, feeling no assurance that it would justly represent the mind of the poet, who might rather have avoided this strong language, as indelicate in the mouth of the chorus here, while they are striving to say what may soothe and gratify Agamemnon. (2) If θράσος ἐκ θυσιῶν stand as it is, then we would certainly suggest σέθεν οἰχομένου as desirable before the closing paroemiac: and (though still doubtful whether the systems should not be reduced to 6 by writing ἐρῶ after τελέσασιν) we incline rather to retain the seven, by suggesting the base αἰνῶ σε λέγων after ἀφίλως. Both these suggested additions are quite colourless, and in no respect at variance with the sense of the existing text. See on 40—106.

741—745. In our first edition we suggested κρίνοντες for κλύοντες, and, after much subsequent consideration, our opinion in favour of κρίνοντες is stronger than ever. (1) Is κλύειν δίκας 'to hear causes (or a cause)' a recognised phrase? We find no authorities for it cited anywhere, while κρίνειν δίκην is one of constant use. Mr Paley quotes Suppl. 911 οὗτοι δικάζει ταῦτα μαρτύρων ὕπο | Ἄρης, and makes μαρτύρων ὕπο = ἀπὸ γλώσσης. But the verb is δικάζει (= κρίνει) not κλύει. Then he cites οὕτω γε ἀπὸ στόματος Plat. Theaet. 142. This is against his view: for there when asked if he can repeat the dialogue, 'no,' says Eucleides, 'not offhand from memory (word of mouth):' so that this phrase is applied to the mouth of the subject; while, as Mr Paley says, the gods κλύουσιν οὐκ ἀπὸ γλώσσης, 'not from verbal evidence;' and the phrase is thus applied to the tongues of others, not of the subject. Yet how probable does it seem that ἀπὸ γλώσσης does refer to the tongue of the gods, when we find it placed in contrast with the silent act of voting by ballot. This argument seems to us very cogent in favour of κρίνοντες δίκας 'giving sentence on our claims:' for δίκαι is used for the process by which the δίκαια (740) were claimed. (2) When we are told, even by Agamemnon, that the gods heard (or judged) the suit of the Greeks, and passed by unanimous vote a sentence of destruction against Troy and its people, we must refer this to the closing events, the entrance of the wooden horse and its fatal consequences. See the following context, 750 etc. We cannot say that the decision of the gods was pronounced by vote at the beginning of the war: for this would be in the strongest contradiction to Homer, the great authority on the whole legend. In the Iliad we see the gods divided against one another, the cause of the Trojans being favoured by Hera, Apollo, Aphrodite, and other deities. But, in the final struggle, that cause was deserted by all, as Virgil represents in Aen. ii.:

> Excessere omnes adytis arisque relictis
> Di quibus imperium hoc steterat. 351—2.
> . . . Divom inclementia, divom
> Has evertit opes, sternitque a culmine Troiam. 602.

How then (especially when κλύειν δίκας is not a technical Attic phrase) can the gods be said 'to hear' at all a suit on which their minds were made up after much experience and much pleading in Olympus during ten years of war? Nay more: how can anybody be said *to hear* a suit 'without verbal evidence or pleading'? Being sufficiently informed they might pass their sentence without hearing; and this, we think, is implied: but, as to οὐκ ἀπὸ γλώσσης, referring to Plato's οὐκ ἀπὸ στόματος as authority on our side, we suppose it means, 'not by tongue-sentence,' not by delivering their verdict in words,' but by casting ballots silently, unanimously, into 'the bloody urn,' so called because it was the urn of condemnation. So much in proof of the superior claim of κρίνοντες. (3) We pass on to the construction of ἀνδροθνῆτας Ἰλίου φθοράς. This we take in connection with δίκας κρίνοντες. If we may render δίκας 'righteous claim,' it would be possible to regard φθορὰς as in simple apposition to it, for what the Greeks claimed was the destruction of Troy. But if we render κρίνοντες δίκας 'giving sentence in the suit,' then φθορὰς is the matter of that sentence, and the construction at full means 'awarding, by their verdict in the case, the

747 (a)   θυέλλαι   (β) θυηλαὶ Herm.
751 (a)   ἐπραξάμεσθα   (β) ἐφραξάμεσθα Herm.
759 (a)   ταῦτα   (β) ταὐτὰ Aur.
766 (a)   ἐξεπίσταμαι,   (β) comma delevit Ed.
767 (a)   σκιᾶς   (β) versum excidisse credimus, qualis sit
          ἀνδρῶν φανέντας τῶν ξυνορμένων τινὰς Ed.
778 (a)   πήματος τρέψαι νόσον.
     (β)   πῆμ' ἀποστρέψαι νόσον. Pors.
791 (a)   ἡδονὰς   (β) κληδόνας Aur.
797 (a)   ἐπλήθυνον   (β) ἐπλήθυον Pors.
799 (a)   πολλὴν κ.τ.λ.   (β) hunc versum expunximus.
800 (a)   λαβὼν   (β) λαβεῖν Ed.
831 (a)   τοίνυν   (β) τοί νιν Schü.
858 (a)   πράσσοιμ' ἂν   (β) πράσσοιμεν Dind.

destruction of Troy with the massacre of its men.' Mr Paley makes
φθορὰs to depend on ψήφους ἔθεντο, which, he says = ἐψηφίσαντο. And he
refers to two passages in which he considers a phrase (verb with accus.)
as = a transitive verb on which depends an accus. object. Be it observed that in both those places the accus. object *follows* the phrase
supposed to govern it, whereas here ἀνδροθνῆτας Ἰλίου φθορὰs *precedes*
ψήφους ἔθεντο, and is divided from it by a whole line containing two
adjuncts of ψήφους ἔθεντο. This makes a great difference: the more so as
one of the adjuncts is εἰς αἱματηρὸν τεῦχος, which hampers Mr Paley's construction in a very awkward manner, more readily felt than easily described.
Ψηφίσασθαι θάνατον εἰς αἱματηρὸν τεῦχος would be a startling expression.
Mr Paley has here advocated (not, we think, successfully) a construction of
the same nature as that which he has rejected at 213, where we maintained
it as justly poetic (στόματος φυλακὰν κατασχεῖν φθόγγον).

766—768. This passage, as it stands in codd., is ungrammatical, δοκοῦντας having no just construction: and line 766 is absurdly tautological.
We can have no doubt that 766 should be written εἰδὼς λέγο:μ' ἂν· εὖ γὰρ
ἐξεπίσταμαι (without comma), and that after 767 a line is lost to this effect,
                ἀνδρῶν φανέντας τῶν ξυνορμένων τινὰς
Angl. 'I can speak from knowledge: for well do I know that some of the
men who sailed with me, seeming to be my very loyal friends, proved to be
(φανέντας) a mere image of friendship, the shadow of a shade.'

859—862. On the interpretation of these lines see Translation and
Supplementary Notes.

862 (a) ἐξεῖπον   (β) ἐξειπεῖν Ed.

871 (a) μέντοι πάρες γ'   (β) πάρες γε μὴν Ed.

876 (a) σωματοφθορεῖν   (β) δωματοφθορεῖν Schü.

887 (a) εἰς ἄργυρον   (β) ἰσάργυρον Salm.

889 (a) οἴκοις   (β) ἅλις Ed.

893 (a) τῆσδε   (β) σῆς γε. Ed.

897 (a) μολών   (β) μολόν Bl.

898 (a) Ζεύς τ' ἀπ'   (β) Ζεὺς ἀπ' Herm.

904 (a) δεῖγμα Fl. Vict. Pors.   (β) δεῖμα F. Herm. Bl.

906 (a) ἀκέλευστος ἄμισθος ἀοιδά,
    (β) ἀκέλευστον ἄμισθον ἀοιδάν, Ed.

907 (a) ἀποπτύσας Fl. Vict.   (β) ἀποπτύσαι F.

909 (a) ἵξει   (β) ἵζει Scal. Pors. Herm.

910 (a) ἐπεὶ Fl.   (β) ἐπὶ F. Herm.

911 (a) ξυνεμβόλοις   (β) ξυνεμβολαῖς Herm.

913—14 (a)   εὖθ' ὑπ' Ἴλιον | ὦρτο ναυβάτας
       (β)   εὖτε ναυβάτας | ὦρθ' ὑπ' Ἴλιον Ed.

917 (a) ὅπως   (β) ὅμως St.

— (a) ὑμνῳδεῖ   (β) μονῳδεῖ Dav.

921 (a) οὗτοι   (β) οὔτι Cas.

922—3 (a)   τελεσφόροις | δίναις κυκλούμενον κέαρ
       (β)   κυκλούμενον | δίναις κέαρ τελεσφόροις Ed.

889. *οἴκοις.* This is adopted for ms. *οἶκος* by Pors. Dind. Bl. Pal. The last translates 'it belongs to the house to have (enough, μέρος τι) of these purple vestments.' Liddell and Scott, 'there is store of these things to the house.' Such a construction is dubious. Later (1586) we find πημονῆς ἅλις γ' ὑπάρχει. Considering that *οἶκος* stands in codd., and δόμος at the close of the next line, we believe *οἶκος* to be a gloss, or rather a careless corruption, and the true word to be ἅλις.

893. *ψυχῆς τῆσδε.* Τῆσδε is defensible, a deictic motion being supposed : yet, as Clyt. addresses her husband before (ἄναξ 889) and after (σοῦ 896), we think Aesch. wrote σῆς γε, the emphasis being suitable.

906. We read ἀοιδὰν for ἀοιδά. It is quite as good in lyric Greek to say δεῖμα μαντιπολεῖ ἀοιδὰν as to say ἀοιδὰ μαντιπολεῖ.

913—914. Our simple transposition of the words in this passage removes the discrepancy between Ἰλίον and πεσεῖν in the antistr.

922—923. Here also transposition corrects the discrepancy between

924 (a) ἐξ ἐμᾶς Fl. ἀπ' ἐμᾶς τοι F.

    (β) ἀπ' ἐμᾶς τοιαῦτ' Ed.

927 (a) μάλα γάρ τοι τᾶς πολλᾶς ὑγιείας Fl. Vict.

    μάλα γέ τοι τᾶς πολλᾶς ὑγιείας F.

    (β) μάλα γέ τοι τὸ μεγάλας ὑγείας Pal.

928 (a) ἀκόρεστον (β) ἀκόρετον in v. praeced. Ed.

— (a) γὰρ (β) γὰρ ἀεὶ Bl.

931 (a) ἀνδρὸς ἔπαισεν......ἄφαντον ἔρμα.

    (β) ἀνδρὸς †ὑπὲρ βιότου | κύματ'† ἔπαισεν ἔρμ' ἄ-
φαντον Ed.

κέαρ and ξυνεμβολαῖς, and also avoids that jumble of dative cases in
922, which has caused Mr Paley to fall into the error of supposing
τελεσφόροις to be an epithet of φρεσίν, whereas it manifestly belongs to
δίναις.

924. For the corrupt τοι of F., Herm. conjectures τὸ πᾶν. This
Mr Paley edits, but unwisely suggests ὅμως, which, being not specially
demanded on any ground, is surely to be rejected on account of ἐμᾶς before
it. To us τοιαῦτ' (ψύθη) seems in every way preferable.

927—928. Accepting Mr Paley's constitution so far as ὑγείας, we read
ἀκόρετον, and add it in 927 to the three foregoing paeons : constituting the
next lines either as two dactylic trimeters, τέρμα, νόσος γὰρ ἀεὶ γεί | των
ὁμότοιχος ἐρείδει, or as one hexameter.

931—932. Comparison with the antistrophe shews a loss of seven
syllables, which attempts have been made to supply. H. L. Ahrens reads
ἀνδρὸς ἔπαισεν †ἄφνω πολλάκι δὴ πρὸς† ἄφαντον ἔρμα. Mr Paley,
citing this, offers ἀνδρὸς †ἐν εὐτυχίᾳ ναός† ἔπαισεν ἄφαντον ἔρμα, not
noticing our conjecture ἀνδρὸς †ὑπὲρ βιότου κύματ'† ἔπαισεν ἔρμ' ἄφαντον. In such cases no scholar can pretend that he has certainly restored
the phrase of Aeschylus ; but we should try to suggest one of a poetic yet
colourless character. We have a metaphor already in πότμος, *fate,*
voyaging on a straight (i.e. apparently safe) course : to say that this voyage
is 'over the billows of life' carries on that metaphor naturally : the word
εὐθυπορῶν does not require any such addition as that which Mr Paley
suggests. Hermann allows no lacuna, but reads ἀνδρὸς ἔπαισεν ἄφαντον
ἔρμα, cutting down the antistr. to correspond with this :

        Ζεὺς δὲ τὸν ὀρθοδαῆ
        τῶν φθιμένων ἀνάγειν ἔπαυσεν.

933—4 (a) ὄκνος βαλὼν | σφενδόνας ἀπ' εὐμέτρου
     (β) ἀπ' εὐμέτρου | σφενδόνας ὄκνῳ βαλὼν Ed.

941 (a) τὸ δ' ἐπὶ γᾶν (β) ἐπὶ δὲ γᾶν Ed.

— (a) πεσόνθ' (β) πεσὸν Pauw.

942 (a) πρόπαρ Fl., προπάροιθ' F.
     (β) τὸ πρόπαρ in v. 941 Ed.

943 (a) πάλιν (β) τοῦτ' in v. 942 Ed.
     (a) αὗτ' ἔπαυσ' (β) κατέπαυσ' Ed.
     (a) ἐπ' ἀβλαβείᾳ γε F.
     (β) ἐπ' εὐλαβείᾳ Fl.

969 (a) ἂν οὖσα (β) ἀλοῦσα Haupt.

933—934. By reading ὄκνῳ for ὄκνος, and interchanging the places of ἀπ' εὐμέτρου and ὄκνῳ βαλών, this passage is rescued from corruption at small cost.

942—944. We write in the antistrophe, to correspond with strophe :

    ἐπὶ δὲ γᾶν πεσὸν ἅπαξ θανάσιμον τὸ πρόπαρ ἀν-
    δρὸς μέλαν αἷμα, τίς ἂν τοῦτ'
    ὀγκαλέσαιτ' ἐπαείδων ;

Or the two latter lines may form a dactylic hexameter.

Cod. Fl. gives πρόπαρ, which F. has altered to προπάροιθε. Τὸ πρόπαρ ...αἷμα means the heart's blood: hence the place of τὸ is fully justified. The comma at αἷμα indicates that we treat the word and its clause as having an absolute, or half-absolute construction: 'when a man's black heart's blood has once fallen on the ground with mortal effect, who can recall this by incantation?' Τοῦτ' replaces the manifest gloss πάλιν.

945—947. Here we are disposed to read, in a corrupt place,

    οὐ δὲ τὸν ὀρθοδαῆ
    τῶν φθιμένων ἀνάγειν
    Ζεὺς κατέπαυσ' ἐπ' εὐλαβείᾳ ;

'Did not Zeus put down and silence for precaution one who possessed the true skill of raising from the dead?' Compare 1454, οὐδὲ γὰρ οὗτος δολίαν ἄτην οἴκοισιν ἔθηκ';

969. ἐντός δ' ἂν οὖσα κ.τ.λ. Mr Paley renders, 'and now that you are within the toils of fate.' This is ungrammatical: for ἂν οὖσα cannot be written so that οὖσα shall be other than conditional, as Hermann justly says. Mr Paley adds: 'The ἂν in ἐντός δ' ἂν is used to introduce the hypothetical proposition, and is repeated with the verb as 336—8.' His citation is not in his favour. It is, θεοῖς δ' ἂν ἀμπλάκητος εἰ μόλοι στρατὸς ... γένοιτ' ἂν, where the place of the hypothetical conjunction εἰ makes all

976 (a)   σχολὴ   (β) σχολὴν Wies.
977 (o)   μεσομφάλου   (β) intercidisse versum credimus,
qualis sit

      ἡγισμέν' ἡμῖν ἐστι, ποιμνίων δ' ἄπο Ed.
982 (a)   σὺ δ'   (β) ἀλλ' Ed.
992 (a)   ἐκοῦσ' ἀνάγκῃ   (β) εἴκουσ' ἀνάγκῃ R.
1005 (a)   παρ' ἐν M., παρὲν Fl., παρὸν F.
   (β)   περ ἐν Schü.
1011 (a)   ἃ ἃ omittunt Fl. F.   (β) inserit M.
1012 (a)   ξυνίστορα M., συνίστορα Fl. F.   (β) συνίστορ' Ed.
1013 (a)   αὐτοφόνα   (β) αὖ | τοκτόνα Ed.
   (a)   κακὰ κάρτάναι M. R.   (β) κακὰ κάρτάναs F. Herm.
1014 (a)   ἀνδρὸς σφάγιον   (β) ἀνδροσφαγεῖον Do.
— (a)   καὶ πέδον   (β) θ' αἱμάτων Ed.
1015 (a)   εὖρις   (β) εὗρις Pors.
1016 (a)   μαντεύει M.   (β) ματεύει Fl. F.
— (a)   ὧν ἂν εὑρήσῃ M., ὧν ἐφευρήσει Fl. F.
   (β)   ὧν ἀνευρήσει Pors.
1017 (a)   lacuna in codd.   (β) ἃ ἃ Bl.
1018 (a)   μαρτυρίοις γὰρ M., μαρτυρίοις μὲν γὰρ Fl. V. F.
   (β)   μαρτυρίοισι γὰρ Pauw.
— (a)   τοῖσδε πεπείθομαι   (β) τοῖσδ' ἐπιπείθομαι Abr.
1019 (a)   τάδε βρέφη M., τὰ βρέφη Fl. F.
   (β)   βρέφη Kar.

the difference by placing the particle ἂν outside the condition. Not so here, where, as in ηὔξω δείσας ἂν 861 the position of ἂν with the participle binds it under the same condition as the verb, though there it follows, here it precedes the verb. We think Haupt's conj. ἀλοῦσα true.

976—979. We now simply adopt in 977 Wieseler's conj. σχολὴν for σχολή, rendering (οὔτοι πάρα ἐμοὶ) ' it is not in my power, you see, (τρίβειν τήνδε θυραίαν σχολήν) to waste time in this out-door converse.' And we retain our conviction, that a verse, to the effect above suggested, has been lost after v. 977.

1012, 1013. We now read συνίστορ' αὐ- | τοκτόνα κακὰ κάρτάναs, making συνίστορα transitive, *conscious of*. Our other readings in this part of the drama remain generally the same, and are shown in *Consp. Lect.*

1019. Mr Paley, keeping τάδε βρέφη with M., fails to mention that the

1022 (a) ἦμεν (β) ἦσμεν Pors. Bl. Herm.

— (a) μαστεύομεν (β) ματεύομεν Schü. Herm.

1024 (a) νέον ἄχθος μέγα ; M. νέον ἄχος μ. ; Fl. V. F.

     (β) νῦν ἄχος νέον ; Ed.

1033 (a) χεῖρ' ἐκ χειρὸς ὀρεγομένα M., χεὶρ ἐκ χερὸς ὀρεγμένα
        Fl. F.

     (β) χεὶρ ἐκ | χερὸς ὀρέγματα Herm.

1038 (a) ἦ (β) μὴ Ed.

1044 (a) φόνου. (β) λοιγοῦ. Ed.

     (a) ἀκόρεστος (β) ἀκόρετος Bo.

1045 (a) ἄτε καὶ δορία M., ἄτε καὶ δωρία Fl., ἄτε δωρία F.

     (β) ἄτε καιρία Dind.

1050 (a) μελαγκέρως M., μελάγκερων Fl. F.

     (β) μελαγκέρῳ Herm.

1051 (a) ἐνύδρῳ (β) ἐν ἐνύδρῳ Schü.

     (a) τεύχει. (β) κύτει Bl.

1060 (a) ἐπεγχέασα ; (β) ἐπεγχέασ' ; Ed.

1061 (a) ποῖ δή με (β) ἆ ποῖ με Ed.

other codd. have τὰ βρέφη. We reject both τάδε and τά, of which τὰ is impossible, and τάδε a gloss on account of τοῖσδε preceding. The apposition of accus. to dat. from excited lips in a scene like this is quite possible.

1022. ἦμεν mss. Pal. ἦσμεν Pors. Herm. ἴσμεν Cobet. ἐσμέν, a gloss in F. The choice is doubtful. We now take ἦσμεν. For μαστεύομεν with Schütz and Herm. we read ματεύομεν.

1024. The corruption of μέγα is proved by the μέγ' which follows. The reading, τί τόδε νῦν ἄχος νέον; is a slight and easy correction.

1038. We now read μὴ for ἦ or ἤ.

1041. Φόνου in 1044 is unmetrical, and would be used too soon. We therefore read λοιγοῦ, which two parallel passages signalise as the just word in this place: Suppl. 679, μηδέ τις ἀνδροκμῆς λοιγὸς ἐπελθέτω, and Cho. 402, βοᾷ γὰρ λοιγὸν 'Ερινύς.

1051. We cannot be satisfied to leave the unmetrical word τεύχει to which γένει corresponds, instead of editing κύτει with Bl. and Herm.

1061. By writing ἆ ποῖ here, as in 1008, we enable ἐπεγχέασ' to stand as it ought, in 1061.

1065 (a)   ξουθὰ   (β) ξουθᾶς Ed.
1066—67 (a) φρεσὶν | Ἴτυν   (β) Ἴτυν | φρεσὶν Ed.
1069 (a)   ἀηδόνος μόρον.   (β) μόρον ἀηδόνος. Herm.
1070 (a)   περεβάλοντο M., περιβαλόντες Fl.
      (β) περίβαλον Bl.
1073 (a)   θεοφόρους τ’   (β) θεοφόρους Herm.
1087 (a)   νεογνὸς ἀνθρώπων μάθοι.
      (β) καὶ παῖς νεόγονος ἂν μάθοι Herm. (Ed. καί τις).
1097 (a)   θερμόνους   (β) θερμὸν οὓς Can.
1098 (a)   προτέροισι τάδ’ ἐφημίσω.
      (β) προτέροις τάδ’ ἐπεφημίσω. Pal.
1099 (a)   κακοφρονεῖν   (β) κακοφρονῶν Schü.
1100 (a)   ὑπερβαρὴς Fl., ὑπερβαρὺς F.
      (β) ὕπερθεν βαρὺς Pal.
1101 (a)   θανατόφορα Fl., θανατήφορα F.
      (β) θανάσιμ’ ὧν Ed.
1102 (a)   τέρμα δ’   (β) τέρματ’ Ed.

1065. ξουθᾶς. Codd. have ξουθά. But as there is no doubt that this adj. sometimes signifies *clear-voiced* or *melodious*, we venture to write ξουθᾶς. For βοᾶς, used of the nightingale's voice, needs a qualifying epithet much more than the distant word ἀηδών itself, and in such a position it seems poor to place an epithet merely calling the nightingale 'yellowish-brown.' The first meanings, out of many, assigned to ξουθὸς by Photius are λεπτός, ἁπαλός. And when Aristophanes makes the Bird-chorus say (*Av.* 726) δι’ ἐμῆς γέννος ξουθῆς μελέων Πανὶ νόμους ἱεροὺς ἀναφαίνω, we cannot believe that he meant to ascribe one and the same colour to the γέννυς of all birds, but rather a delicate utterance of notes.

1087. Mss. have the corrupt νέογνος ἀνθρώπων μάθοι. Herm. emends καὶ παῖς νεόγονος ἂν μάθοι, which we follow, but with καί τις for καὶ παῖς.

1097. Mss. have θερμόνους. Canter wrote, with the fullest justice, θερμὸν οὓς, which no succeeding editors, save Hermann and ourselves, have had the wisdom to adopt. We wrote a long defence of it in our first edition, which we do not repeat here, satisfied with referring to Madvig's admirable correction at 1154, φαιδρὸν οὓς for ms. φαιδρόνους.

1101, 1102. Our emendation here θανάσιμ’, ὧν τέρματ’ for θανατόφορα, τέρμα δ’ has our full confidence, though Mr Paley has not made it known to his readers. The corruption of θανατόφορα, compared with the strophic θρεομένας, is manifest. The fitness of θανάσιμα in its stead is shown by

1107 (a) κλύειν   (β) κλύζειν Aur.
1119 (a) τηρῶ   (β) κυρῶ Ahr.
1121 (a) τό μ' εἰδέναι   (β) see note below.
1123 (a) πῆμα   (β) πῆγμα Aur.
1136 (α) πῶς δῆτ' ἄνακτος
        (β) πῶς δῆτ' ; ἄνατος Can.
1137 (a) οὐδὲν οὐδέν   (β) οὐδέν' οὐδέν Can.
1141 (a) φροιμίοις ἐφημίοις   (β) φρ. ἐπισσύτοις. Ed.
1152 (a) ἄπαρχος   (β) ἔπαρχος Can.
1153 (α) οἶα   (β) οἷα Madv.
        (a) μισητῆς   (β) μισήτης Madv.
1154 (a) λέξασα   (β) λείξασα Tyr.
        (a) καὶ κτείνασα Fl. F. V.   (β) κἀκτείνασα Can.
        (a) φαιδρόνους   (β) φαιδρὸν οὒς Madv.
1155 (a) τεύξεται   (β) δήξεται Madv.
1156 (a) τοιάδε   (β) τοιαῦτα Vict.

θανάσιμον γόον 1374, and that of plur. τέρματα (τῶν μελέων) by plur. ὅρους (the same sense) 1077. The attempts of Triclinius and Hermann to emend by correcting the strophic θρεομένας are intolerable.

1121. Dobree's conj. τὸ μὴ εἰδέναι has been largely received. But we now keep τό μ' εἰδέναι, thinking that λόγῳ παλαιὰς ἀμ., *old traditional sins*, is sustained by Soph. *Oed. T.* 1395, τὰ πάτρια λόγῳ παλαιὰ δώματα.

1141. The ms. ἐφημίοις (which grew out of ἐφημένους in next line) is obviously corrupt, and editors have left a lacuna, which may be probably supplied by ἐπισσύτοις.

1152—55. These stand thus in previous editions:

νεῶν τ' ἔπαρχος Ἰλίου τ' ἀναστάτης
οὐκ οἶδεν οἶα γλῶσσα μισητῆς κυνὸς
λέξασα κἀκτείνασα φαιδρόνους, δίκην
Ἄτης λαθραίου, τεύξεται κακῇ τύχῃ.

where κἀκτείνασα is Canter's certain correction of the ms. καὶ κτείνασα.

In our first edition we failed to suspect the genuineness of these words for the following reasons.

(1) In the application of the term κυὼν to Clytaemnestra there is nothing which should lead us to expect an extension of the metaphor to the next word. Shameless women (and men too) are again and again so named : see Liddell and Scott (*Lex.* in v. κυων); and Aesch. might bear in mind

1160 (a)   ἀρὰν   (β) Ἄρην Herm.
1165 (a)   μῆν   (β) μ᾽ ἐν Aur.

that Clyt. had called herself κύων in the good sense of a faithful guardian
(566), and now from Cassandra's point of view supply the epithet μισήτη.
The context would confirm this notion.   Having just before described
Aegisthus as a cowardly lion, why should Aesch. call Clyt. κύων in a strictly
material sense, and superadd simile within simile, δίκην Ἄτης λαθραίου,
capping all by giving her other titles, ἀμφίσβαινα, Σκύλλα, Ἅιδου μήτηρ?

(2) Hence we did not suspect λέξασα as referred to γλῶσσα.   That 'a
tongue' should *speak*, what more natural?   'Εκτείνασα in the sense of
lengthening speech we took to be a reference to what Agamemnon said,
in Cassandra's hearing, to Clytaemnestra (844), μακρὰν γὰρ ἐξέτεινας. while
φαιδρόνους might either express the outward semblance of joy, or that real
joy which the designing murderess felt in the prospect of her vengeance.

(3) The phrase τεύξεται κακῇ τύχῃ, though poor as English, is not so in
Greek idiom, the emphasis falling entirely on the epithet κακῇ.   See 1413,
αἰνεῖς ... κακὸν αἶνον.   We saw some difficulty in the accus. οἷα, but as
this case sometimes occurs with τυγχάνειν in Homer, considering also the
distance from its verb, the objection seemed not insuperable.

The lines, as read by Tyrwhitt and Madvig, are as follows, their
changes being marked by asterisks: λείξασα is Tyrwhitt's conj., the rest
are Madvig's.

> νεῶν τ᾽ ἔπαρχος Ἰλίου τ᾽ ἀναστάτης
> οὐκ οἶδεν *οἷα γλῶσσα *μισήτης κυνὸς
> *λείξασα κἀκτείνασα *φαιδρὸν οὖς,* δίκην
> Ἄτης λαθραίου, *δήξεται κακῇ τύχῃ.

In English:

> 'he, the fleet's captain, Ilion's wasting conqueror,
> knows not the nature of a wanton hellhound's tongue,
> which licking *first* and stretching out a jocund ear
> shall, as some lurking Ate, bite with dire success'.

These ingenious, and, it must be owned, probable readings, exhibit Clyt.
as a treacherous dog, which, after receiving its master with apparent joy,
by licking his hand and pricking up its ears, takes the first opportunity
to attack and bite him.

That 'a tongue' should lick is in rule: that it should 'stretch out an
ear' and 'bite' are crotchets in language, which may have for their apology
that a wild prophetess speaks, from whom the ' tongue of a dog ' may be
taken for the dog itself.   Equally strange is the parenthetic simile, by which
Aesch. seems to embody an Ate lying in wait to injure as a dog that goes
mad and bites its master.

1166 (a) ἄγαν γ᾽ (β) ἄγαν Bo.
1167 (a) παιδίων (β) παιδείων Schü.
1177 (a) κάρτ᾽ ἄρ᾽ ἂν (β) κάρθ᾽ ὅρον Dind.

Nevertheless, after much thought, we believe that these emendations are right. And what determines this opinion is, that φαιδρὸν οὖς (the admission of which would involve λείξασα at least) obtains an all but decisive support from Aristoph. *Pax.* 150—3:

> ἀλλ᾽ ἄγε, Πήγασε, χώρει χαίρων,
> χρυσοχάλινον πάταγον ψαλίων
> διακινήσας φαιδροῖς ὡσίν.

That the comic poet imitates tragedy here would be obvious, even without the words before, 135,

> οὐκοῦν ἐχρῆν σε Πηγάσου ζεῦξαι πτερόν,
> ὅπως ἐφαίνου τοῖς θεοῖς τραγικώτερος ;

Whence, then, did he take his φαιδροῖς ὡσίν *jocund ears* (so strange an expression), if not from this passage of Aeschylus? We can hardly suppose it occurs elsewhere; and the unmerciful parodist would seize such an ἅπαξ λεγόμενον as he seized ἱππαλεκτρύων *Av.* 800 (see ἱπποκάνθαρος, *Pax* 1581), ἀξύστατος, *Nub.* 1367, and others in the *Frogs.* Οἴα and δήξεται are somewhat less strongly supported, but, when the signs of joy are admitted, the picture is more justly and vigorously completed by the act of biting than by such an expression as τεύξεται.

1177. We dislike all the old readings (including our own) of this troublesome verse which take a gen. χρησμῶν with παρεσκόπεις. But we like almost anything better than what Mr Paley gives in his new edition, ἦ κάρτ᾽ ἀραίων παρεκόπης χρησμῶν ἐμῶν. Hartung, he says, has happily restored παρεκόπης, 'you have missed.' Whence is this meaning obtained, which, if we mistake not, may truly be called παρακεκομμένον, *a spurious coinage,* though its learned inventor may not be παράκοπος, like Io (*Prom.* 596)? Mr Paley says: 'for ἀραίων, the same as ἀρῶν, the fatal import, see inf. 1369.' Thus he renders: 'you have missed the fatal import of my oracles,' ἀραίων becoming virtually a substantive. We deem this notion erroneous, based upon a groundless crotchet of Herm. The place to which he refers is 1338, in our text 1322—3, which he edits τοσῶνδε κρατῆρ᾽ ἐν δόμοις κακῶν ὅδε | πλήσας ἀραίων αὐτὸς ἐκπίνει μολών, where Blomf. reads, rightly, τοσόνδε. Herm. here is pleased to say: ' πλήσας, ἀραίων per se constant. Male jungunt κακῶν πλήσας ἀραίων.' No reason does he assign for this dictum. Mr Paley comes to his support by writing "ἀραίων does not go with κακῶν but stands for ἀρῶν...the poet would (α)   παρεσκόπης   (β) παρεσκόπεις V.

1180 (α)   δυσπαθῆ   (β) δυσμαθῆ Can.

1183 (α)   δίπλους   (β) δίπους V.

1187 (α)   ἐπεύχεται, θήγουσα φωτὶ φάσγανον,

(β)   ἐπεύχεται δέ, φωτὶ θήγουσα ξίφος Ed.

1191 (α)   σὲ   (β) σφὲ Aur., σφώ Ed.

1192 (α)   ἀγαθῷ δ᾽ ἀμείψομαι.

(β)   ἐγὼ δ᾽ ἄμ᾽ ἔψομαι. Herm.

1193 (α)   ἄτην   (β) ἄταις Schü.

rather have said τοσῶνδ᾽ ἀραίων οὗτος ἐν δόμοις κακῶν | κρατῆρα πλήσας."
We can accept the reason as little as the dictum. 'Αραίων is a very emphatic epithet exaggerating the force of κακῶν, and if so, its position is
better after, than before, its substantive. Mr Paley translates : 'so huge
a bowl of evils in the house has this man filled with curses.' He reads
τοσῶνδε (a bowl of *so many* evils) and yet he renders (as if he read τοσόνδε)
'*so huge* a bowl!' But, in either case his version contains its own confutation, and overthrows Hermann's dictum. What is 'a bowl of evils?'
Is it, like a teapot or a water-jug, a vessel specially destined and kept in
the house to hold 'evils?' The idea is too grotesque to be received.
A 'bowl of evils' must mean a 'bowl full of evils.' How then could
Agamemnon fill with 'curses' (or 'fatal imports') a bowl *already full* of
'evils?' Undoubtedly the right translation of 1322—3 is 'so huge a bowl
in the house had this man filled with accursed evils.' For the adj.
ἀραῖος, see 214, 1494. Coming back to 1177, we read with Dindorf ἦ
κάρθ᾽ ὅρον παρεσκόπεις χρησμῶν ἐμῶν, 'verily you quite misconceived the
purport of my oracles.'

1186—1188. These lines are difficult. Herm. and Mr Paley follow F.,
reading ἐνθήσειν for ἐνθήσει without period after κότῳ. We prefer the old
reading, with some correction in 1188. Cassandra seems to speak here as
if her death preceded that of Agamemnon, and there is nothing to determine the order of these acts. But probably it is implied that Clytaemnestra committed the execution of Cassandra to Aegisthus or some other
agent, while she was engaged in the murder of Agamemnon. Ὡς δὲ...
'like a woman preparing a poison she will infuse into her wrath a requital
of me also :' i. e. while she requites Agam. for the slaughter of Iphigeneia,
she will requite him also for the introduction of me, his paramour, into the
house. In the next line probably φάσγανον is a gloss for ξίφος, and the
line should be ἐπεύχεται δέ, φωτὶ θήγουσα ξίφος. A scribe altered it who
did not see the length of α before ξ.

1195 (a) δέ με (β) δ' ὅμως Ed.
1196 (a) μέτα (β) μ' ἔτλη Ed.
1197 (a) ἐχθρῶν οὐ (β) ἐχθρῶν τ' οὐ Ed.
1203 (a) κοπείσης (β) *κοπείσῃ
1211 (a) κάτοικος (β) κάτοικτος Scal.
1213 (a) εἶχον (β) εἶλον Musgrave.
1216 (a) τὰς λέγω (β) τάσδ' ἐγὼ Aur. Can.
1224 (a) χρόνῳ πλέω. (β) χρόνον πλέω. Herm.
1234 (a) φόβον (β) φόνον Aur. Can.
1242 (a) ἀλλ' ὡς θανούσῃ (β) ἄλλως· θανούσῃ Herm.
1247 (a) ἢ (β) οὐ Herm.
1249 (a) ἐμοῖς (β) φίλων Ed.
1250 (a) ἐχθροῖς—τοῖς ἐμοῖς.
     (β) ἐχθροὺς—τὸν φόνον Ed.

1195—1197. All attempts to construe the uncorrected codd. are merely absurd : ἐποπτεύσας δὲ has no construction, and μετὰ | φίλων is monstrous. For μετὰ Hermann badly reads μέγα, and for μάτην the amazing word μάτηρ. Our corrections are very slight and give excellent sense.

1191. σφὼ μὲν. We now read σφώ, the dual accus. of σύ, rather than σέ, which we much dislike after such words as καὶ σκῆπτρα καὶ μαντεῖα περὶ δέρῃ στέφη.

1249—1251. We have restored this text to its original purity from a state of foul corruption. The words in codd. are :

ἡλίῳ δ' ἐπεύχομαι
πρὸς ὕστατον φῶς, τοῖς ἐμοῖς τιμαόροις
ἐχθροῖς φονεῦσι τοῖς ἐμοῖς τίνειν ὁμοῦ
δούλης θανούσης εὐμαροῦς χειρώματος.

Our restoration is

ἡλίῳ δ' ἐπεύχομαι
πρὸς ὕστατον φῶς, τοῖς φίλων τιμαόροις
ἐχθροὺς φονεῦσι τὸν φόνον τίνειν ὁμοῦ
δούλης θανούσης εὐμαροῦς χειρώματος.

The emendation of this passage is founded on a logical process, which to our own mind is conclusive. Assuming the corruptness (which is obvious), and then looking for the words in which this lies, our attention is first drawn to the repeated pronoun τοῖς ἐμοῖς, and we see that the scribes, misled by dwelling altogether on l. 1251, imagined

1253 (a) σκιά τις ἀντρέψειεν,

    (β) σκιᾷ τις ἂν πρέψειεν, Con.

1257 (ᾱ) βροτοῖς, (β) βροτοῖσιν, Pauw.

    (α) δακτυλοδεικτῶν (β) δακτυλοδείκτων Schü.

1259 (a) μηκέτι δ' εἰσέλθῃς (β) μηκέτ' ἐσέλθῃς Herm.

1265 (α) ἐπικρανεῖ Fl., ἄγαν ἐπικρανεῖ F.

    (β) ἀπάνευθε κρανεῖ Ed.

that Cassandra speaks throughout of *her own* murderers and *her own* avengers. Hence they thrust in the pronouns, and then, having obscured the meaning of ἐχθρούς, they changed it into ἐχθροῖς, as an epithet of φονεῦσι. Thus they succeeded in depriving τίνειν of an object, ὁμοῦ and the gen. δούλης of all propriety, and the whole passage of a construction. When we come to the work of restoration, we observe these things : (1) the presence of ὁμοῦ and of l. 1251 prove that the avengers are, as Herm. perceived, in the *first* instance, those of Agamemnon, in the *second* only, of Cassandra : (2) we see that τίνειν must have a subject, and that the only way to give it one is to take ἐχθροὺς for that purpose, instead of using the adj. as a stupid epithet to φονεῦσι. (3) We see that τίνειν must have an object, and that this object must take the place of τοῖς ἐμοῖς, while the nature of the case determines it to be either τὸν φόνον or αἷμ' ἐμόν, either of which would be suitable, though we prefer the former. (4) Finally the presence of ἐχθροὺς is sufficient to convince us that its antithetic word φίλων must take the place of the corrupt ἐμοῖς in 1250. Compare 1208, ἄτας τάσδε θριγκώσων φίλοις. By these three emendations we gain a perfect construction and an admirable sense. '*I pray that to the slayers avenging friends* (i.e. to Orestes and Electra avenging their father), *foes* (i.e. Clytaemnestra and Aegisthus) *may at the same time atone for the slaughter of a female slave who died an easy conquest.*'

For comparison with this reasoned commentary, thoughtful scholars may compare the guesses of Hermann, and the note of Mr Paley, which roams from surmise to surmise without any conclusion.

1265—1266. The constitution of this place is difficult. Of the three codd. containing it F. has ἄγαν ἐπικρανεῖ, V., Fl. have ἐπικρανεῖ without ἄγαν. Herm. thinks ἄγαν was added by Triclinius, in order to form a dimeter, which it does not effect. On the other hand Fl. is very prone to omit words, perhaps V. also. Voss conjectured ἄταν τε κρανεῖ, which Bl. adopted, thinking that ἄγαν represented something. Herm. reads ἐπικραίνει, and says that ἄλλων θανάτων ποινὰς means 'retribution consisting of other deaths,' i. e. his own death. Mr Paley says the same, but includes

1266 (a) τίς ἂν (β) τίς ποτ' ἂν Ed.
1272 (a) ἂν πως (β) ἂν πως Herm.
1281 (a) τῆς μελλούσης Fl. V., μελλούσης F.
       (β) τῆς μελλοῦς Herm.
1282 (a) πέδον (β) πεδοῖ Herm.

also the (future) death of Clytaemnestra (why does he not add that of
Aegisthus?). This view seems to us very harsh and questionable, when we
see that a gen. dependent on ποινὴν or ποινὰς universally expresses that of
which the penalty *is paid*, not that of which *it consists*. We are therefore
unwilling to accept this view if it can be avoided. Besides which θανὼν
already expresses Agamemnon's death and makes ἄλλων θανάτων the
merest tautology. Again, we do not see why the future ἀποτίσει (1263)
should here have passed into a present ἐπικραίνει, when the death of
Agamemnon is not only a future contingency, but one which the Chorus
cannot at this moment picture to itself as present. Cassandra, indeed, had
said, 'Αγαμέμνονός σέ φημ' ἐπόψεσθαι μόρον, but Cassandra was a prophetess
doomed to be disbelieved, and the Chorus repel her prophecy with horror.
In these anapaests, therefore, though they express a disturbed and anxious
mind, which entertains the possibility (on the point of being realised) of
the king's death, we nevertheless regard the future κρανεῖ of codd. as far
more suitable, and therefore more probable than the present κραίνει. These
combined considerations lead us to entertain a conjecture which (if it can
be received) will avoid all the objections above stated. The reading which
occurs to us as possible, and well worth considering, is

ποινὰς
ἄλλων θανάτων ἀπάνευθε κρανεῖ,

This gives, as a translation of the words from νῦν δ' to κρανεῖ, 'but now, if
he is to repay the blood of former victims, and for the dead by dying to
complete retribution without other deaths,' i. e. without being himself
guilty of murder : for the Chorus do not here regard the sacrifice of Iphigeneia as a crime demanding retribution. The adverbial preposition ἀπάνευθε (=ἄνευ, as ἀπάτερθε=ἄτερ) is an Homeric word, but no doubt Aesch.
could use it in anapaests. This supposes that ἀπάνευθε κρανεῖ had been
corrupted into ἄγαν ἐπικρανεῖ, and that the transposition of ἄλλων and
ποινὰς was the result of a false conception of the sense at a later time.

1266. We are now satisfied to correct this verse by merely inserting
ποτ',

τίς ποτ' ἂν εὔξαιτο βροτῶν ἀσινεῖ

the rhythm corresponding to that of 1265.

1287 (a) κτείνοντες (β) τείνοντες Can.
1293 (a) μυθοῦσθαι (β) μυθεῖσθαι Pal.
1300 (a) πημονὴν ἀρκύστατον
     (β) πημονῆς ἀρκύστατ' ἂν Aur. Elm.
1303 (a) νίκης. νείκης Heath. (β) εὐχῆς Ed.
1306 (a) ἀμύνασθαι (β) ἀμύνεσθαι V.
1308 (a) περιστοιχίζων, Fl. (β) περιστιχίζω, F.
1309 (a) οἰμώγμασιν (β) οἰμωγμάτοιν Elm.
1310 (a) αὐτοῦ (β) αὐτοῦ Schü. (?).
1316—17 (a) Διὸς νότῳ | γᾶν εἰ
     (β) διοσδότῳ | γάνει Pors.
1322 (a) τοσῶνδε (β) τοσόνδε Bl.
1336 (a) ἀπέταμες (β) ἀπέταμές τ' Ed.
1337 (a) ἄπολις (β) ἀπόπολις Seid.
1341 (a) τόδ' (β) τότ' Voss.
1345 (a) θρηκίων τε λημμάτων.
     (β) θρηκίων ἀημάτων. Can.
1346 (a) χρὴ (β) χρῆν Pors.
1356—7 (a) εὖ πρέπει | ἀντίετον Fl., εὐπρέπειαν | τίετον
     V., εὖ πρέπει | ἀτίετον F.
     (β) ἐμπρέπειν | ἀτίετον Herm. al.
1359 (a) τύμμα τύμμα τῖσαι.

1303. νίκης. This ms. reading is kept by Mr Paley. He explains 'the victory as that which Agamemnon gained over Clytaemnestra by the sacrifice of their daughter Iphigeneia.' Those who have read the first Ode in this play, belonging to the Parodos, will hardly wish to call that event *a victory* gained by Agamemnon. Therefore νείκης, *quarrel*, is a better reading, though not thoroughly satisfactory. We suspect that Aesch. wrote εὐχῆς, *vow*—meaning a vow which Clyt. made ten years before, to avenge her daughter's death. See 1459—1460.

1320. We now read with Stanley εἰ δ' ἦν, πρεπόντως ὥστ' ἐπισπένδειν νεκρῷ, 'were it possible to pour libations over a dead man with decency.'

1322—3. See note above on 1177 respecting ὁραίων.

1336, 1337. ἀπέδικες. Mr Paley accepts the notion of those who remove the interrogation after ἀρὰς and place it after ἀπέδικες. We cannot follow him.—The triple ἀπὸ in composition convinces us that ἀπέδικες, ἀπέταμες, ἀπόπολις, are closely joined, supplying a 'lusus verborum.'

(β) τύμμα τύμματι τῖσαι. Voss, Pors.

1363 (a) ἐμπατεῖ (β) ἐμπατεῖν Herm.

1367 (a) λυμαντήριος (β) post hunc v. intercidisse alterum
        verisimile est, qualis sit

        ἀνήρ, ὁ πασῶν ἐκφανὴς ἰδεῖν στρατῷ Ed.

1371 (a) ναυτίλων (β) ναυτίλοις Herm.

1372 (a) ἱστοτριβής. (β) ἰσοτριβής. Pauw.

1375 (a) τοῦδ' (β) τῷδ' Herm.

1376 (a) εὐνῆς (β) εὐναῖς Ed.

1382 (a) καὶ πολλά (β) καὶ πολύ γε Ed.

1384 (a) ἰὼ παρανόμους (β) ἰὼ ἰὼ παράνους Herm.

1388—91 De Strophe γ' quae corrupta est et mutila cf. Not.

1398 (a) ἐμπίπτεις (β) ἐμπίτνεις Can.

— (a) διφνεῖσι (β) διφυίοισι Herm.

1400 (a) κράτος ἰσόψυχον
      (β) κράτος τ' ἰσόψυχον Herm.

1401 (a) καρδία δηκτὸν (β) καρδιόδηκτον Abr.

1402 (a) ἐπὶ δὲ (β) ἴδ' ἐπὶ Ed.

1367, 1368. That corruption exists here appears from the adj. λυμαν-τήριος, which has no masc. substantive to agree with. We would not conjecture λυμαντὴρ ὅδε, which after τῆσδε would be inelegant. We therefore think a line is lost, such as we have suggested.

1371. We kept ναυτίλων in our first edition. But now we cannot resist the superior claim of Hermann's conjecture ναυτίλοις.

1388—1391. Mr Paley justly says that it is hardly worth while to try to emend lines so corrupt and so devoid of context as this nominal strophe γ'. He has however made an attempt to do so, which we cannot accept, as it proposes δόμοισῖν in correspondence with λάπτων. We should also wish to keep the phrase δι' αἷμ' ἄνιπτον, before which we suppose something lost. The following may be suggested as possible:

> καὶ †πολύμναστον ἐπηνθίσω
> Πλεισθενίδαισι μίασμα† δι' αἷμ' ἄνιπτον,
> τάν τ' ἔριν, ἃ δόμοισιν
> τότ' ἦν ἄδματος, ἀνδρὸς οἰζύς.

This implies that in antistr. γ' a lost line must be indicated, answering to καὶ πολύμναστον ἐπηνθίσω. The other three severally correspond.

1402—1404. For ἐπὶ δὲ we suggest ἴδ' ἐπὶ with comma at κρατύνεις.

1403 (a) σταθεὶς (β) σταθεῖσ' Herm.

      (a) ἐννόμος Fl. V., ἐκνίμως F. (β) ἐκνόμοις Ed.

1404 (a) lacuna (β) νόμοις Ed.

1409 (a) νείρει (β) νείρᾳ Cas.

1411 (a) οἴκοις τοῖσδε (β) ἐν μελάθροις Ed.

1440 (a) δὲ καὶ (β) δίκαν Bu.

1441 (a) προσβαίνων (β) προβαίνων Can.

1456—7 (a) τὴν πολύκλαυτόν τ' Ἰφιγένειαν

          ἀνάξια δράσας

      (β) τὴν πολύκλαυτον ἀνάξια δράσας

          Ἰφιγένειαν Weise.

1457 (a) ἄξια πάσχων (β) πάσχων ἄξια Ed.

1462 (a) εὐπάλαμνον μέριμναν

      (β) εὐπαλάμων μεριμνᾶν Eng.

1465 (a) ψεχὰς (β) ψαχὰς Bl.

1466 (β) δίκη (δίκα) (β) δίκην (δίκαν) Bl.

      (a) θήγει (β) θηγάνει Herm.

1477 (a) ἐπιτύμβιος αἶνος (β) ἐπιτύμβιον αἶνον St.

1482 (a) κάππεσε, κάτθανε (β) κάππεσεν, ἡμεῖς Pal.

1484 (a) Ἰφιγένειαν ἵν' (β) Ἰφιγένειά νιν Jac.

1488 (a) χεῖρα (β) χεῖρε Pors.

1492 (a) μίμνει (β) μένει Ed.

1494 (a) ῥᾶον (β) ἀραῖον Herm.

1495 (a) προσάψαι. (β) πρὸς ἄτᾳ. Bl.

1496 (a) ἐνέβη (β) ἐνέβης Can.

In the following line ἐκνύοις for ἐκνόμως, and νόμοις to fill up the antistrophe. 'O demon, that fallest heavy on the houses and double-raced
children of Tantalus, and by dint of women exercisest an equal-souled
sway, heart-stinging to me, behold, perched on the corpse before me like
a hateful crow, she boasts to chant a hymn in ill-tuned strains?'

1411. It is clear that οἴκοις τοῖσδε comes from a marginal gloss: and
the metre of antistr. ὡς μὲν ἀναίτιος εἶ suggests either οἰκονόμον, which we
wrote in the first edition, or ἐν μελάθροις, perhaps better.

1456, 1457. If we changed our reading here, it would be to substitute

        τὴν πολυκλαύτην Ἰφιγένειαν

        δοάσας ἔκδικα πάσχων ἄξια

1504—6 (a) μοι δ' | ἀλληλοφόνους | μανίας μελάθρων
(β) μοι | μανίας μελάθρων | ἀλλ. Erf.

1515 (a) αὐτοῦ τ' (β) αὐτοῦ δ' Elm.

1519 (a) αὐτοῦ (β) αὐτός Bl.

1524 (a) ἔθρυπτ' (β) ἔκρυπτ' Tyr.

1525 (a) ἄσημα δ' αὐτῶν (β) hic excidisse videtur aliquid
huiusmodi ;

μόρια τῷ δυσδαίμονι | φαγεῖν ἔπεμψ'· ὁ δ' Ed.

1528 (a) ἂν. πίπτει (β) ἀμπίπτει Can.

(a) ἐρῶν, (β) ἐμῶν, Aur.

1530 (a) ἀρᾷ (β) ἀρὰν Abr. Herm.

1504—6. Here codd. give

βαιὸν ἐχούσῃ πᾶν ἀπόχρη μοι δ'
ἀλληλοφόνους
μανίας μελάθρων ἀφελούσῃ.

It is manifest that the scribes, knowing the law of anapaestic rhythm
(συνάφεια) which precludes the hiatus μοι—ἀλληλοφόνους, foisted in the
unmeaning δ' to save the metre. Herm. for μοι δ' reads τάσδ', which
weakens the expression. We, casting out δ', transpose, as Erf., μανίας
μελάθρων and ἀλληλοφόνους, observing how often in the mss. of Aesch.
words are dislocated. Canter's reading καλληλοφόνους, edited by Klausen,
must not be forgotten. It is specious, and so tenable that, were it in
codd., we would not alter it. But we prefer the transposition, as giving
the hypothetical sense, 'I am content with less wealth, *if I shall have
removed*' &c.

1519. We are not fully satisfied with αὐτοῦ, which seems superfluous,
while αὐτός, Blomfield's reading, stands in effective contrast to the children
whose blood was spilt.

1525—6. The obscure manner in which Thyestes here becomes the
subject, without name or pronoun to mark the change from Atreus, as well
as the jingling concurrence αὐτῶν αὐτίκ', assures us that words are lost.
Aesch. may have written to this effect :

ἄσημα δ' αὐτῶν †μόρια τῷ δυσδαίμονι
φαγεῖν ἔπεμψ'· ὁ δ'† αὐτίκ' ἀγνοίᾳ λαβὼν κ.τ.λ.

1530. We now agree with Hermann and Paley in reading ἀρὰν, and
we take συνδίκως to be an Aeschylean adverb for σὺν δίκῃ, which he may
have written : 'making, with full justice, his kicking-down of the dinner-
table (the symbol of) a curse, that even so &c.'

1534 (a) ὄντα μ' ἐπὶ δέκ' (β) ἐπὶ τοῖνδ' ὄντα μ' Ed.
1550 (a) δεσμὸν Fl. V. (β) δεσμὸς F. Vict.
1553 (a) πήσας (β) πταίσας Bu., παίσας Pal.
1554—5 (a) γύναι, σὺ τοὺς ἥκοντας ἐκ μάχης νέον
         οἰκουρὸς εὐνὴν ἀνδρὸς αἰσχύνουσ' ἅμα
      (β) εὐνὴν σὺ τοῦδ' οἰκουρὸς αἰσχύνας ἅμα
         γυναικὶ τοὺς ἥκοντας ἐκ μάχης τρέων Ed.
1556 (a) τόνδ' ἐβούλευσας μόρον.
      (β) τ' αἰσχρὸν ἔρραψας φόνον Ed.
1560 (a) ἠπίοις (β) νηπίοις Jac.
1563 (a) οὐκ (β) οὐδ' Pal.
1566 (a) ἢ (β) ἢ Pors.
1570 (a) νότῳ (β) σκότῳ Aur.
1572 (a) τί (β) σὺ Ed.
1578 (a) καὶ (β) κοὐ Herm.
1579 (a) lacuna.
      (β) οὐ γάρ, εἰ γέροντές ἐσμεν, τοῖς κακοῖς ὑπείξομεν Ed.
1582 (a) κἀγὼ μὴν (β) μὴν κἀγὼ Pors.
1583 (a) ἐρούμεθα. (β) αἱρούμεθα. Aur.
1584 (a) δράσομεν (β) δράσωμεν Vict.
1585 (a) ὁ ἔρος (β) θέρος Schü.
1586 (a) δ' ἅλις γ' (β) ἅλις γ' Ed.
      (a) ὕπαρχε—ἠματώμεθα.
      (β) ὑπάρχει—αἱματώμεθα Aur.
1587 (a) στείχετε δ' οἱ γέροντες

1534. We read for this line, believing ἐπὶ δέκ' to be corrupt,

τρίτον γὰρ ἐπὶ τοῖνδ' ὄντα μ' ἀθλίῳ πατρὶ

1554—1556. Our reading of this passage contains, in the first two lines, all the ms. words, emended and replaced, but with τοῦδε for ἀνδρὸς and τρέων for νέον, ἀνδρὸς and νέον being manifestly corrupt. In 1556 we have suggested τ' αἰσχρὸν ἔρραψας φόνον chiefly to avoid the recurrence of the same phrase within a few lines. See 1563.

1579. The line, which we have suggested in the place where a verse is lost, represents, we believe unobjectionably, what Aeschylus might have written.

(β) στεῖχε καὶ σὺ χοῖ γέροντες Fr.

1588 (a) καιρὸν χρῆν (β) ἀρκεῖν χρῆν Herm.

1589 (a) τῶν δ᾽ ἅλις γ᾽ ἐχοίμεθ᾽ ἄν

(β) τῶνδ᾽ ἅλις, δεχοίμεθ᾽ ἄν Mar.

1593 (a) δαίμονας (β) δαίμονος Cas.

1594 (a) ἁμαρτῆτον κρατοῦντα

(β) ἁμαρτεῖν, τὸν κρατοῦντά Cas.

θ᾽ ὑβρίσαι add. Bl.

1601 (a) θαρρῶν (β) θαρσῶν Pors.

(a) ὥσπερ (β) ὥστε Scal.

1602 (a) deest pes in fine. (β) ἐγὼ suppl. Heath

1603 (a) deest pes in fine. (β) καλῶς suppl. Can.

1603. This Conspectus shows that the editor has received about 286 corrections of the ms. text made by other scholars, and 134 for which his own judgment is responsible; the latter including 16 suggested additions which supply good poetic sense in places manifestly defective. These additions are in the text itself carefully distinguished from the adjoining context. The editor admits that many of his emendations are of an unusually bold character in places which seemed to him to require the ἄκος τομαῖον. If he is censured, as by some he probably will be, for undue audacity, he can only reply, ἀλλ᾽ εἰ τὸ κάλλος ἐξέσωσ᾽ οὔ μοι μέλει. His endeavour has been to exhibit such a text of this noblest Greek drama, as the scholar may read or the actor recite without having to flounder through many a puddle of grammatical, logical and metrical corruption. If he has done this, he is content: if he has failed to do it, his failure is complete.

APPENDED NOTES ON INTERPRETATION.

80. Τό θ' ὑπέργηρων. Mr Paley (Ed. 4, l. 79), editing ὅ θ' ὑπέργηρως, the conjecture of Franz, says in his note: 'the preservation of the termination in ως is in favour of Franz's emendation': alluding to the corrupt readings of most codd. τιθιπεργήρως, τόθιπερ γήρως, while Cod. F. has τόθ' ὑπέργηρων. But it is not surprising that scribes should corrupt γήρων into γήρως, being familiar with the words γῆρας, γήραος, γήρως. The τ with which all begin would be very surprising, if it did not represent an original reading τό. There could be nothing else suggestive of that letter at the beginning of their corrupt word. This argument is decisive in favour of τό θ' ὑπέργηρων[1]. See also note on *Consp. Lect.*

542. Νικώμενος λόγοισιν οὐκ ἀναίνομαι. Mr Paley's note here (566) by rendering 'I do not reject or disdain the feeling of joy,' seems to suggest that ἀναίνομαι requires an accus. object to be mentally supplied. This would be an error. The verb, like αἰσχύνομαι, admits three constructions (1) accus., (2) infin. as 1582, (3) participle, as here, οὐκ ἀναίνομαι νικώμενος. So Bl. Gloss. 'cum participio loquentis construitur. Eurip. *Iphig. A.* 1512, θανοῦσα δ' οὐκ ἀναίνομαι. *Herc. F.* 1235, εὖ δράσας δέ σ' οὐκ ἀναίνομαι.'

859—862. We regret, on every ground, that in his 4th edition (904—907) Mr Paley should persist in combating the

---

[1] We also think that the abstract expression τό θ' ὑπέργηρων comes in sequence to ὅ τε γὰρ νεαρὸς μυελὸς with far more fitness and probability than the concrete ὅ θ' ὑπέργηρως. Our emendation οὔ τις ἀρείων for οὐδὲν ἀρείων, gets rid of the only grave objection to τό θ' ὑπέργηρων.

interpretation of these lines, which we gave in the *Journal of Philology*, and repeat in this edition; and that he should substitute a version, which the logic and context of the place, the laws of language and taste, and the facts of Greek archaeology concur in rebutting. A thoughtful student of the Greek drama cannot suppose that Clytaemnestra in this στιχομυθία merely resumes an entreaty which she had made already (ἔκβαιν' ἀπήνης τῆσδε κ.τ.λ. 834), and which Agamemnon had answered with a reasoned denial, 846 κ.τ.λ. She returns indeed to the charge, but it is by a questioning ἔλεγχος that she now tries to carry her point, and this change of form is introduced and indicated by the transitional particles καὶ μήν¹, *well now.* Mr Paley renders τόδ' εἰπὲ μὴ παρὰ γνώμην ἐμοί, 'do speak on this matter not contrary to my will'—wrongly in all but μὴ παρά. Εἰπὲ τόδε cannot mean what he gives, nor anything but (with ἐμοί) 'tell me this (which I am going to ask),' i.e. 'answer me this question.' Γνώμην ought not to be rendered 'will': it means '*opinion*' or '*judgment.*' Again μὴ παρὰ γνώμην ἐμοὶ is bad Greek in the sense 'not against my opinion.' Aesch. had already given the true Greek for this phrase, as well as the true sense of γνώμην, in *Suppl.* 448, γένοιτο δ' εὖ παρὰ γνώμην ἐμήν, 'may it turn out well contrary to my opinion.'

Evidently Clytaemnestra says: *well now* (καὶ μὴν) εἰπὲ τόδε ἐμοί *tell me this* μὴ παρὰ γνώμην *not contrary to your opinion*, i.e. give me a sincere answer to this question: or, as it stands in our verse translation,

'Well now, thy true thought not evading, answer me.'

Coming to the next line, we have Agamemnon replying

γνώμην μὲν ἴσθι μὴ διαφθεροῦντ' ἐμέ.

¹ We find καὶ μὴν 20 times used by Aeschylus; here alone with an imperative; and we doubt whether all Greek literature will supply a second example of such use. It is manifestly due here to nothing but the necessity of στιχομυθία, which required an introductory line before the actual question.

Which Mr Paley renders: 'as for will, be assured that I am not the man to alter mine for the worse.' We could proceed on his lines here, only correcting his renderings of γνώμην and διαφθεροῦντα. We could write: 'as for opinion, be assured that I am not the man to misstate mine.' Διαφθείρω can take the sense given by Mr Paley: it can equally well take the sense we give. And ours is right, because we cannot suppose that Aesch. means Agamemnon simply and brutally to reply here: 'I am not the man to change my will, I can tell you.' His language is the sentiment of a true gentleman: 'be sure I will say what I really think.' Mr Paley seems to suppose he has found an argument against our view when he says 'the pronoun (ἐμὲ) is clearly emphatic.' But it is used with exactly as much emphasis in our rendering as in his[1]. In our verse translation it stands:

'My true thought be assured I shall not falsify.'

Then Clyt. puts her first question:

ηὖξω θεοῖς δείσας ἂν ὧδ' ἔρδειν τάδε;

Mr Paley does not edit this as a question. He prints it with a full stop, though it finds a manifest reply (εἰδώς γε) from Agam., and is followed up by an undoubted question in the next speech of Clyt. Yet he himself gives the question-form as an alternative in his note; thereby showing that the right

[1] Let us say a few words here about the pronominal forms ἐμοῦ, ἐμοί, ἐμέ. It seems to be often assumed (because there exist μου, μοι, με, which as enclitics are, *eo nomine*, less emphatic) that ἐμοῦ, ἐμοί, ἐμέ are therefore always essentially emphatic. This is an error: and the proof is, that they gain emphasis by an appended γε. They are no more emphatic than their first person ἐγώ or their congeners σοῦ, σοί, σέ. In short their more or less emphasis, or indifference, depends on their position relatively to other words: and a poet, swayed by the claims of metre, will often place them for convenience where some may suppose an emphasis to be designed. Such we believe to be the case with ἐμοί in 859. Aesch. would willingly have written εἰπέ μοι τόδε. 'Εμοί falling to the close gains some force and goes near to represent our idiomatic 'please,' or 'pray.'

version to his mind is doubtful. To our mind it is not doubtful in the smallest particular. But let us hear Mr Paley.

906. 'You would have vowed to the gods to act thus in a time of fear,'
i.e. you are pursuing a course more like one in peril than a victor....Or
interrogatively: ' Did you make a vow to the gods that you would so act (ὅτι
ὧδε ἔρδοις ἄν) in a time of fear?'

Of these two widely divergent renderings we could not
have been 'happy with either' were the other away. They
both imply something novel in archaeology, that a Greek
warrior in a dangerous crisis of battle could make a vow to
some god or gods, that, if rescued and victorious, *he would not*
on returning home *walk on purple tapestry to his palace.* What?
Are we anywhere told that Greek warriors in time of danger
vowed to the gods *that they would refrain from doing something?* Do we not read everywhere, that their vows were *to do
something involving expenditure*, to offer victims, to build shrines,
or, as here, to walk on purple embroideries in honour of the
propitious deity? This certainty sets aside both Mr Paley's
suggestions. The former, if made interrogative, by writing
'Would you' instead of 'you would,' becomes correct. The
second is on every ground wrong. (1) That the words ηὔξω
ἂν δείσας are to be taken together is certain (see ἂν ηὐξάμην
891). (2) The nature of the question suggested by Mr Paley
carries its own confutation with it. Could any one be supposed
to *make a vow, that, if a dangerous crisis occurred, he would
not walk on purple after being saved?* We render in our verse
translation:

'Would'st thou in fear have vowed unto the gods
    such act?'

i.e. 'would you in some fearful crisis have vowed that you
would do the thing I am now inviting you to do?' Clyt.
herself afterwards says (891) 'I would have vowed the treading
under foot of many a broidered cloth, if an oracle had declared
such expenditure to be the necessary ransom of your life.'

Agamemnon's reply stands in codd. thus:

εἴπερ τις εἰδώς γ' εὖ τόδ' ἐξεῖπον τέλος,

where τόδε τέλος, '*this performance,*' means '*this vow,*' my future execution of what I promised. We have, without hesitation, edited ἐξειπεῖν for ἐξεῖπον, and our verse translation is

'Yes, skilled as well as any man to speak this vow,'

i. e. 'nobody knew better than I, as an experienced commander, when the time was come to proclaim aloud a vow such as this.' Mr Paley edits ἐξεῖπεν and annotates thus:

907. εἴπερ τις—γε must, it seems, stand for εἴπερ γέ τις, the γε having no other meaning in this position. It follows that for ἐξεῖπον we must read ἐξεῖπεν, 'if any one ever did make this vow with a knowledge of what would befall him.' He means that he did not make such a vow, because a knowledge of the future was impossible; a sentiment very appropriate to the present position.

This remarkable note might perhaps be left to the judgment of most Greek scholars without further notice. As we write, however, for learners of every grade, we will simply observe:

(1) γε emphasises the word which it follows, and may happen to stand in almost any part of the sentence. It is habitually used in replies, emphasising the word to which it is joined as important in such reply. Thus in Plato, φῂς ἢ οὔ; πάνυ γε. Eurip. *Hec.* 246. H. ἤψω δὲ γονάτων τῶν ἐμῶν ταπεινὸς ὤν; Ul. ὥστ' ἐνθανεῖν γε σοῖς πέπλοισι χεῖρ' ἐμήν. Thus, if the answer is affirmative, γε is properly rendered '*yes*'. So we render it here; and its right place is after εἰδώς. Εἴπερ τις is an adverbial phrase further strengthening the affirmation εἰδώς γ' εὖ, 'knowing well, if anybody (does know well)' = knowing as well as anybody. This phrase might naturally stand after 'εἰδώς γ' εὖ, but, as metre required it to precede, Aesch. so placed it with perfect right.

(2) As to the suggestion that εἴπερ γέ τις is the true construction, we read it with surprise; but we merely reply

that in no place of any Greek author (as we firmly believe) will the phrase εἴπερ τις be found so divided by γε. Obviously our version implies that ηὐξάμην ἄν is to be mentally supplied as the principal verb of this sentence. Clyt. had asked, ' Would you have vowed' &c.? Agam. replies, ' Yes, I would have vowed, knowing as well as any man how to do so.' As to Mr Paley's final words, ' He means' &c., we leave them to the consideration of logical interpreters. They make Agam. to say, ' He did *not* address a vow to the gods, that he would *not* walk on purple, because a knowledge of the future was impossible' ! And 'that sentiment' Mr Paley considers 'very appropriate to the present position.' We cannot agree.

Quitting this painful discussion, which nothing but the regard due to our younger readers would have prevailed on us to insert, we refer them, for the just view of this στιχομυθία, to the analysis of Epeisodion III., which they will find on p. 96.

1554—1556. Admitting that our restoration of this marvellously corrupt passage is extensive and apparently bold, we firmly believe it to be correct in the main (as regards 1554, 1555), allowing the final words of 1556 to be a purely conjectural improvement. As to γύναι with which codd. start, we say that it is simply ridiculous to suppose that the queen is here addressed. She cannot be supposed present before the place where she speaks.

1557—1561.

καὶ ταῦτα τἄπη κλαυμάτων ἀρχηγενῆ·
'Ορφεῖ δὲ γλῶσσαν τὴν ἐναντίαν ἔχεις·
ὁ μὲν γὰρ ἦγε πάντ' ἀπὸ φθογγῆς χαρᾷ,
σὺ δ' ἐξορίνας νηπίοις ὑλάγμασιν
ἄξει· κρατηθεὶς δ' ἡμερώτερος φανεῖ.

In this speech Aegisthus replies to the upbraidings of the Chorus thus : ' For these words again you will smart hereafter. The tongue of Orpheus is the converse of yours. He dragged all things in the wake of his song for joy , you for the provocation of your silly howlings will be dragged (to prison): and under that control you will show yourself a tamer creature.'

Here Mr Paley annotates:

1609. ἄξει appears to be the middle voice,—'You forsooth, after irritating people by your senseless barkings, think to lead them to your own purposes.' But Prof. Kennedy, with Peile and Butler, supposes the antithesis to be this,—'he led captive by his songs, you shall *be* led captive (δεσμὸς, v. 1599) in consequence of your insolence.' The poet however merely speaks of the γλῶσσα ἐναντία, or two opposite kinds of eloquence, viz. that which soothed and that which irritated. The object of both was the same, but the latter was a mistaken way to effect it.

When Mr Paley cites Butler and Peile along with ourselves as taking ἄξει for a middle-passive, *you will be dragged,* he has omitted to say that Pauw, Voss, Conington, Plumptre, Nägelsbach, Jenisch, Enger, Linwood, &c., do the same : while Hermann, Blomfield, Scholefield, Bothe, Dindorf, Weil, Karsten, Keck, Van Heusde, who are silent about ἄξει, must be ranked on the same side. For, if they had taken the view of Klausen and Mr Paley, they must have said so, and have written in its defence. Few scholars will for a moment doubt, that the 'iusta interpretatio,' declared rightly by Karsten to be 'fundamentum critices,' points with unerring finger to the fact, that ἄξει, middle future, is here used in a passive sense. 'Απάγειν in Attic procedure was the technical word for 'arresting or committing to prison:' and ἄξει here = ἀπάξει or ἀπαχθήσει. The word ἡμερώτερος is used in allusion to the wild beasts tamed by Orpheus : 'mulcentem tigres' Verg.

1569. ζεύξω βαρείαις, und. ζεύγλαις. οὔτι μὴ σειραφόρον κριθῶντα πῶλον, *far from being a trace-harnessed high-fed colt.* The σειραῖος or σειραφόρος ἵππος of a chariot resembled the leader in a modern 'tandem.' It was attached by traces to the chariot, and would often be a young and spirited animal, whose function was to pull on and quicken the yoked pair. Hence it is spoken of as κριθῶντα (κριθάω), *barley-fed,* i.e. *high-fed.*

CONSPECTUS METRORUM
CHORICORUM.

1. For general information on this subject, the student is referred to Linwood's 'Greek Tragic Metres.' There, or in any equivalent treatise on the subject, he will find an explanation of the names of the so-called 'Feet,' the laws of Arsis, Thesis and Ictus, as constituting the Rhythm of Verse, those of Metre in general, and of the particular metres used in Greek tragic composition. With this knowledge, he will have no difficulty in reading and comprehending the subjoined metrical exposition of the choric verses in the Agamemnon, with their appended names.

2. As the terms Anacrusis and Basis (Base) often occur, let it be observed that Anacrusis is a syllable, usually short (‿), prefixed to a rhythm of which it does not constitute a part. Anacrusis may also be a long syllable or resolved into two short (‿‿); but either instance is comparatively rare. In

$$\check{\iota} \mid \grave{\omega} \ \gamma\epsilon\nu\epsilon\alpha\grave{\iota} \ \beta\rho\sigma\tau\hat{\omega}\nu$$

ῐ is an anacrusis.

A Base is a disyllabic foot, spondee (– –), iambus (‿ –) or trochee (– ‿), prefixed to a rhythm of which it does not constitute a part. Two feet so prefixed are called a double base. The long syllable of a base may be resolved into two short: thus in

$$\delta\iota' \ \ \check{\epsilon}\rho\iota\nu \mid \alpha\check{\iota}\mu\alpha\tau\acute{o}\epsilon\sigma\sigma\alpha\nu$$

δι' ἔριν is a trochaic base with first syllable resolved.

A verse may have anacrusis and base.

$$\cup \mid -- \mid -\cup-\cup--$$
πα | λιμμή | κη χρόνον τιθεῖσαι

3. Trihemimeris (trihem.)   means 1½ foot (3 half feet).
     Penthemimeris (penthem.)   ,,   2½ feet (5   ,,   ).
     Hephthemimeris (hephthem.) ,,   3½ ,, (7   ,,   ).
The trochaic hephthemimer is a verse of frequent occurrence
in this play.

The Cretic foot $(-\cup-)$ is a trochaic trihemimer.

4. Dipodia (2 feet), tripodia (3 feet), pentapodia (5 feet),
are used to express recurrence of the same foot: thus pentapod. troch. means a sequence of 5 trochees.

A spondee at the close of a line is treated as equivalent to
a trochee in verses to which the latter foot properly belongs,
but such a trochaic verse is called impure.

5. Conspectus.

PARODOS.

Anapaestorum systemata novem; 40—106.

PRO-ODE, 107—150.

στροφή, 107—20.   ἀντιστρ. 121—34.

1. $-\cup\cup \ -\cup\cup \ -\cup\cup \ -\cup\cup \ -\cup\cup \ --$
2. $-\cup\cup \ -\cup\cup \ -\cup\cup \ -\cup\cup \ --$
3. $-- \ --$
4. $-- \mid -\cup\cup \ --$
5. $\cup-\cup- \mid -\cup\cup \ -\cup\cup \ -\cup\cup \ --$
6. $-\cup\cup \ --$
7. $-- \ -\cup\cup \ -\cup\cup \ -\cup\cup$
8. $-\cup\cup \ -- \ -\cup\cup \ -\cup$
9. $-- \ -\cup\cup \ -\cup\cup \ -\cup\cup \ -\cup\cup \ -\cup\cup \ -\cup\cup \ --$
10. $\cup-\cup- \mid -\cup\cup \ -\cup\cup \ -\cup\cup \ --$

11. — — — ◡◡ — ◡
12. — ◡◡ — ◡◡ — ◡◡ — ◡◡ — ◡◡ — —
13. ◡ — ◡ — ◡ — ◡ —
14. — ◡◡ — ◡◡ — ◡◡ — — — —

1 (12). dact. hexam.
2. dact. pentam.
3. spond. dim.
4. bas. spond. † dact. dim.
5 (10). bas. dupl. iamb. † dact. tetram.
6. dact. dim.
7. dact. tetram.
8. dact. tetram. cat.
9. bini dact. tetram.
11. dact. dim. cat.
13. iamb. dim.
14. dact. pentam.

Not. 1. versus 4, 11 bas. (spond. v. troch.) † dact. c. troch. appellatur 'pherecrateus.' Idem versus, si augetur syllaba post troch. ad finem, appellatur glyconeus. Ita latine ap. Horat.

> et te | saepe vocanti (pherecr.)
> duram | difficilis mane (glycon.)

Not. 2. v. 13 disponi potest ut sit anacr. br. † troch. hephthem.

> βλᾰ|βέντα λοισθίων δρόμων.

ἐπῳδός, 135—150.

1. — — ◡ — — — ◡ —
2. ◡ — ◡ — | — ◡◡ — ◡ — —
3. — — — ◡◡ — ◡◡ — —
4. — — | — ◡◡ — ◡ — —
5. — — — — — ◡◡ — —
6. — ◡◡ — ◡◡ — ◡◡ — ◡◡ — ◡
7. ◡ — ◡ — | — ◡◡ — — — ◡
8. — ◡◡ — ◡◡ — ◡◡ — ◡◡ | — ◡◡ — ◡◡ — —
9. — — — ◡◡ — ◡◡ — ◡◡ | — ◡◡ — ◡◡ — —
10. — — — ◡◡ — ◡◡ — — — ◡◡ — —
11. — ◡◡ — ◡◡ — ◡
12. — ◡◡ — ◡◡ — — — — — ◡◡ — —

13. $-\cup\cup$ $--$ $-\cup\cup$ $-\cup\cup$ $-\cup\cup$ $--$
14. $-\cup\cup$ $--$ $-\cup\cup$ $--$ $-\cup\cup$ $--$
15. $-\cup\cup$ $-\cup$
16. $-\cup\cup$ $-\cup\cup$ $-\cup\cup$ $--$ $--$

1. iamb. dim.
2. bas. dupl. iamb. † dact. c. dipodia troch. impur.
3 (5). dact. tetram.
4. bas. sp. † dact. c. dipodia troch. impur.
6. dact. pentam. cat.
7. bas. dupl. iamb. † dact. trim. cat.
8 (9). dact. tetram. † dact. trim.
10 (12, 13, 14). dact. hexam.
11. dact. trim. cat.
15. dact. c. troch.
16. dact. pentam.

ODE, 151—234.

στροφὴ α΄, 151—156. ἀντιστρ. α΄, 157—162.

1. $--$ | $-\cup$ $-\cup$ $-\cup$ $-$
2. $-\cup$ $-\cup$ $-\cup$ $-$
3. $-\cup$ $-\cup$ $-\cup$ $-$
4. $-\cup$ $-\cup$ $-\cup$ $-$ | $-\cup$ $-\cup$ $-\cup$ $-$
5. $-\cup\cup$ $-\cup\cup$ $-\cup\cup$ $-\cup\cup$ $--$
6. $-\cup$ $-\cup$ $-\cup$ $-$

1. bas. spond. † troch. hephthem.
2 (3, 6). troch. hephthem.
4. bini troch. hephthem.
5. dact. pentam.

στροφὴ β΄, 163—168. ἀντιστρ. β΄, 169—174.

1. $-\cup$ $-\cup$ $-\cup$ $-$ | $-\cup$ $-\cup$ $-\cup$ $-$
2. $-\cup$ $-\cup$ $-\cup$ $-$
3. $--$ | $-\cup$ $-\cup$ $-\cup$ $-$
4. $-\cup-$ $-\cup-$ $-\cup-$ | $-\cup$ $-\cup$ $-\cup$ $-$
5. $-\cup$ $-\cup$ $-\cup$ $-\cup$ $-\cup$
6. $-\cup$ $-\cup$ $-\cup$ $-$

1. bini troch. hephthem.
2 (6). troch. hephthem.
3. bas. spond. † troch. hephthem.
4. trini troch. trihem. † troch. hephthem.
5. pentapodia troch.

στροφὴ γ΄, 175—185.　ἀντιστρ. γ΄, 186—196.

1.　∪ – ∪ –　– | ∪ – ∪ –　–
2.　∪ – ∪ –　– | ∪ – ∪ –　–
3.　∪ –　∪ –
4.　∪ – ∪ –　– | ∪ – ∪ –　–
5.　∪ | – –　| – ∪　– ∪　– –
6.　∪ –　– ∪ | – ∪　– –　– ∪　–
7.　∪ –　∪ –　∪ –　(or ∪ | – ∪　– ∪ –)
8.　– ∪ ∪　– ∪　– –
9.　– ∪ ∪　– ∪　– –
10.　– ∪ ∪ – | – ∪ ∪ –
11.　– ∪ ∪ –　– ∪ ∪ –　– ∪ ∪ –　– ∪ ∪ – | – ∪ ∪　– ∪

1 (2, 4). dochm. dupl. (ex bin. iamb. penthem.)
3. dipod. iamb.
5. anacr. br. † bas. sp. † tripod. troch.
6. antispastus † troch. hephthem.
7. tripod. iamb. (=anacr. br. † troch. penthem.)
8 (9). dact. c. dipod. troch.
10. choriamb. dim.
11. choriamb. tetram. † dact. c. dipod. troch.
Not. in v. 6. antispastus exemplo rariori basis duplex est.

στροφὴ δ΄, 197—205.　ἀντιστρ. δ΄, 206—214.

1.　∪ – ∪ –　– | ∪ – ∪ –　–
2.　∪ – ∪ –　– | ∪ – ∪ –　–
3.　∪ | – ∪ ∪͡∪ ∪　– ∪　–
4.　∪ –　∪ –　– | ∪ –　∪ –　–
5.　∪ –　∪ –　– | ∪ –　∪ –　–
6.　∪ | – ∪ ∪͡∪ ∪　– | – ∪　– –
7.　∪ – | – ∪ – ∪　–

8.   − ∪ ∪ − ∪ − ∪ − | − ∪ ∪ − ∪ − −

9.   − ∪ ∪ − ∪ − −

1 (2, 4, 5). dochm. dupl. (ex bin. iamb. penthem.)
3. anacr. br. † troch. hephthem. (secund. p. solut.)
6. anacr. br. † troch. penthem. † dipod. troch. impur.
7. bas. iamb. † troch. penthem.
8. dact. c. troch. penthem. † dact. c. dipod. troch. impur.
10. dact. c. dipod. troch. impur.

στροφὴ ε΄, 215—224.   ἀντιστρ. ε΄, 225—234.

1.   ∪ | − ∪ − − ∪ − − ∪ −
2.   ∪ − ∪ − − | ∪ − ∪ − −
3.   ∪ − ∪ − | − ∪ − −
4.   ∪ | − ∪ − ∪ − ∪ − −
5.   ∪ − ∪ − | − ∪ − ∪ − ∪ −
6.   ∪ | − ∪ − − ∪ −
7.   ∪ − ∪ − − | ∪ − ∪ − −
8.   ∪ | − ∪ − − ∪ − − ∪ − − ∪ −
9.   ∪ − ∪ − − | ∪ − ∪ − −
10. − ∪ ∪ − ∪ − −

1. anacr. br. † trini troch. trihem.
2 (7, 9). dochm. dupl. (ex bin. iamb. penthem.)
3. dipod. iamb. † dipod. troch. impur. (qui versus periodicus est).
4. anacr. br. † troch. dim.
5. bas. dupl. iamb. † troch. hephth.
6. anacr. br. † bini troch. trihem.
8. anacr. br. † quaterni troch. trihem.
10. dact. c. dipod. troch. impur.

Anapaestorum systemata tria, 332—344.

STASIMON I. 345—447.

στροφὴ α΄, 345—359.   ἀντιστρ. α΄, 360—374.

1.   ∪ | − − | − ∪ − ∪ − −
2.   ∪ | − − | − ∪ − ∪ − −
3.   ∪ | − ∪ − ∪ − ∪ − ∪ − −
4.   ∪ | − ∪ − − ∪ − − ∪ −

5. ∪ | − ∪ − − ∪ −
6. ∪ | − ∪ − − ∪ −
7. ∪ | − − | − ∪ −
8. ∪ | − − | − ∪ −
9. ∪ | − − | − ∪ − ∪ − −
10. ∪ | − − | − ∪ − ∪ − −
11. ∪ | − ∪ − − ∪ − − ∪ −
12. − ∪ − ∪ − | − ∪ | − ∪ ∪ − ∪ − −
13. − − | − ∪ ∪ − −
14. − ∪ | − ∪ ∪ − −
15. − − | − ∪ ∪ − ∪ − | − ∪ | − ∪ ∪ − −

1 (2, 9, 10). anacr. br. † bas. spond. † tripod. troch. impur.
3. anacr. br. † pentapodia troch. impur.
4 (11). anacr. br. † trini troch. trihem.
5 (6). anacr. br. † bini troch. trihem.
7 (8). anacr. br. † bas. spond. † troch. trihem.
12. troch. penthem. † bas. troch. † dact. c. dipod. troch. impur.
13. bas. spond. † dact. c. troch. ⎫
14. bas. troch. † dact. c. troch. ⎬ pherecr.
15. bas. spond. † dact. c. troch. trihem. † bas. troch. † dact. c. troch.

Not. v. 15 = glyconeus † pherecrateus. Tribus his vv. 13, 14, 15 similes
sunt tres ultimi in stroph. β′ et γ′.

στροφὴ β′, 375—389.   ἀντιστρ. β′, 390—404.

1. ∪ | − ∪ − − ∪ − − ∪ −
2. ∪ | − ∪ − − ∪ − | − ∪ − ∪ − −
3. ∪ − ∪ − ∪ − ∪ − ∪ −
†   ∪ − ∪ − − | ∪ − ∪ − − †
4. ∪ | − − | − ∪ ⌢∪∪∪ −
5. ∪ − ∪ − ∪ − ∪ − ∪ −
6. ∪ − ∪ − − | ∪ − ∪ − −
7. ∪ − ∪ − | − ∪ − ∪ − ∪ −
8. ∪ − ∪ − | − ∪ − ∪ − ∪ −
9. ∪ | − ∪ − ∪ − | − ∪ − ∪ −
10. − | − ∪ − ∪ − ∪ −
11. ∪ | − ∪ − − ∪ −

12. $-\cup- \mid -\cup\ -\cup\ --$
13. $-- \mid -\cup\cup\ --$
14. $-\cup \mid -\cup\cup\ --$
15. $-- \mid -\cup\cup\ -\cup- \mid -\cup \mid -\cup\cup\ --$

1. anacr. br. † trini troch. trihem.
2. anacr. br. † bini troch. trihem. † tripod. troch. impur.
3. iamb. trim. (puri).
† (6). dochm. dupl. (ex bin. iamb. penthem.)
4. anacr. br. † bas. spond. † troch. penthem. (altero pede soluto).
5. pentapodia iamb.
7 (8). bas. dupl. iamb. † troch. hephthem.
9. anacr. br. † bini troch. trihem.
10. anacr. br. † troch. hephthem.
11. anacr. br. † bini troch. trihem.
12. troch. trihem. † tripod. troch. impur.
13. bas. sp. † dact. c. troch. ⎫
14. bas. tr. † dact. c. troch. ⎬ pherecr.
15. bas. spond. † dact. c. troch. trihem. † bas. tr. † dact. c. troch.

στροφὴ γ′, 405—419.   ἀντιστρ. γ′, 420—434.

1. $\cup \mid -\cup-\ -\cup-\ -\cup-$
2. $-\cup- \mid -\cup\ -\cup\ -\cup-$
3. $\cup \mid -\cup-\ -\cup-$
4. $\cup \mid -\cup-\ -\cup-$
5. $-\cup\ -\cup\ -\cup\ - \mid -\cup\ -\cup\ -\cup\ - \mid -\cup\ -\cup\ -\cup\ -$
6. $\cup \mid -\cup\ -\cup\ -\cup-$
7. $\cup \mid -\cup\ -\cup\ -\cup-$
8. $- \mid -\cup\ -\cup\ -\cup-$
9. $-\cup\cup\ -\cup\ -\cup\ --$
10. $\cup\cup \mid -\cup-\cup--$
11. $\cup\cup \mid -\cup-\cup--$
12. $\cup\cup \mid -\cup--$
13. $-- \mid -\cup\cup\ --$
14. $-- \mid -\cup\cup\ --$
15. $-- \mid -\cup\cup\ -\cup- \mid -\cup \mid -\cup\cup\ --$

1. anacr. br. † trini troch. trihem.
2. troch. trihem. † troch. hephthem.

3 (4). anacr. br. † bini troch. trihem.
5. trini troch. hephthem.
6 (7). anacr. br. † troch. hephthem.
8. anacr. long. † troch. dim.
9 (10, 11). anacr. soluta † tripod. troch. impur.
12. anacr. soluta † dipod. troch. impur.
13 (14). bas. spond. † dact. c. troch.
15. bas. sp. † dact. c. troch. trihem. † bas. tr. † dact. c. troch.

ἐπῳδός, 435—447.

1. ∪ | − ∪ − − ∪ −
2. ∪ | − ∪ − − ∪ −
3. − ∪ − ∪ − ∪ −
4. ∪ − ∪ − ∪ − ∪ − ∪ − ∪ −
5. ∪ − ∪ − ∪ − ∪ − ∪ − ∪ −
6. ∪ | − ∪ − − ∪ −
7. ∪ − ∪ − | − ∪ − ∪ − ∪ −
8. − ∪ − ∪ − ∪ −
9. ∪ | − ∪ − − ∪ −
10. ∪ − ∪ − | − ∪ − ∪ − ∪ −
11. ∪ ∪̑ ∪ ∪ − ∪ − ∪ ∪̑ ∪ ∪̑ ∪ ∪ ∪ −
12. ∪ ∪̑ ∪ ∪ − ∪ ∪̑ ∪ ∪ −
13. ∪ − ∪ − | − ∪ − ∪ − ∪ −

1 (2, 6, 9). anacr. br. † bini troch. trihem.
3 (8). troch. hephthem.
4 (5). iamb. trim. (puri).
7 (10, 13). bas. dupl. iamb. † troch. hephthem.
11. iamb. trim. (tribus ped. solutis).
12. iamb. dim. (duob. ped. solutis).

STASIMON II. 640.

στροφὴ α΄, 640—652. ἀντιστρ. α΄, 653—665

1. − ∪ − ∪ − ∪ − | − ∪ − ∪ − ∪ −
2. − ∪ − ∪ − ∪ − | − ∪ − | − ∪ − ∪ − ∪ −
3. − ∪ − ∪ − ∪ −
4. − | ∪ ∪ − ∪ − ∪ − −

K. A.   14

5. ⏑⏑–⏑ –⏑––
6. ⏑⏑ | –⏑ | –⏑⏑ –⏑⏑
7. –– | ⏑⏑––
8. ⏑⏑–⏑ –⏑––
9. ⏑⏑–⏑ –⏑ ––
10. ⏑⏑–– ⏑⏑–⏑ –⏑––
11. ⏑⏑–⏑ –⏑ ––
12. –– | –⏑⏑ –⏑– | –⏑⏑ –⏑––
13. ⏑⏑⏑ | –⏑⏑ –⏑

1. bin. troch. hephthem.
2. troch. hephthem. † troch. trihem. † troch. hephthem.
3. troch. hephthem.
4. anacr. l. † ion. a min. dim. (cum anaclasi).
5 (8, 9, 11). ion. a min. dim. (cum anaclasi).
6. anacr. sol. † bas. tr. † dact. dim.
7. bas. sp. † ion. a min. mon.
10. ion. a min. trim. (cum anaclasi).
12. bas. sp. † dact. c. troch. trihem. † dact. ´c. dipod. troch. impur.
13. bas. tr. soluta † dact. c. troch.

Not. vv. 1 † 2 ita fieri possunt quattuor:

   1 α. troch. hephthem.
   1 β. troch. hephthem.
   2 α. troch. hephthem.
   2 β. troch. trihem. † troch. hephthem.

    στροφὴ β΄, 666—672. ἀντιστρ. β΄, 673—679.

1. ⏑– | –⏑⏑ –⏑–
2. –⏑ | –⏑⏑ –⏑– ¦ –⏑ | –⏑⏑ ––
3. –⏑⏑ –⏑⏑ ––
4. –⏑⏑ –⏑⏑ –⏑⏑ –⏑⏑ –⏑⏑ ––
5. ⏑͡⏑⏑ –⏑ –⏑–
6. ⏑͡⏑⏑ –⏑ –⏑–
7. –– | –⏑⏑ –⏑– | –⏑ | –⏑⏑ ––

1. bas. iamb. † dact. c. troch. trihem.
2. bas. troch. † dact. c. troch. trihem. † bas. troch. † dact. c. troch.
3. dact. trim.

4. dact. hexam.
5 (6). troch. hephthem. (prim. pede soluto).
7. bas. sp. † dact. c. troch. trihem. † bas. troch. † dact. c. troch.

στροφὴ γ΄, 680—688. ἀντιστρ. γ΄, 689—697.

1. ∪− ∪− | −∪ −∪ −∪ −∪ −−
2. ∪− ∪− | −∪ −∪ −−
3. ∪ | −− | −∪ −∪ −−
4. −∪∪ −∪ −−
5. −∪ | −∪∪ −∪ −−
6. ∪∪−− ∪∪−− ∪∪−∪ −∪−−
7. ∪∪−− ∪∪−− ∪∪−− ∪∪−−
8. − | −∪ | −∪∪ −
9. −∪ | −∪∪ −−

1. bas. dupl. iamb. † pentapodia troch. impur.
2. bas. dupl. iamb. † tripod. troch. impur.
3. anacr. br. † bas. sp. † tripod. troch. impur.
4. dact. c. penthem. troch.
5. bas. tr. † dact. c. dipod. troch. impur.
6. ion. a min. tetram. (cum anaclasi).
7. ion. a min. tetram.
8. anacr. l. † bas. tr. † dact. c. syll.
9. bas. tr. † dact. c. troch.
Not. De ἀνακλάσει in Ion. a min. rhythmo vid. Linwood (Trag. M.)
p. 87.

στροφὴ δ΄, 698—704. ἀντιστρ. δ΄, 705—711.

1. ∪− ∪− | −∪− −∪− −∪−
2. −∪ | −∪ −∪ −∪ −
3. ∪− ∪− ∪∪͡∪ ∪− ∪− ∪−
4. ∪− ∪− | −∪−
5. − | ∪͡∪∪ ∪͡∪∪ ∪͡∪∪
6. ∪͡∪∪ −∪ −∪− | −∪∪ −∪ −⌐
7. −∪∪ −∪ −−

1. bas. dupl. iamb. † trini troch. trihem.
2. bas. tr. † troch. hephth.

3. iamb. trim. (tert. pede soluto).
4. anacr. br. † bini troch. trihem.
5. anacr. l. † tres troch. soluti.
6. troch. hephthem. (pr. p. sol.) † dact. c. dipod. troch. impur.
7. dact. c. dipod. troch.

Anapaestorum systemata septem, 712—737.

STASIMON III.   903.

στροφὴ α´, 903—914.   ἀντιστρ. α´, 915—926.

1. — ∪ — ∪ — ∪ —
2. — ∪ — ∪ — ∪ —
3. — ∪ — ∪ — ∪ — ∪ — —
4. — ∪ ∪ — ∪ ∪ — ∪ ∪ — ∪ ∪ — —
5. — ∪ — ∪ — ∪ —
6. — ∪ — ∪ — ∪ —
7. — ∪ | — ∪ ∪ — —
8. ∪ — ∪ — ∪ — ∪ — ∪ —
9. — | — ∪ — ∪ — ∪ —
10. — ∪ | — ∪ ∪ — ∪ —
11. — ∪ — ∪ — ∪ —
12. — ∪ — ∪ — ∪ —

1 (2, 5, 6, 11, 12).   troch. hephthem.
3.   pentapod. troch. impur.
4.   dact. pentam.
7.   bas. tr. † dact. c. troch.
8.   pentapod. iamb.
9.   anacr. l. † troch. hephthem.
10.   bas. tr. † dact. c. troch. trihem

στροφὴ β´, 927—940.   ἀντιστρ. β´, 941—955.

1. ∪ ∪ ∪ — ∪ ∪ ∪ — ∪ ∪ ∪ — ∪ ∪ ∪ —
2. — ∪ ∪ — ∪ ∪ — —
3. — ∪ ∪ — ∪ ∪ — —
4. — ∪ ∪ — ∪ ∪ —
†   — ∪ ∪ — ∪ ∪ — †

5. $-\cup\cup \ -\cup\cup \ -\cup \ --$
6. $-\cup \ -\cup \ -\cup \ -$
7. $-\cup \ -\cup \ -\cup \ -$
8. $-\cup \ -\cup \ -\cup \ -$
9. $-\cup \ -\cup \ -\cup \ -$
10. $-\cup \ -\cup \ -\cup \ -$
11. $-\cup \ -\cup \ -\cup \ -$
12. $-- \ -\cup\cup$
13. $-\cup\cup \ -\cup\cup \ -\cup\cup \ -\cup\cup \ -\cup\cup \ --$
14. $-\cup \ -\cup \ -\cup \ -$

1. paeon. tetram.
2 (3). dactyl. trim.
4 (†). dact. penthem.
5. dact. c. troch. tripod.
6 (7, 8, 9, 10, 11, 14). troch. hephthem.
12. dact. dim. (pr. p. spond.)
13. dact. hexam.

Commatica, 993.

στροφὴ α΄, 993—994. ἀντιστρ. α΄, 997—998.

1. $\cup\cup\cup- \ \cup--$
2. $--\cup \ -$

1. bacchiac. dim. (pr. p. solut.)
2. palimbacchiac. dim.

στροφὴ β΄, 1001—1003. ἀντιστρ. β΄, 1016—1018.

1. $\cup-- \ \cup--$
2. $\cup-- \ \cup-- \ \cup-$
3. $\cup- \ \cup- \ \cup- \ \cup- \ \cup- \ \cup-$

1. bacchiac. dim.
2. bacchiac. trim. cat.
3. iamb. trim. (purus).

στροφὴ γ΄, 1011—1014. ἀντιστρ. γ΄, 1017—1020.

1. $--$
2. $-\widehat{\cup\cup}-\cup \ - \ | \ -\widehat{\cup\cup}-\cup \ -$

3. $-\cup$ $\overset{\frown}{\cup\cup}\cup$ $-\cup-$

4. $--$ $\cup-$ $--$ $\cup-$ $--$ $\cup-$

1. spondeus.
2. dochm. dupl. (syll. secund. solut.)
3. troch. hephthem. (ped. sec. solut.)
4. iamb. trim.

στροφὴ δ΄, 1023—1027. ἀντιστρ. δ΄, 1030—1034.

1. $\cup-$ $\cup-$ | $\overset{\frown}{\cup\cup}\cup$ $-\cup-$

2. $\overset{\frown}{\cup\cup}\cup$ $-\cup$ $-\cup-$

3. $\cup-$ $\cup-$ $\cup-$ $\cup-$ $\cup-$ $\cup-$

4. $\cup--$ $\cup--$ $\cup--$ $\cup--$

5. $\overset{\frown}{\cup\cup}\cup$ $-\cup-$

1. bas. iamb. † troch. penthem. (pr. p. solut.)
2. troch. hephthem. (pr. p. solut.)
3. iamb. trim. (purus).
4. bacchiac. tetram.
5. troch. penthem. (pr. p. solut.)

στροφὴ ε΄, 1037—1041. ἀντιστρ. ε΄, 1048—1052.

1. $\overset{\frown}{\cup\cup}\cup-\cup$ $-$ | $\overset{\frown}{\cup\cup}\cup-\cup$ $-$

2. $--$ $\cup-$ $\cup-$ $-$

3. $--$ $\cup-$ $\cup-$ $\cup-$ $\cup-$ $\cup-$

4. $--$ $\cup-$ | $\overset{\frown}{\cup\cup}\cup-\cup$ $-$

5. $\overset{\frown}{\cup\cup}\cup-\cup$ $-$ | $-\cup--\cup$ $-$

1. dochm. dupl. (ex duob. troch. penthem. pr. p. sol.)
2. iamb. hephthem.
3. iamb. trim. (pr. spond.)
4. bas. dupl. † dochm. (troch. penthem.)
5. dochm. (troch. penthem.) † bini troch. trihem.

στροφὴ στ΄, 1042—1047. ἀντιστρ. στ΄, 1053—1058.

1 (2). iambici trimetri quibus non respondent antistrophici.

3. $\overset{\frown}{\cup\cup}\cup-\cup$ $-$ | $\overset{\frown}{\cup\cup}\cup\overset{\frown}{\cup\cup}\cup$ $-$

4. $\cup--\cup$ $-$ | $\cup--\cup$ $-$

5. ⏑͜⏑⏑– ⏑–– ⏑––
6. ⏑ | –⏑– –⏑–

3. dochm. dupl. (strophico κρỏκὄ- respondet antistr. θᾱ).
4. dochm. dupl.
5. bacchiac. trim. (pr. p. solut.)
6. anacr. br. † bini troch. trihem.

στροφὴ ζ', 1059—1062. ἀντιστρ. ζ', 1069—1072.

1. ⏑– | ⏑–⏑– – | ⏑⏑⏑–⏑ –
2. ⏑͜⏑⏑–⏑ – | ⏑͜⏑⏑– ⏑–

1. bas. iamb. † dochm. dupl.
2. dochm. dupl.
3 (4). iamb. trim. (non respondent antistrophici).

στροφὴ η', 1063—1068. ἀντιστρ. η', 1073—1078.

1. ⏑͜⏑⏑–⏑ – | ⏑͜⏑⏑–⏑ –
2. ⏑––⏑ –
3. ⏑⏑ | ⏑͜⏑⏑ –⏑ –– –
4. ⏑͜⏑⏑–⏑ – | –⏑– –⏑–
5. ⏑͜⏑⏑–⏑ – | –⏑͜⏑–⏑ –
6. ⏑––⏑ –

1. dochm. dupl.
2 (6). dochm.
3. anacr. sol. † troch. penthem. † spond.
4. dochm. † bini troch. trihem.
5. dochm. dupl.

στροφὴ θ', 1079—1085. ἀντιστρ. θ', 1091—1097.

1. ⏑– ⏑– ⏑–
2. ⏑͜⏑⏑ ⏑͜⏑⏑ –⏑–
3. ⏑– ⏑– | –⏑⏑–⏑ –
4. ⏑͜⏑⏑–⏑ – | –⏑͜⏑–⏑ –
5. –⏑͜⏑–⏑ –

1. tripod. iamb. (vel anacr. br. † troch. penthem.)
2. troch. hephthem.
3. bas. iamb. † dochm.
4. dochm. dupl.
5. dochm.
6 (7). bini iamb. trim.

στροφὴ ἱ, 1086—1090.   ἀντιστρ. ἱ, 1107—1111.

1. ◡◡◡◠◡ – | ◡◡◡–◡ –
2. – – ◡◠◡ ◡– ◡–
3. ◡– –◡ – | –◠◡–◡ –
4. ◡– –◡ – | ◠◡◡◠◡◡ –
5. –◠◡–◡ –

1. dochm. dupl.
2. iamb. dim.
3. dochm. dupl.
4. dochm. dupl.
5. dochm.

Anapaestorum systemata tria, 1256—1267.

Commatica, 1332.

στροφή, 1332—1338.   ἀντιστρ. 1353—1359.

1. ◠◡◡–◡ –
2. ◡ | ◠◡◡ ◠◡◡ –◡–
3. ◠◡◡–◡ – | –◠◡–◡ –
4. ◠◡◡–◡ – | –◡–◡ –
5. ◡ | ◠◡◡ ◠◡◡ –
6. ◠◡◡–◡ –
7. –◡ | –◡◡ – –

1. dochm.
2. anacr. br. † troch. hephthem.
3 (4). dochm. dupl.

5. anacr. br. † troch. penthem.
6. dochm.
7. bas. tr. † dact. c. troch.

στροφὴ α′, 1377—1383. ἀντιστρ. α′, 1398—1404.

1. $- \overarc{\cup\cup} - \cup \ - \ | \ - \overarc{\cup\cup} - \cup \ -$
2. $- \cup \ | \ - \cup\cup \ - -$
3. $\cup - \cup - \ - \ | \ \cup - \cup - \ -$
4. $- \cup\cup \ - \cup\cup \ - \cup \ - -$
5. $\overarc{\cup\cup}\cup \ - \cup \ - \cup -$
6. $- \overarc{\cup\cup}\cup - \ - \ | \ \cup - - \cup \ -$
7. $- \cup - \ | \ - \cup \ - \cup \ - \cup \ -$

1. dochm. dupl.
2. bas. tr. † dact. c. troch.
3. dochm. dupl.
4. bin. dact. c. dipod. troch.
5. troch. hephthem.
6. dochm. dupl.
7. troch. trihem. † troch. hephthem.

στροφὴ β′, 1384. ἀντιστρ. β′, 1466—1474 faciunt anapaest. system. duo, sed in stropha perierunt vv. aliquot.

στροφὴ γ′, 1388, ἀντιστρ. γ′, 1475, corruptae sunt.

στροφὴ δ′, 1392—1397. ἀντιστρ. δ′, 1405—1410 faciunt anapaestorum systemata duo.

στροφὴ ε′, 1411—18. ἀντιστρ. ε′, 1435—42.

1. $- \cup\cup \ - \cup\cup \ -$
2. $- \cup\cup \ - \cup\cup \ - \cup \ - -$
3. $- \ | \ - \cup\cup \ - \cup \ - - \ | \ - \cup \ | \ - \cup\cup \ - -$
4. $\cup - \ \cup - \ \cup - \ \cup -$
5. $\cup - \ \cup - \ \cup - \ \cup -$
6. $\cup - \ \cup - \ \cup - \ \cup -$
7. $\cup - - \cup \ -$
8. $- \cup\cup \ - \cup \ - -$

1. dact. penthem.
2. bin. dact. c. dipod. troch. impur.
3. anacr. l. † dact. c. dipod. troch. † bas. tr. † dact. c. troch.
4 (5, 6). iamb. dim. (puri).
7. dochm.
8. dact. c. dipod. troch.

στροφὴ στ΄, 1419—1423. ἀντιστρ. στ΄, 1443—1447 faciunt anapaestorum systemata duo.

 στροφὴ ζ΄, 1424—1426. ἀντιστρ. ζ΄, 1448—1450.

  1. ⏤ ⏤ ⏤ ⏤ ⏤ | ⏤ ∪ ∪ ⏤ ∪ ⏤
  2. ∪ ∪ | ⏤ ∪ ⏤ ∪ ⏤
  3. ⏤ ∪ ∪ ⏤ ∪ ∪ ⏤ ∪ ⏤ ⏤

 1. dochm. dupl.
 2. anacr. sol. † troch. penthem,
 3. bin. dact. c. dipod. troch.

στροφὴ η΄, 1427—1434. ἀντιστρ. η΄, 1451—1458 faciunt anapaestorum systema.

  στροφὴ θ΄, 1459—1465. ἀντιστρ. θ΄, 1488—1494.

  1. ∪ ⏤ ∪ ⏤ ⏤ | ∪ ⏤ ∪ ⏤ ⏤
  2. ⏤ ∪ ∪ ⏤ ∪ ⏤ ⏤
  3. ∪ ⏤ ∪ ⏤ ⏤ | ∪ ⏤ ∪ ⏤ ⏤
  4. ∪ ⏤ ∪ ⏤ | ⏤ ∪ ⏤ ∪ ⏤ ∪ ⏤
  5. ∪ ⏤ ∪ ⏤ ⏤ | ∪ ⏤ ∪ ⏤ ⏤
  6. ∪ ⏤ ∪ ⏤ ∪ ⏤ ∪ ⏤ ∪ ⏤ ∪ ⏤
  7. ∪ | ⏤ ⏤ | ⏤ ∪ ⏤ ∪ ⏤ ⏤

 1 (3, 5). dochm. dupl. (ex bin. iamb. penthem.)
 2. dact. c. dipod. troch. impur.
 4. bas. dupl. iamb. † troch. penthem.
 6. iamb. trim. (purus).
 7. anacr. br. † bas. sp. † tripod. troch.

  στροφὴ ι΄, 1479. ἀντιστρ. ι΄, 1495—1505 faciunt anapaestorum systema : in stropha perierunt duo vv.

INDEX.

[Numerals refer to the lines in our Greek text : but after p. to page.]

ἀναίνομαι, *refuse* 542, see note p. 194
ἀνδροθνής, *with death of men* 742
ἀνδροσφαγεῖον, *human - slaughter - house* 1014
ἀνθαλῶναι, *be taken in return* 317
ἀνθέω, *bloom, abound* 618
ἄνομος νόμος, *music unmusical* 1065
ἀντέλλω, *to rise* (of stars) 7
ἀντερῶ, *will refuse* 498
ἀντήνωρ, *instead of a man* 409
ἀντί (prep. with gen.) *instead, against* 14, 403, 982, 1193, 1203, 1473, 1488
ἀντίμολπον ἄκος ὕπνου, *musical remedy for sleep* 17
ἀντιρρέπω, *to counterpoise* 533
ἀντιτίεσθαι φόνον 1188
ἀνύτομαι, *grow up* 1083
ἀξιόω, *dignify* 831; ἀξιόομαι, *deign* 348
ἀξύστατος, *unexampled* (?) 1397
ἀπαλλάσσω, *come off* 1214
ἀπανθίζω γλῶσσαν ματαίαν, *shed the flowers of a rash tongue* 1592
ἀπαρκέω, *suffice* 356
ἀπειπεῖν, *forbid* 1258
ἀπήμαντος, *free from harm* (or *wrong*) 355
ἀπό (prep. with gen.), *from ;* ἀπὸ γλώσσης, *by word of mouth* 741, ἀπ' ἐμᾶς ἐλπίδος, *contrary to my expectation* 924, ἀπὸ ψυχῆς κακῆς, *through cowardice* 1572, ἀπὸ φθογγῆς 1559, see note p. 199
ἀποθαυμάζω, *admire fully* 295
ἄπτερος φάτις, *wingless voice* (not conveyed by a bird) 253

ἄπυρα ἱερά, *fireless rites* 71, note p. 150
Ἄρης, *manly vigour* 79 ; Ἄρη πνεῖν *to breathe war* 352
ἀρκύστατα (pl.), *space between nets, toils* 1300
ἄτη, *madness, crime, curse,* see Introduction
ἀτολμήτως, *in a way not to be dared* 352
αὖθις, *at another time* 294
αὐτοκτόνος, *mutually slaying* 1013
αὐτότοκος, *young and all* 132
αὐτόχθονος, *land and all* 499
Ἀφροδίτη, *loveliness* 389
ἀχηνία, *destitution, want* 389

Βαρύς, *heavy, dangerous, sullen, painful* 187, 408, 420, 1548 ; βαρείαις (ζεύγλαις) 1569
βαφή, *stain, dye,* κρόκου βαφαί, *saffron-dyed veil* 216, χαλκοῦ βαφαί, *dyeing of brass* 571
βιάζομαι, *force, constrain* (midd.) 722, (pass.) 1438
βιάομαι, *constrain* 360
βλαβείς (βλάπτω), *hindered, stopped,* with gen. 119
βοὴν (= βοήθειαν) κηρύσσειν, *to cry for aid* 1274
βουκολέω, *mitigate, console* 628
βοῦς ἐπὶ γλώσσῃ (proverb) 35
βραβεύς, *umpire, chief* 208

Γάρ, *for* 10, 14 &c.[1]
γε[2] (emphatic particle)

---

[1] Aesch. often places one γὰρ in close sequence to another, as Prom. 333, πάντως γὰρ οὐ πείσεις νιν, οὐ γὰρ εὐπιθής. Two such instances in the Agam. are well explained by Linwood (Lex.) (1) 517 : τὰ δ' αὖτε χέρσῳ, καὶ προσῆν πλέον στύγος· εὐναὶ γὰρ ἦσαν δηΐων πρὸς τείχεσιν· ἐξ οὐρανοῦ γὰρ κ.τ.λ. The first γάρ, he says, refers to the first clause, τὰ δ' αὖτε χέρσῳ, and explains why they were on the land ; the second shows why this condition was one of more odious annoyance (πλέον στύγος). (2) 694 τὸ δυσσεβὲς γὰρ ἔργον μέτα μὲν πλείονα τίκτει......οἴκων γὰρ εὐθυδίκων καλλίπαις πότμος αἰεί. The first γὰρ declares why the Chorus does not agree with an old proverb: 'for,' they say, 'one crime gives birth to many:' then adding '(crime, we say) for as to righteous houses, their lot is to have virtuous offspring.'

[2] The simpler character of Aeschylean style, as compared with that of Sophocles, appears, for instance, in his more sparing use of the expressive

particle γε, which is used in the Agam. about 20 times only, while in the Oedipus T., a shorter play, we find it in about 90 places. As it is specially suited to the tone of lively and disputative dialogue, Aesch. uses it five times in the short stichomuthia which we have discussed in pp. 194—199. (1) Affirmatively with εἰδώς, 'yes, knowing well:' (as in answer to the question, '*were you harassed by the desire of your fatherland?*' the herald replies, ὥστ' ἐνδακρύειν γ' ὄμμασιν χαρᾶς ὕπο, '*yes, so that tears are in my eyes for joy*,' 500): (2) the three next examples show γε throwing emphasis on nouns: φήμη γε μέντοι—ὁ δ' ἀφθόνητος γε—τοῖς δ' ὀλβίοις γε—ὁ δ' ὕστατός γε. So ἅλις γε. In that which follows it modifies a verb, πάρες γε μήν, *give up at least*. In a few places it has its frequent use of emphasising pronouns, τοῦτό γε, ἡμῖν γε, ἔγωγε, and others. Finally it follows other particles with a word between, to which the emphasis belongs; as ἦ μαίνεταί γε, καὶ μὴν πεπωκώς γε, καὶ μὴν ἄγαν γε, οὐκ εἰ παρέσται γε, μὴ δίκτυόν τι γ' Ἀιδου; In one place we have confidently introduced it (ἔν γε τοῖς 701) with a preposition: and it stands in two other emendations, σῆς γε 893 and καὶ πολύ γε 1382; but, though we think these probable, we should not insist on them, against any who may prefer τῆσδε and καὶ πολέα.

after hand 1033; ἐξ αἰνιγμάτων,
after riddles; ἐκ θυσιῶν 103, 731;
ἐκ τῶν ὁμοίων, on equal terms
1350
ἐκπάτιος, out of the path, lonely (?) 49
ἐκπράσσω, accomplish, make 1200;
Peile and Linwood take it to
mean here, *unmake*. This view
deserves consideration : but we
are not convinced of its truth.
ἐκφάτως, distinctly, loudly 657
ἑλέναυς, ἕλανδρος, ἑλέπτολις, see p.91
ἐλεύθερος, free, οὐκέτ' ἐξ ἐλευθέρου
δέρης, with neck no longer free 305
Ἑλλάς (subst.), Greece: (adj. fem.)
Grecian 111, 398
ἔμβασις, that in which we tread; ἀρβύλας πρόδουλον ἔμβασιν ποδός,
shoes, the foot's slave-like walking-
dress 873
ἔμμορφοι, in their own forms.   See
notes on pp. 79, 165
ἐν (prep. with abl.) in, on, among;
ἐν μέρει 309; ἐν Ἅιδου 1456
ἐν τέμνων ἄκος, pp. 146—7
ἐνδακρύω 500
ἔνι for ἔνεστι 79
ἐξεικάζω, liken; οὐδὲν ἐξηκασμένα,
not mere semblances 1169
ἐπεί, from the time when 40, 197;
when 181, 229, 617; since 220,
367, 644
ἐπί (prep. with three cases) : gen.
upon 1356, 1364, 1402; dat. upon
36, 76, ἐπ' ἐξειργασμένοις, on a finished work 1304; against 341;
after 232; for 946; over 1476;
acc. towards, to, against 114
ἐπινέμομαι, advance, encroach 445.
See note at p. 80
ἐπιξενοῦμαι, claim kindness (as a
stranger) 1245
ἐπιρρέπω, incline to, devolve on 228,
658
ἐρικύμων, pregnant 118
εὖ, well; τὸ εὖ, the good 120; εὖ πεσόντα, successful: note p. 58
εὐθνήσιμος, giving easy death 1218
εὐπειθής, persuasive 251
εὐπιθής, easily persuaded 909
εὐσεβέω 315
εὐφημέω, use auspicious words 28,
555

εὔφημος, of good omen, auspicious
595, 1172
εὔφρων, cheerful, favourable 240,
744

Ζεύγνυμι, to yoke 1569
ζεῦγος Ἀτρειδῶν, the two sons of
Atreus 44
ζευκτήριον, yoke 488
Ζεύς 151; ξένιος 61; σωτήρ 1312
ζυγός, central bench (in a vessel)
containing the ζυγῖται or middle
rowers, the most active: meaning
Aegisthus and Clytaemnestra 1547

*Η, surely 985, (or interrog. particle)
245, &c.
ἡδονή, delight; πρὸς ἡδονήν 264
ἥκω, am come 564
Ἥφαιστος, fire-god (Vulcan) 258

Θανάσιμος, deathful 931, 1101, 1201,
1374
θάνατος, death 1392, 1423, 1460, pl.
675, 1265, 1501
θεῖος, divine, heaven-sent 438, 678,
1005
θέμις, right, justice, lawful 100, 196,
1360
θερμὸν οὖς 1097
θυμός, life 1313
θυοσκινέω, promote incense-burning
89
θυραῖος, outside, foreign 765, 976,
1537

Ἰατρόμαντις, medical seer, mediciner
1552
ἵζω (with accus.), sit on 909
ἶνις, son, cub 666
ἰσάργυρος, worth silver 887
ἰσόπαις, childlike 76
ἰσόπρεσβυς, like an old man 79
ἰσοτριβής, wearing out together 1372
ἰσόψυχος, equal in spirit 1400

Καινίζω, handsel 992
καίριος, seasonable 954; mortal
1045, 1217, 1268; καιρίως 1269
καλλίπαις, having noble children
697
καλλίπρωρος, fair-visaged, beautiful
213

INDEX. 223

καλῶς, well, nobly; τὸ μὴ καλῶς ἔχον,
what is not good 774
κάμνω, to be weary, to faint 442;
καμών, worn out 629
κάρα, head; φίλον κάρα, dear one
833
κάρβανος, foreign, barbarous 982
καρπόομαι, enjoy 580
κάρτα, very, exceedingly 254, 551,
1177, &c.
κασίγνητος, brother 304; κάσις ξύνουρος 453
κατά (prep.) with accus. κατ᾽ ἄνδρα,
as a man 328, 853; κατ᾽ ἦμαρ,
in the day-time 627; κατ᾽ ἴχνος,
on the track: with gen. but not in
Ag.
κεκομμένος φρενῶν, deprived of reason, insane 439
κῆδος, marriage (care, mourning, p.
91) 653
κληδών, invocation 206; report 791,
802; fame 855
κοιμᾶν φλόγα, to extinguish flame
556
κοιμᾶσθαι φρουράν 2
κόμιστρα (pl.), price of recovery, ransom 893
κόρος, arrogance, insolence 368, 701
κρεουργὸν ἦμαρ, feast-day 1521
κριθάω, be high-fed (with barley)
1570
κρίνω, to select 432
κτήσιος, in possession 333; κτήσιος
βωμός, altar of Ζεὺς κτήσιος 959
κτίζω, found, make 427
κύριος, empowered, entitled 107, 806;
τὸ κύριον, the appointed time 700;
κυρίως, with full power, fully
κύρω, κυρέω, obtain, hit 1119; κυρέω, be 1126, 1296 (κυροῦνθ᾽ ὅπως)

κύτος, saucer, urn, vessel (shallow)
299, 744, 1051

Λάκτισμα δείπνου 1530
λαμπαδηφόρων νόμοι 289
λαμπτήρ 22
λαμπτηρουχία, beacon-watch 818.
We cannot agree with those who
strive to explain this as meaning
the 'chamber-lights.' See 22
λαπάζω (or ἀλαπάζω), lay waste 128
λάσκω, cry out 516, 555, 793. We
now find that our conjecture at
516 (λάσκοντες for λαχόντες) had
been anticipated by Linwood
λέγοις 296
λείχω, lick 756, 1154
λιγύς, melodious 1069
λοιγός, destruction 1040
λυμαντήριος 1367

Μεθύστερον, at a later time, afterward 394
μείλιγμα, darling 1368
μείρω, allot; εἱμαρμένος, allotted,
fixed 841
μέλω, care for, mind 348; μέλειν,
impers. 528, 544, 1075
μετά (prep.) with acc. after 209; gen.
with 959; dat. not in Ag. In
comp. means (1) change, (2) sharing, (3) pursuit
μεταγιγνώσκω, change the mind 200
μεταίτιος, cause in part 739
μεταμανθάνω 660
μέτειμι, pursue 1596
μέτοικος 57
μή¹, not (subjective negative)
μῆχαρ, remedy 182
μηχαρίζομαι, provide, enlarge 281
(conjectural reading)

¹ Μή, with its compounds μηδέ, μήτε, μηκέτι, μηδαμῶς, μηδέν, &c., is
found in Ag. as follows :—
(1) With opt. verb expressing wish, 433, 1174, 1377: (2) with imperative of prohibition, 840, 850, 960, 980, 1553, and with participle after
imperative, 469, 714, 834 : (3) with subjunctive of prohibition, 129 (οἶον
μή), 142 (ἐκκαλέω μή), 318, 807, 848, 1259, 1584, 1586; μὴ lest, 1553:
(4) with conjunction (εἰ, εἴπερ, ὅπως), 238, 324, 971, 981, 342 ; with participle (=εἰ with verb) 250: (5) with infin. 326, 691, (after τὸ) 187, 528,
(after ὥστε, ὡς) 185, 335, 624, 1303: (6) with abstract adj. τὸ μὴ τελέσφο-
ρον, 926.

μίμνω (μι-μένω=μένω), *remain, await*
144, 1072
μινύρομαι, *hum a tune* 18
μισητός, *hateful ; μίσητος, lascivious*
1153

Νυκτηρεφής, *night-wrapt* 423
νυκτίπλαγκτος, *nightly-restless* 12
νυμφόκλαυτος, *bride-deplored* 688
νυμφότιμος, *bridal-honouring* 656
νωμάω, *direct* 711
νωτίζω, *skim* 263

Ξένιος, *hospitable* 374 ; Ζεὺς ξένιος,
guardian of guest-law 61
ξένια, (pl.) *hospitable entertainment*
1520
ξιφοδήλητος, *sword-destroying* 1457
ξουθός, *brown, melodious* 1065

Οἰκουρός, *house-guard* 1150, 1555
οἶον, *only* 129
ὁμοιοπρεπής, *taking semblance* 721
ὁμότοιχος, *having a party wall* 929
ὄναρ 84 ; ὄνειρον 13, 25, 1149 ; (ὀνει-
ραρ) -ατος 450, 819, 908, *dream.*
ὅπη, *as* 68 ; ὅποι, *whither* 1440;
ὅπως, *how* 110, 775, 1296, with
superl. 559, 564, 632, 1285; οὐκ
ἔσθ' ὅπως with opt. 579; ὅπως,
in order that 1576 ; ὅπως ἄν (with
opt. rare) 342
ὁρμαίνειν θυμόν, *pant forth life* 1313
ὅρος, *limit, boundary, definition*
1077, 1177; ὁ θῆλυς ὅρος 445 we
have rendered '*the feminine decision*,' making πιθανός *credulous.*
Linwood and Schütz render
it, *the opinion laid down by a
woman*, and πιθανός *persuasive*,
making ἐπινέμεται deponent, as
we do. This is favoured by the
context which follows, not by that
which precedes. See note at p. 80
οὐ, οὐκ, οὐχί, *not* (objective negative)
ὀφλεῖν δίκην, *to be condemned in a
suit* 493

Παγκαίνιστος; *ever renewable* 888
παγκρατής, *victorious* 1577
Παιάν, Παιών, *healer, healing god*
(Apollo) 141, 1173
παιάν, *hymn* 223, 604

πάλαι, *long ago* (with past) 546, 1110,
(with pres.) 507
παλαιστής, *wrestler, suitor* 1131
παλαίφατος, *spoken of old* 689
παλίγκοτος, *hostile, odious* 797, 802
παλιμμήκης, *doubly long* 179
παλίνορτος, *returning, recoiling* 145
παλίντροπος, *averted* 705
παλιντυχής, *reversed* 425
παλίρροθος, *tide-reciprocating* 173
πάμπροσθε, *long before* 664
πανάλωτος, *all-capturing* 338
παρά (prep. takes 3 cases : not dat.
in Ag.) : with gen. *from* (pers.
usually) 242, 290: with acc. *to*
166 : *beside, beyond, against* 827,
859 : παρ' οὐδὲν θέσθαι, *to make no
account of, disregard* 208
πάρα, for πάρεστι, *it is possible* 976,
1532, 1599
παραθέλγω, *soothe away* 72
παρακλίνω, *turn aside* 685
παρακοπή, *madness* 202
παραλλάσσω, *pass away* 449
παράνους, *distracted* 1430
παρασκοπέω, *overlook* 1177
παραυτά, *in like manner* 680
παρέσται, *shall come to pass* 1174
παρεστῶτα (τὰ), *present conditions*
974
παρηβάω, *leave youth behind, decline*
912
παρηγορία, *suasion* 96
πάρηξις, *putting to land* 515
παρίημι, *omit, neglect* 268
παροψώνημα, *side-dish, relish* 1376
πᾶς, *all ; τὸ πᾶν, the whole* 162, *ἐς τὸ
πᾶν, on the whole*
πατέω, *walk* 1227, *trample* 350, 885,
1118, 1282
πάτριος, *of one's country* 1081
πατρῷος, *of father, of fathers* 1202,
see note on 191
πάχνη, (hoar-frost) *clotted blood* 1441
πέδον, *ground ; πέδον πατεῖν, tread to
the ground* 1282
πειράομαι, *attempt* (with inf.) 1567,
try (with gen.) 1593
πένομαι, *be poor* 890
πεπαίτερος, *softer, milder* 1290
πεπαμένος (πάσασθαι), *possessing* 763
πεπρωμένος, *appointed* 1592; τὸ πεπρωμένον, *destiny* 69

ὑπό (prep. with 3 cases): gen. *under,
by, attended with* 434—5, 1482;
dat. *under, by* 788, 952; acc.
under 914, ὑπ' ἄλγος ἔρπει by tmesis for ἄλγος ὑφέρπει 415. Other
examples of tmesis are περὶ χεῖρε
βαλοῦσα 1487, πρὸ...βαλών 932;
ὑπὸ...στροβεῖ 1141, ὑπαὶ...λύοι 873
ὑποκαίω, ὑπολείβω 70
ὑπτίασμα κειμένου πατρός, 1210,
seems to mean πατέρα κείμενον
ὕπτιον, *his father lying on his back*,
i. e. prostrate in death, as Clyt.
flung him (ἀποταμοῦσ' ἀπέδικε
1340). The mental image of the
crime shall prey on the mind of
Orestes by divine judgment, until
it obliges him to return and avenge.

Φαιδρός, *bright, cheerful, jocund* 479;
    φαιδρὸν οὓς 1154
φαίνω 104
φέρειν πλέον, *prevail* 949
φεύγω, *cry* φεῦ 1233
φιλήτωρ, *darling* 1375
φόβου μέλαθρον 1363
φρήν, φρένες 922
φυλακὰν κατασχεῖν 213

Χάρις δαιμόνων, *a blessing from the
gods* 167 (see note in Consp. L.);

χάρις Διὸς 340; εὐμόρφων κολοσσῶν χάρις 387; χάριν ματαίαν
391; see 964;—χάριν ξυναινέσαι
444; πνέων χαριν 1131;—Ἅιδου
εὐκταίαν χάριν 1312; ἀθίκτων χάρις 349; ἄχαρις χάρις 1472; καιρὸν
χάριτος 715;—χάριν τίνειν 749;
χάρις οὐκ ἄτιμος πόνων 331; χάριν
τροφεῦσιν ἀμείβων 674
χάριν, *on account of* 24
χέρνιψ, *lustral water* 658
χλιδή, *luxury* 1376
χρέος, *occasion* 87, *office* 421

Ψύθος, *falsehood* 438

Ὥς, (1) *as*, passim; accented after the
word it modifies, τοξότης τίς ὣς
1119; idiomatic with abs. particip.,
ὡς ὧδ' ἐχόντων, *such being the facts*
1318; intensifying adjectives and
adverbs, positive or superl., ὡς
τάχος 27; γένοιτο δ' ὡς ἄριστα 633,
see ὅπως: abs. with infin. ὡς εἰπεῖν,
ὡς τορῶς φράσαι 1513. (2) for ὥστε,
so as, so that, with infin. 335, 624,
1306. (3) *how*, ὡς λέγοις 1306.
(4) *that* 455. (5) ὡς ἄν[1] (see ἄν).
(6) *from the time when*, ὡς τάδ'
ἤμπλακον 1137. (7) Note ὡς δὴ
as if forsooth 1562.

---

[1] The potential particle ἄν, when (not in junction with a relative) it
modifies a verb, is used (1) with opt. (pres. or aor.), infin. (pres. or aor.),
and, in past sense, with indic. (aor. or imperf.); as λέγοιμ' ἄν, *I would say,*
δοκεῖ ἂν βῆναι, *he seems likely to have walked,* ηὐξάμην ἄν, *I would have
vowed.* As ἄν in these uses is (normally) the apodosis of a conditional
sentence, it has a protasis *if* expressed or supposed, and, when the verb
is past, that protasis is always apparent, either as εἰ, or as contained in
a participle, as ηὔξω ἂν δείσας; *would you have vowed if you had been
alarmed?* But ἄν with the opt. is often used as a modest or modified
future, where no protasis appears: as λέγοιμ' ἄν, *I would (or will)* say.
This idiom is more frequent than any other use of ἄν in this play: see 252,
257, 296, 511, 581, 680, 766, 824, 1053. 1087, 1123, 1437, 1158, 1253,
1300, 1379, 1493, 1507, 1595. The regular protasis (εἰ with opt.) is rare:
see 38, 970, 1319, 1589. Ἄν is used before and again after a protasis with εἰ
324, and doubled (after a present with εἰ) 317. At 229 (if the reading is
true) ἐπεί with opt. forms the protasis. A participial protasis is shown
900, 941, 1266. Ἄν with infin. occurs 864, and in the previous line an
infin. (δρᾶσαι) is to be mentally supplied with ἄν. See also 356, where αν
is a conjectural insertion. With a past indic. ἄν occurs five times: four of

these places have the regular protasis, εἰ with past indic. 800, 891, 951, 1321 : one (cited above) has a participial protasis 861.

Ἄν compounded with relative particles takes subjunctive : of such use we find these instances : ὅταν five times, 7, 16, 597, 898, 1493 ; εὖτ᾽ ἄν twice, 12, 392 ; ὡς ἄν 829 ; ἕως ἄν 1364. The reading αν=ἃ ἄν 1364, cannot be relied on as certain. The construction of ἄν σκήψειεν following ὅπως, 344, is peculiar : and ἄν must not be regarded as in composition with ὅπως.

POSTSCRIPT.

Since this Edition was printed, I have received from Mr Munro a valuable note, containing a new conjectural reading and interpretation of the lines at p. 39, 1153—1155 (1228—1230). His words are :

"The following would be, I think, a simple restoration of this much disputed passage:

οὐκ οἶδεν οἷα γλῶσσα μισήτης κυνός,
λέξασα κἀκτείνασα φαιδρόνους δοκὴν
ἄτης λαθραίου, τεύξεται κακῇ τύχῃ.

'Knows not what the tongue of a lustful she-hound, speaking as it spoke and lengthening out with a gay heart the ambush of dark crime, will achieve—with foul success.' The correction is of the slightest, ι for ο, the substitution of a very uncommon for a very common word. The *neut. plur.* accus. of a *pronoun* after τεύξεται is quite idiomatic: Aeschylus, Euripides and Sophocles all supply more than one example: Ellendt gives at least 4 instances from Sophocles: (Phil. 506 πόνων ἆθλ' ὅσσα μηδεὶς τῶν ἐμῶν τύχοι φίλων). ἐκτείνασα calls for an accus. as μακρὰν μὲν ἐξέτεινας, and in Eurip. μακρὰν δ' ἔτεινας = μακρὰν ῥῆσιν. Then 'like dark Ate' is manifestly out of place in such a context. For δοκήν comp. Hesych. δοκαί· ἐνέδραι, παρατηρήσεις: and again ἐν δοκῇ· ἐν ἐπιβουλῇ. The word therefore meant 'ambush,' 'hostile watching for,' 'deliberate plot,' 'insidious conduct,' 'any form of dark secret treachery' like the Latin *insidiae*, the

K. A.

AGAMEMNON.

French *guet-apens*, which comes from our *wait, laying a wait*. Plato and Demosthenes both use ἐνέδρα in the same sense as δοκή has here: Plat. Laws x, p. 908 D, εὐφυὴς δὲ ἐπικαλούμενος, δόλου δὲ καὶ ἐνέδρας πλήρης. Homer has ἐν προδοκῇσιν, and is fond of δοκεύω, the verb of δοκή, using it of a hound watching by what part to seize an animal; of a warrior spying out another's weak point; of a charioteer waiting to *jockey* the man in front of him: Euripides uses this verb in the Bacchae. I would not personify Ate, but take ἄτης λαθραίου for the murder of Agamemnon, just as in 1427 δολίαν ἄτην refers to the death of Iphigenia.

The above reading depicts well, I think, the appalling equanimity of Clytaemnestra, the long-protracted dissimulation, through hundreds of verses, of her never-wavering tongue. And 1156—1159 thus perhaps afford a more symmetrical and Greek-like parallel to the four lines preceding: it was Clytaemnestra's tongue that led Agamemnon slowly on from his chariot to the bath and shirt of death. See Jerem. 9. v. 8: Their tongue is an arrow shot out; it speaketh deceit: one speaketh peaceably to his neighbour with his mouth, but in heart he layeth his wait." H. A. J. M.

Mr Munro adds many examples of compounds like φαιδρόνους, as κουφόνους, ταχύνους, κρυψίνους and others: but on this point no doubt exists.

My own impression in favour of the Tyrwhitt and Madvig readings οἷα, λείξασα, φαιδρὸν οὖς, δήξεται, was caused to a great extent by the apparent likelihood that the jocular φαιδροῖς ὠσίν of Aristophanes was drawn from the φαιδρὸν οὖς suggested here. But in another note Mr Munro argues that Euripides, not Aeschylus, was the tragic poet parodied in that passage of the Pax. He says:

"The scholiast on Aristoph. Pax 154—156 ἀλλ᾽ ἄγε, Πήγασε,...φαιδροῖς ὠσίν, distinctly informs us that the poet is quoting from, or closely parodying, the Bellerophon of Euripides; and this we might have inferred from the term Πήγασε applied to the κάνθαρος. The φαιδροῖς ὠσίν therefore may be the actual words of Euripides: 'playful,' 'frisking ears' (? 'glancing in the sunshine'); or ὠσίν may be a parody of a different substantive in the original. Xenoph. Apol. 27 εἰπὼν δὲ ταῦτα μάλα ὁμολογουμένως δὴ τοῖς εἰρημένοις ἀπῄει καὶ ὄμμασι καὶ σχήματι καὶ βαδίσματι φαιδρός. The scholiast of Aristophanes refers to the Agamemnon oftener than to any other extant play of Aeschylus. His silence here is perhaps a proof that he, or his authorities, did not refer φαιδροῖς ὠσίν to the Agamemnon."

That Aristophanes parodies the Bellerophon is quite clear: but there was nothing to prevent him from parodying Euripides and Aeschylus in one passage—two birds with one stone. And have not the lines χρυσοχαλίνων πάταγον ψαλίων | διακινήσας φαιδροῖς ὠσίν the ring of Aeschylus more than of Euripides? And does the silence of the scholiast about the Agamemnon prove anything but that φαιδρόνους was written in the MS. which he used?

POSTSCRIPT.

Whatever the final judgment of criticism may be, it is remarkable that so many words (γλῶσσα, κυνός, λέξασα, φαιδρόνους, and even τεύξεται) should have concurred in leading Madvig to conjectures so nearly coherent as those received in my text. But Mr Munro justly says (what I have always felt) that 'like dark Ate' is out of place. I ask then whether his fine conjecture δοκὴν may not be received along with λείξασα and φαιδρὸν οὖς, as an accusative apposition. Admirable as I confess Mr Munro's defence of λέξασα to be, I find a painful hitch in the word φαιδρόνους. Such terrible dissimulation must be a heavy burden to the worst *mind*, not a *cheerful* stimulant.

If my suggestion holds, the three lines become—

> οὐκ οἶδεν οἷα γλῶσσα μισήτης κυνός,
> λείξασα, κἀκτείνασα φαιδρὸν οὖς, δοκὴν
> ἄτης λαθραίου, τεύξεται κακῇ τύχῃ.

> knows not what issues a lascivious she-hound's tongue,
> licking with playful ear outstretch'd—a wily snare
> of secret mischief—will achieve with foul success.

This I could gladly accept.

For EU product safety concerns, contact us at Calle de José Abascal, 56–1°, 28003 Madrid, Spain or eugpsr@cambridge.org.

www.ingramcontent.com/pod-product-compliance
Ingram Content Group UK Ltd.
Pitfield, Milton Keynes, MK11 3LW, UK
UKHW020320140625
459647UK00018B/1938